THE LOST
TREASURE
OF THE
KNIGHTS
TEMPLAR

THE LOST TREASURE

OF THE

KNIGHTS TEMPLAR

• • • •

*Solving
the Oak
Island
Mystery*

• • • •

STEVEN SORA

Destiny Books
Rochester, Vermont

Destiny Books
One Park Street
Rochester, Vermont 05767
www. InnerTraditions.com

Destiny Books is a division of Inner Traditions International

Library of Congress Cataloging-in-Publication Data
Sora, Steven, 1952–
      The lost treasure of the Knights Templar : solving the Oak Island mystery /
Steven Sora.
          p.   cm.
      Includes bibliographical references and index.
      ISBN 0-89281-710-0 (alk. paper)
      1. Oak Island (N.S.)—Antiquities.   2. Treasure-trove—Nova Scotia—Oak
Island.   3. Oak Island Treasure Site (N.S.)   4. Templars—History.   5. America—
Discovery and exploration—Scottish.   I. Title.
      F1039.O35 S67   1999
      971.6'23—dc21   98-48741
                                                                              CIP

Printed and bound in the United States

10 9 8 7 6 5 4 3 2

Text design and layout by Kristin Camp
This book was typeset in Centaur with Greco Deco as the display typeface

To my wife and best friend, Terry, and our sons, Christian and Mike

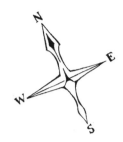

CONTENTS

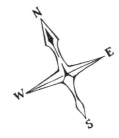

ACKNOWLEDGMENTS

Thanks first to my family: my wife, Terry, for her unflagging support and generosity over the miles and the years, my sons, Christian and Mike, for their initial patience and later their interest. Thanks to Bob Meledandri for his assistance in translating, editing, and critiquing the manuscript from the earliest stages and for his friendship and support from the very beginning.

Thanks to the staff of numerous libraries and bookstores from New York to Pennsylvania to Nova Scotia who helped in procuring hard to find books and materials. Special thanks to the staff at the Public Library in Bethlehem, Pennsylvania, to the J. V. Fletcher Library in Westford, Massachusetts, and the Douglas N. Harding Rare Book Shop in Wells, Maine.

My appreciation for those who bring history alive and keep it alive, notably Dr. Regis Courtemanche of C. W. Post and H. S. "Pete" Cummings, Jr., of the Prince Henry Project.

Particular gratitude to everyone at Inner Traditions, especially Ehud Sperling, Jon Graham, Rowan Jacobsen, Peri Champine, Lee Wood, and Blake Maher, and to copyeditor Marcia Merryman Means for her careful work.

And finally a word of tribute to the historians and writers who risk intellectual adversity while inspiring new discovery, notably Michael Baigent, Barry Fell, Charles Hapgood, Richard Leigh, Henry Lincoln, and Frederick Pohl.

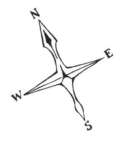

INTRODUCTION

$\mathcal{A}$n agent of the English king is stabbed and left to bleed to death on the altar of remote Grey Friars chapel in Scotland.

A parish priest in a mountainous village in southern France suddenly becomes immensely wealthy as a result of parchments he finds hidden in an old altar. Kings, Church leaders, and the elite of Paris take an interest as he uses his wealth to restore his church, employing such a bizarre pagan motif that few would recognize the building as Christian. The circumstances of his death are as inexplicable as his wealth.

A secret cabal meets in the dark forests of the Ardennes to hatch a scheme to loot a very specific treasure from Jerusalem. They hide their elite group within a military organization, but once their mission is complete, the cover organization is outlawed and its leaders sentenced to death.

A fog-shrouded bay becomes the center of the most massive treasure hunt in history. The project unites business leaders, a president of the

United States, Hollywood actors, and assorted American and Canadian millionaires in an undertaking that will cost millions of dollars as well as human lives.

What do all these events have in common? They are all linked through time and space by a single thread. A secret society formed a thousand years ago that has survived official persecution and is still on its way to reaching its goal. This society at times has controlled the greatest amount of wealth amassed in the world, owned the world's largest navy, started revolutions, and undermined governments. The society still exists today.

In this book you will learn of an extremely complex construction located on an island off the coast of Nova Scotia that has defied humans and modern science for two hundred years. Tiny Oak Island, only 128 acres in size, is one of 350 islands in Mahone Bay. Today it lies about one hour away from Halifax on the southern half of Nova Scotia. Well before modern times, the surrounding land had hardly been settled when evidence of a hidden treasure was discovered. The evidence is a two-hundred-foot vertical shaft protected by oaken platforms as well as cement and metal barriers. The shaft itself is booby-trapped by diagonal shafts running underground, designed to bring in thousands of gallons of ocean water. Their purpose is to stop anyone from finding the pit's treasure. The water shafts run hundreds of feet to a false beach, where imported fiber and eelgrass were used to cover and protect the drains that supply the ocean water. The intricately designed system stops all invaders who trespass below a certain depth.

Somehow, someone managed to construct this repository hundreds of years ago. It was discovered more than two hundred years ago, but carbon dating tells us it may be much older. Somewhere under Oak Island there may be an immense treasure: buried treasure of pirates, hidden bounty of Spanish plunderers, or sacred artifacts carried overseas from Europe. No one is certain. Very little has been brought to the surface over the years except more clues. Attempting to find the treasure has already consumed an amount of money that would rival the greatest hoard ever found from a pirate treasure. The effort has cost several individuals their own fortunes and has cost several more their lives. To date, no one is wealthier for having attempted to recover the treasure.

Welcome to the Money Pit.

The past, it is said, is history. Today, two things are certain. At present, even greater technology and resources are available to those willing to spend the money to uncover the Money Pit's secrets. And there is someone willing to make the commitment. A wealthy Canadian businessman has formed what is called the Triton Alliance with fifty-two Canadian and American investors who are underwriting the current excavation. Under the leadership of David Tobias, even the highly respectable Woods Hole Oceanographic Institute has become involved. Oak Island is under siege to give up its secrets. And what might be the value of the treasure? According to Mr. Tobias, it is worth billions.

There is a treasure lying under the surface of Oak Island. There is evidence that this treasure has a thousand-year provenance and is so valuable that to someone (we know not who), there is no price too great to pay to protect it from being discovered. Concealed in the Money Pit along with a cache of immense monetary value may be secrets that hold crucial importance for the world, even centuries after being hidden. To some, these secrets should stay hidden. To others, no price is too steep to uncover the hoard.

The premise of this book is that a secret society that has existed under several names and for more than a thousand years was responsible for gathering together what is concealed underneath Oak Island. This group, once wealthy and powerful, fell out of power and was forced to go underground. In their darkest hour they had to give up possession of their wealth, although the organization has survived. The treasure and secrets protected by the group passed to an elite Scottish family, which inherited the guardianship of the secret society. This family was instrumental in designing and building the massive underground complex and in using this remote island in the New World as their private bank.

Just what is being protected? To be certain, it is massive wealth—in the form of gold and silver, sacred artifacts, and the crown jewels pledged to the first banking organization in Europe as collateral for loans. In addition, there are documents—some from ancient texts that hold secrets protected for more than a thousand years (genealogies of the family of Jesus—from David to Jesus to "heirs" of Jesus). These secrets were perceived both then, when they were concealed, and now as possibly threatening to the Catholic Church. What are these secrets and what implications do they have for us all? To find out we must head into uncharted territory.

The sea charts of ancient mariners often included small notes in the borders to indicate where the territory was unknown. Here the known truths had not been uncovered. No clues were offered to aid the explorer as to the possibility of lands lying ahead or a sheer drop off the edge of the Earth. Instead, there were depictions of sea serpents and mermaids and the dire warning *There Be Monsters Here.*

Chapter 1

THE MYSTERY OF OAK ISLAND

$\mathcal{N}$ova Scotia in the late eighteenth century offered few diversions. One of them was hunting for buried treasure, since the island was a known haunt of buccaneers and privateers. On a summer afternoon in 1795, three young men decided to go digging for pirate treasure.[1] One of them, Daniel McGinnis, had been wandering through the woods of Oak Island and noticed a spot that gave the appearance of having recently been cleared. Red clover and other plants foreign to the island were growing in the cleared area. There was also a ship's tackle hanging from a sawed-off tree branch, fifteen feet above the ground. The tree itself had strange markings on it.

The real tip-off was a depression McGinnis saw in the ground. It appeared that someone might have buried something there. Sixteen-year-old Daniel had no trouble persuading two of his friends to return to the uninhabited island with him. This may not have been the first time the boys had hoped and labored to find a chest full of gold, but this particular day would end differently from the others. With shovels and pickaxes, Daniel McGinnis, teenager Anthony Vaughn, and John Smith, aged twenty, went to work. The excavation was started in the center of the depression, and they found the ground softer than they had expected.

Two feet down they reached a layer of carefully laid flagstones that were not indigenous to the island. (Later it was decided that they came from Golden River on the mainland of Nova Scotia, two miles away.) When they removed the stones they realized they were digging into a previously dug shaft. Ten feet down into the shaft they came upon a platform constructed of oak logs. The logs were rotted and therefore easy to remove. These fitted logs were embedded into the sides of the thirteen-foot-wide shaft, and their poor condition gave them the appearance of having been there for a long time. The clay walls of the shaft had preserved markings that indicated previous digging. The young men removed the logs and continued digging. At twenty feet a second platform of oak logs impeded their progress but fortified their belief that something very valuable was buried further down in the shaft.

After removing the second platform, they continued working, only to reach another platform at the thirty-foot level. At this point they realized additional help was needed, both in terms of manpower and machinery. Persuading hardworking farmers to abandon their chores was difficult, and little work was done on the shaft for years. Another obstacle to enlisting workers for the project was that few of them would come to the island in the first place. The 128-acre island was just one of 350 islands in Mahone Bay, but it had a reputation. Years before, strange lights had been seen on the island at night, and a few of the mainlanders had rowed out to investigate. It is said that they were never heard from again. The island was haunted.

Without the support they needed, the young treasure hunters temporarily gave up on further excavation. Before the year was over, John Smith bought property on the island, and when he married, he moved there to farm it. Daniel McGinnis also farmed part of the island. When John's wife was pregnant with their first child, they went to the mainland to visit the family doctor. Smith told Dr. Simeon Lynds, a relative of his fellow treasure hunter Anthony Vaughn, about the discovery, and Dr. Lynds became interested—so much so that he decided to invest money into excavating the shaft.

In 1801 Dr. Lynds formed the first syndicate that tried to conquer the Money Pit.[2] He raised the necessary capital from thirty other prominent Nova Scotians and went to work. Using ropes and pulleys, workers first removed the mud that had settled into the shaft after the teenagers' aborted attempt, and then dug further. Again they encountered oak platforms at ten-foot intervals. The Onslow Syndicate, so named for Dr. Lynd's hometown, also came upon layers of charcoal, putty, and a brown fibrous material, which was enough to keep everyone involved excited. Apparently someone had taken a lot of trouble to hide what must be a very important treasure.

At ninety feet, just over the expected oaken platform, they encountered another flagstone with an inscription. The flagstone's symbols were not immediately deciphered. When they were shown to a professor of languages at a nearby Halifax college, he said that the inscription told of treasure buried another "forty feet below."[3] The code was a very common one, also used by Edgar Allan Poe in his story "The Gold Bug," in which a simple cipher is used in a search for buried treasure. It was cracked by substituting the most frequently used symbol for the most commonly used letter in the English language, an *E*. The inscribed stone was made into a part of John Smith's fireplace and later found its way to a bookstore in Halifax, where another syndicate used it to raise money. It disappeared when the store closed.

Ninety-three feet below the surface, the treasure seekers discovered a new problem. After one more platform, they found that for every bucket of earth being raised, they had to bail out two buckets of water. Still their optimism held. It was late in the day, and they went home excited that the next day they surely would be breaking into the treasure trove. When they returned the next day they found that water had seeped in and flooded the shaft. Bailing took the place of digging, but water kept filling into the ninety-foot hole. Efforts were made to bail out the shaft with a pump, to no avail. The pump burst, and work was grudgingly discontinued. The flooding tunnel was a booby trap that would never cease defeating the treasure seekers. Had the inscription been a ruse? The excavators found no treasure, and forty feet below might well have been forty miles below because of the flooding.

The next year the syndicate dug the second of the many shafts that would eventually be sunk. They reached one 110 feet and then started to tunnel over to the first shaft. But again, water flooded the new tunnel and, in turn, the new shaft. Patience and funds were quickly exhausted. Work would not resume again for forty years, although the "treasure" was not forgotten. In 1845 a new company was formed to reach the treasure in the pit. This second major venture included another Dr. Lynd, of Truro, Nova Scotia, and a mining engineer, James Pitbaldo. Anthony Vaughn and John Smith were nearing seventy years of age by the time the digging was started, but the pit had lost none of its appeal for them, and both assisted.

It took twelve days to reach sixty-eight feet again (both of the other pits had since caved in), and they dug until a Saturday. On Sunday, before church, the pit was inspected, there was no water. After church, however, they found that the pit was again flooded. The syndicate had prepared for this contingency, which had caused the previous expeditions to fail. A platform was erected, and a horse-driven drill put in place. At ninety-eight feet the drill went through a platform that was found to be made of five-inch-thick spruce. Another foot down was a platform of oak. Surely they had reached the treasure. Then, after going through twenty-two inches of metal, they discovered still another oak platform.

The drillers thought they had pierced a box and were into a second box. After another level of spruce, they reached clay. A second boring reached the oak "box," which they now believed was the treasure trove, but the drill was bringing up only the brown fibrous material that had been encountered previously. The fiber later turned out to be coconut husks. Nothing besides the metal fragments that had already been brought up by the drill was found. According to Jotham McCully who was in charge of the drilling, these fragments resembled "links of watch chain," and the drillers attempted to recover as much of the material as possible.[4] During this operation there was a disturbance among the workers who were sorting through the salvaged material. One noticed the foreman, James Pitbaldo, pocket something he would not show the others. Although he said that he would not reveal it until the next meeting of the syndicate directors, he didn't reveal it even then. He did try, through another businessman, Charles Archibald, of Acadia Iron Works, to buy the pit from the other directors, who refused to sell. The foreman was killed shortly after in another mining accident, taking his secret discovery to his grave.

In 1850 the syndicate drilled still another shaft to 109 feet and made another attempt to tunnel to the original shaft. This new tunnel led the drillers to a significant discovery. The tunnel was being flooded by seawater. In fact, by watching the water in the pit and the water off-shore, they discovered that the water level in the pit was rising and falling with the tides of the bay. The only conclusion they could draw was that there was a natural channel from the nearby beach that was the cause of the flooding. The beach, Smith's Cove as it is called, was searched for signs of such a channel, and a spot where water rushed out from the sand was discovered. Surrounding this channel was more of the brown fibrous material.[5] Under one layer was eelgrass, and under the eelgrass they found a mass of beach rock, free of sand. To the disbelief of all, the "natural" channel was confirmed to be artificial.

The syndicate then built a coffer dam to reduce the water that flowed into the cove, allowing further investigation. The effort proved that this was truly the channel that flowed into the pit. Weeks of work went into building the stone and clay dam, and the men found that a total of five drains had been constructed into what now appeared to be an artificial beach. Even today, this would be considered a complex undertaking. The builders had dug a five-hundred-foot tunnel that was capable of channeling six hundred gallons of ocean water per minute, complete with a filter system that prevented the basins from becoming clogged after years or centuries of operation. In addition, they further disguised their work with an artificial beach that would protect the workings of this elaborate flooding system. In 1850 the idea was nothing short of remarkable and served as further proof that something very important was concealed under Oak Island.

The men dismantled the five drains. Each of these five drains was spaced far apart from the others at their closest point to the ocean, but they converged closer to the shore. Each was constructed of twin rows of rock, eight inches apart, covered with stone slabs. Then more bad luck hit the expedition. An Atlantic storm destroyed the dam that had been built to hold back the waters. Because it was too late in the year to reconstruct it, the men decided to sink still another shaft between the shore and the pit, which would absorb any water from the destroyed drain system. After one shaft missed, a second was dug, which also became flooded. Just south of the original shaft, they dug out what would be the fourth shaft within fifty feet and were faced with another setback. The new shaft collapsed into a cave and then was flooded. Fortunately, it happened during a break in work, and no one was killed. The men refused to enter the shafts, however, and all work was suspended.

By 1859 the syndicate again had raised the funds needed to resume work. Sixty-three men were hired, more shafts were dug, manual pumps were replaced by steam pumps. Still the Money Pit held its own against then-modern technology. A boiler explosion killed one of the men, and the work stopped again. The land surrounding the Money Pit was owned by John Smith and several others, but after the failure of what came to be called the Truro Syndicate, most of Oak Island was sold to Anthony Graves. Graves was a local farmer who never took part in the excavations, although he leased the land to the treasure hunters. A new syndicate was formed to lease the land and try to drill again, but this syndicate failed to raise the necessary money.

In 1866 another company was formed with the goal of building a larger dam. Work started, but the Atlantic Ocean refused to cooperate, and the second dam was flooded. This short-lived company sank a few more shafts, which came to complicate matters for later ventures, but nothing new was found. Meanwhile, the land owned by Anthony Graves reverted to famland. In 1880 the owner was plowing when just eighty feet away from the original pit, the earth gave way. Excavators later guessed that a tunnel lying underneath caused the cave-in, but no one came forward to explore further. It was also said that a coin bearing the unlikely date of A.D. 1317 was discovered, but like the inscribed stone, the coin also disappeared. No modern numismatist was given the chance to study the discovery.

In 1891 twenty-four-year-old Frederick Blair of Amherst, Nova Scotia, was next to take on the Money Pit. His firm, the Oak Island Treasure Company, was founded with sixty thousand dollars' worth of shareholders' money, half of which was needed to lease the land. Using modern technology to stop the water trap from flooding the shafts, the men drilled into the tunnel system and exploded 160 pounds of dynamite. The shafts still flooded. Experimenting with red dye, it was discovered that another water tunnel system existed, this time extending from a beach on the other side of the island. A deeper, six-hundred foot tunnel from the south side of the beach was a second trap to protect whatever was concealed in the Money Pit.

Besides disappointment, the 1890s brought new discoveries. A drill had consistently veered off in one spot at a depth of 151 feet. Deciding the obstacle must be a chest, the drillers pierced whatever was deflecting their drill and brought up what appeared to be parchment. The drill had mangled the parchment, and only the letters "V.I." could be read. Other efforts brought up a pick, a seal-oil lamp, and an axe head, items that Blair decided dated to at least the 1680s. The Blair expedition also suffered the second fatality in the history of the pit—a worker fell to his death from a hoisting platform.

In 1897 more metal and concrete believed to be from a vault were brought up. Analysis in Halifax agreed that the substance was concrete and therefore man-made. Similarly, analysis of the "puddled clay" confirmed that it was not unlike the clay used by miners from the sixteenth and seventeenth centuries. Despite being more convinced than ever that a great treasure lay just below, personal bankruptcy threatened members of the company, and a new infusion of money proved elusive.

In 1909 Franklin Delano Roosevelt, then a young lawyer with the establishment firm of Carter, Ledyard, and Milburn, was summering off the coast of New Brunswick. Having heard of the activity in nearby Nova Scotia, he joined the search. He, too, invested in Blair's syndicate and brought in other well-heeled establishment figures, including Duncan Harris, Albert Gallatin, and John Shields (wealthy family members and friends) to invest alongside him. Roosevelt personally visited the site and even participated in the work. Surprisingly, Roosevelt was no stranger to treasure hunting. In 1896, as a young man, he had spent four days digging on Grand Manan Island for Captain Kidd's treasure. As president, he once had a navy cruiser land on Cocos Island, 350 miles southwest of Costa Rica, where the privateer Edward Davis reputedly stashed loot from his adventures along the Spanish Pacific coast.[6]

Franklin Roosevelt was not the last celebrity to become fascinated by Oak Island. Future syndicates organized to search for the treasure claimed investments from John Wayne, Admiral Richard Byrd, Errol Flynn, and Vincent Astor but left these notable investors no richer.[7] The efforts of Blair's group continued. Dynamite was again used, and more cement was discovered; as ever, no money and no treasure were given up by the Money Pit. Blair's head engineer, Harry Bowdoin, claimed that "any competent engineer could clear up the affair in no time."[8] He was accused of using the expedition as a means of getting publicity for his own salvage company, and after his failure he declared in an article that he believed the Money Pit was nothing but an elaborate hoax.

Smaller operations continued over the years until, in 1922, a major investor-participant was found. William Chappell of Sydney, Nova Scotia, and his son, Mel, joined Fred Blair. Mel was an engineer, and he decided that an open pit and a centrifugal pump would be used. Again the latest equipment that modern technology could muster failed to open the secret of the pit. Still, the open pit gave up an ancient anchor fluke and more concrete. Away from the pit another tantalizing clue was found by Chappell as he walked around the island. A stone triangle had been set up as a marker, which came to be regarded twenty years later as very significant. In 1937 Charles Roper, a Halifax-based land surveyor hired by Hedden, checked the measurements between certain drilled rocks and the triangle, but his survey offered no explanation for the marker. In the 1950s Fred Nolan, a surveyor from Bedford, Nova Scotia, agreed that numerous stones had been set in place as measurement markers. Nolan, who now owns part of the island, believes this triangle is a key to determining where the treasure actually lies.

To date, the marker has been just a clue; however, it has not helped

Nolan, or anyone else, find answers. The Chappell expedition, too, ran out of money, as all the preceding ventures had. The Depression of the 1930s did not stop two more minor attempts, but the Money Pit yielded no new secrets to the treasure seekers. In 1934 Gilbert Hedden, who had been the manager of a family-owned steel business in New Jersey, an auto dealer, and the mayor of Chatham in his home state, was just the wealthy investor Blair and Chappell were seeking. Chappell, who died in 1946, was sixty-seven, and his time was running out. Partnership with Hedden brought electricity to the island and a contract drilling team from the coal mining districts of Pennsylvania, but no results. After three years the expedition's failure as well as business needs back home sent Hedden packing.

Chappell and Hedden had not found any treasure, but they did add to the body of research on mysterious Oak Island. In addition to rediscovering the stone triangle, Heddon found other monuments. These included two distant boulders with mooring holes similar to those the Norse sailors left behind in Norway—and even Maine, according to some historians. Hedden brought in a surveyor who found large stones that had been placed there to form of an arrowhead. Working from the highest point of the island, the survey indicated another spot to dig near the original shaft, but nothing came from the new location. After the death of Chappell, his son Mel, who was ten years old when he first came to Oak Island in 1895, continued as owner and treasure hunter until 1975. After Hedden, another engineer, Edwin Hamilton, took over but failed to uncover anything new. By then so many shafts had been dug that the location of the original pit was uncertain. Hamilton's efforts may have been successful in only one respect—he believed he had located one of the two water tunnels and the original shaft.

In the 1950s George Green, a petroleum engineer from Texas, and John Lewis, a gold miner with a ten-thousand-dollar new drill, tried and failed to make new discoveries. In 1960 a stunt motorcycle rider, Robert Restall, his son, and two workers were added to the list of fatalities claimed by the unyielding Money Pit. Restall had devoted five years to trying to cope with the water problem and to compiling measurements of the island. One August day he was overcome by carbon monoxide in the shaft. His son went down to help him but also collapsed. Two others made heroic efforts to save the father and son but were also lost, and the worked again was halted. As always, others came forward to take their places. In 1965 a California geologist, Bob Dunfield, and a Miami contractor, Dan Blankenship, were next. Dunfield brought in heavy equipment, including two bulldozers, to clear the original pit area and a seventy-ton crane to deepen the hole and dig trenches to stop the water flow. He even built a causeway that now leads from the island to the shore of Nova Scotia. His critics were not few in number, and complaining townspeople and unexplained equipment problems plagued his operation. His work covered up the stone triangle, which has since been re-formed.

Chronology

1795   Discovery of Money Pit
1802   Onslow Syndicate
1849   Truro Syndicate
1861   Various Groups (Graves no longer involved)
1893   Blair (in 1897 the Chappells join him)
1909   Henry Bowdoin (Blair still involved)
1931   Chappell/Blair
1934   Hedden first becomes involved
1955   Greene (Chappell still involved)
1959   Restall does extensive work on drainage system
1965   Dunfield constructs causeway to the island and Blankenship takes over excavation
1970   Tobias forms Triton Alliance and starts the current excavation

In 1966 Dunfield's time ran out as his deal with Mel Chappell was not renewed. He tried to buy the island from Chappell but was turned down. Dunfield left but Blankenship was hooked. From the day a *Readers' Digest* article about the treasure captured his attention, he had become obsessed with Oak Island. He sold his successful contracting business in Miami and moved to Nova Scotia permanently. Four years later, in 1970, David C. Tobias of Montreal incorporated the latest syndicate under the name Triton Alliance. Named for a Greek demigod who was the son of the sea god Poseidon, Triton still runs the excavation of Oak Island today. Blankenship was one of the first investors, starting as a minority partner with Dunfield in 1965. With a farmer from New York, Dan Hanskee, the two have been working the pit ever since. In 1990 on my first visit to Oak Island, Dan Hanskee gave me a guided tour of the island while the work continued. Borehole 10X is the name given to the current shaft, which the drillers believe is closest to the original efforts. Borehole 10X was in operation then and until recently was still in operation. Mel Chappell has since died. Tobias, Blankenship, and Nolan all still own lots.

With the excavation of Oak Island four years past its bicentennial, the investment of its most important current backer is keeping the project going. Tobias, a Montreal millionaire who runs more than one business, has the money to invest but not the time. For this reason, Blankenship and Tobias have been in equal partnership over the past several years. Other investors have been invited in through a stock offering, but even after the success of the famed treasure hunter Mel Fisher's limited partnership, which paid off very handsomely, new investors have not always been easy to find. Tobias continues to sink his own funds into the operation, and between the costs of legal wrangling and digging, his personal contribution has passed the million-dollar mark. The Triton Alliance is now a consortium of fifty-two American and Canadian investors, including George Jennison, a past president of the Toronto Stock Exchange; Charles Brown, a Boston developer; Donald Webster, a Toronto-based financier; Bill Sobey, of Canada's largest supermarket chain; Bill Parkin, a weapon systems designer for the Pentagon; and Gordon Coles, Nova Scotia's deputy attorney general.

The Triton group has allied itself with another syndicate to fund the exploration. The newest group is called Oak Island Discoveries, a partnership between a Boston millionaire, David Mugar, and film director William Cosel. Triton and Oak Island Discoveries together are funding a series of tests that will determine their next step. The prestigious Woods

Hole Oceanographic Institute is conducting the testing on the shafts with equipment that is similar to that used in exploring the Titanic in 1991. If the testing is successful, Tobias and Mugar will go on to raise another ten million dollars. The contribution of Tobias goes well beyond the job of fund-raising. Under his leadership the excavation has seen the most scientific approach to date as well as the most extensive historic research into just who is responsible for the elaborate pit and what might be found someday. Tobias used the resources of the National Museum of Natural Science in Ottawa, which confirmed that the fibrous material was coconut fiber. He turned to the Steel Company of Canada to analyze the iron spikes found in the coffer dam and found that the spikes had been forged prior to 1790.[9]

In 1990 Tobias said he was convinced that the English navigator and privateer Sir Francis Drake was the primary candidate for the person responsible for the Money Pit; Drake had raided the Spanish Main for Queen Elizabeth I, sharing in the spoils, and Tobias contended that Drake needed to preserve a portion of his gains outside of England. He believes that the pit was Drake's stash of part of the loot he had taken for Queen Elizabeth I. His well-researched theory, however, is not the only one with merit. After two hundred years of work there are certain facts that have been established without doubt. First, the underground workings exist and are man-made. Second, whoever constructed the Money Pit was knowledgeable about advanced hydraulics. Third, the work, which must have taken a year or longer, was completed before 1750, when settlement would have made such construction impossible to keep secret. Apart from what we know is true, it is possible to make assumptions as well. What was buried had to be of considerable value for someone to go to such lengths to conceal it. The Money Pit has so far defeated any attempts to claim its secret, and there is a very good chance that a treasure of incredible value is still there, awaiting discovery.

Chapter 2

THEORIES AND SUSPECTS: WHO DUG THE MONEY PIT AND WHAT LIES BELOW

The Money Pit has defied engineers and excavators for more than two hundred years, and so has the mystery of just who is responsible for its existence. A complete list of suspects might include any individual or group of people that are known to have inhabited the area. A people referred to by anthropologists as Paleo-Indians, or the Red-paint people, were in the Canadian Maritime Provinces from as early as 8500 B.C. While little is known about them, it is safe to say that they were not aware of advanced hydraulics.

As early as A.D. 700 and as late as A.D. 1100, a more advanced culture inhabited the Atlantic coasts. They are generally referred to as the Micmac peoples, a name derived from their term *nikmaq,* meaning "my kin friends."[1] The Micmac were nomadic, dividing their year between wintering inland and summering along the Atlantic coast. They became skilled at fishing the coastal Atlantic and by the eighteenth century had developed a writing system.[2] Again, we can eliminate this group from the suspect list because they lacked both the motive and the means to construct an underground vault as complex as the Money Pit.

Conventional histories of North America often start with the state-sponsored explorations of the New World. This would leave us with a narrow time frame that would begin in 1497, when the first European explorer reached Canada, and end sometime before 1795, when the area became populated and the pit was discovered. This first explorer was John Cabot, an Italian sailing under the English flag five years after Columbus reached the Caribbean. Cabot is given credit as the first European to have reached the Atlantic coast of Canada. He made landfall on June 24, 1497, which was Saint John the Baptist's feast day. He established no colonies but may have opened up the coast of Newfoundland and Labrador for European fishermen. In all likelihood, they had been fishing the rich banks well before Columbus, although they knew the area as a fishing ground and not as a "New World" or the sought-after passage to Cathay for which Columbus had been searching.[3]

Five years after Cabot's venture, a Portuguese expedition to America took place. Pedro de Barcelos, a landowner from the Azores, led the expedition. On board was a friend and fellow Azorean, João Fernandes.[4] Because Fernandes's time away from the sea was spent farming, his nickname was *lavrador*, meaning "farmer" in Portuguese. Although the exact landfall of this expedition is debated, the Canadian province of Labrador received its name from the nickname of João Fernandes, a farmer on expedition.

The Portuguese, too, were disappointed in finding only icy waters and no exotic trading ports of the Orient. Also sailing under the flag of Portugal was Gaspar Corte Real.[5] He may have reached Newfoundland, but records of his journey are sparse and inexact. Both the date and the length of time of his expedition are debated. On his second voyage his entire expedition was lost. A brother, Miguel, set sail to find him but was also lost. If the rich fishing banks off Newfoundland and Labrador had ever been a secret, they were no longer. Bretons, Basques, French, and English fishing ships did their own unrecorded exploration. Fishermen did not keep logs, but they did leave behind certain clues. Some historians claim the Portuguese were there much earlier than the accepted dates and point to the native North American name for the Grand Banks—*baccaloes*, which is the Portuguese word meaning "cod fish."[6]

By the time another Italian, Giovanni Verrazano, sailing under the French flag, reached the New World, fishing fleets and fishing shacks could be seen along the rivers and bays the Europeans would "discover." His expedition took place in 1524 and lasted for only a few short months. Verrazano received credit for giving Nova Scotia one of its earliest names, which he is said to have put on the maps as "Arcadia."[7] This name will feature prominently in the tale of just how an ancient treasure reached the New World and the Money Pit. While its modern meaning holds little of interest to the uninitiated, for a certain few, the theme of Arcadia and the transmission of an underground stream of knowledge passed through generations is of paramount importance.

Giovanni Verrazano, too, might have been part of an elite group, as were several of the important world explorers. He lived in a world still dominated by the terrifying hold that the Inquisition exerted. New ideas, including the possibility of undiscovered lands, were suspect and could earn a man of science prison and torture as easily as a reward. Explorers, and men of science, had a need to attach themselves to the several societies (which we will meet later) that are known to have existed at this time and that allowed a certain degree of insurance against persecution. Verrazano's family crest included a six-pointed star, which some believe indicated he was not the Christian he was purported to be. Religion played an important role during the Inquisition, and a non-Catholic would be disqualified from leading a mission of such importance. The religion of Columbus is still a matter of nagging debate.[8]

Just where did Verrazano place the name Arcadia? Reports of the early explorers and mapmakers do not always agree. One mapmaker shows Arcadia as being north of the Hudson River. Others say it was the Outer Banks of North Carolina and correctly state that Verrazano derived the name from a very popular piece of literature by Jacobo Sannazaro, set in Greece.[9] Sannazaro's *Arcadia* had been printed fifteen separate times before Verrazano reached America. Because Verrazano correctly noted the latitude, Morison for one believes Maine and the Canadian Maritimes are Arcadia.[10] Arcadia, as defined by Sannazaro, was the idyllic world, a

Garden of Eden lost to the modern (medieval) world. It was life in a pure state, where thought and deed were free to wander away from the threat of official punishment by church and state. The English philosopher Sir Francis Bacon and others believed this world could exist only outside Europe and carried the theme further. They believed in the creation of a new country in which certain freedoms would be guaranteed and all religions would be tolerated. Bacon described this country in his *New Atlantis*. Interestingly enough, the French name for Nova Scotia was L'Acadie, a label they applied from the native Micmac word for the "land." Mapmakers may have made the two names into one, and Nova Scotia was for a while called L'Acadie and Arcadia.

Verrazano's trip to America in 1524 had been short compared to other such European voyages. He left the Madeira Islands off the coast of Africa on January 17th and was back in France by mid-June of the same year. The only place he had spent any time was in the area of what is now Rhode Island, where he described the natives as "the most civilized in customs" and "inclining more to whiteness"—a description that might indicate both previous contact and intermarriage with earlier European explorers.[11] Verrazano was fond of Greek place-names and gave Rhode Island its name after his coastal visit, again taking the name from Sannazaro's work.

The French navigator Jacques Cartier was next to sail to the New World, with a higher purpose than fishing in mind.[12] In 1534 Cartier's fleet encountered a large French fishing vessel, which Cartier claimed was "lost," obviously annoyed that he was not the first to reach the region. He explored the coasts of Newfoundland, Prince Edward Island, and the Gaspé Peninsula. In his travels he met up with two fleets of Micmacs, each consisting of forty to fifty vessels. They wanted to trade with the single French ship, but being outnumbered Cartier was cautious. Finally, he did permit a small convoy of nine large canoes to dock near enough to the French to exchange goods. The incident seems to give evidence of a native understanding of trade that was developed from past experience. As Cartier sailed farther up the Saint Lawrence River, he encountered another fleet of canoes, this time carrying Huron natives. He thought the Huron were like the Micmac, but in appearance they seemed much poorer; he wrote that their only homes were over-turned boats. It is more likely that he encountered a Huron fishing fleet far away from home and making temporary camp. Cartier's trip back to Europe took only three weeks, demonstrating just how easy it is for experienced sailors to cross the North Atlantic.

In 1604 the French explorer Samuel de Champlain reached Nova Scotia and established a temporary settlement at La Have in Nova Scotia, fifteen miles away from Oak Island.[13] He later moved to another settlement on the Bay of Fundy, where he stayed for three years. Champlain's settlements in Nova Scotia were for the most part short-lived, and little activity took place apart from fur trading with the native population. The relationship between France and England in Europe was hostile, and such hostility was carried to the New World. The ownership of the area was contested by the British and the French, but no major military operations took place apart from the building of a fort at Louisbourg on Cape Breton Island, far from the Oak Island area, in 1644. Engineers were imported for the construction of the fort, which gave rise to a theory that an "underground bank" might have been constructed on Oak Island. Military payrolls would often be in the form of gold and silver, and the threat of raids on land and piracy on the seas formed the basis for the need of such a repository. The theory is further based on the availability of labor. It can thus be said that the first suspect, the French military, had both a motive and a means to construct such a complex "bank" as the Money Pit. The theory has merit, but since there is no precedence for such construction, its merit is only that it simply cannot be ignored. The French who built Louisbourg were not in control of Oak Island and the Mahone Bay region for long, however, leaving it to the British in a later treaty.

Between 1606 and 1749 most of the southern half of Nova Scotia was uninhabited. On the northern coast along the Bay of Fundy and the Minas Basin, sixty French Acadian families settled. In 1632 several of these families crossed the southern part of the peninsula and settled at La Have; present day Lunenburg is not far from Oak Island. The continuing hostility between France and England led to the Treaty of Utrecht, which transferred Nova Scotia to England in 1715. It did not stop the growth of the French settlements already in place. Nova Scotia became more rapidly populated by the English after Halifax was founded in 1749, forty miles from Mahone Bay. The British, however, were concerned that the Acadian population was possibly as high as ten thousand, so they induced British colonists to settle in the area. Many of these settlers came from American colonies in New England. Ten years later, in 1759, the Shoreham Grant gave land to these settlers from New England. At that time, Oak Island, one of 350 islands in Mahone Bay, was divided and deeded but not settled. By 1795, when the three adolescents went digging for treasure, it was still uninhabited. Interestingly enough, to those who believe pirates built the Money Pit, the name Mahone derives from the French word *mahonne,* meaning a low-lying pirate ship mostly used in Mediterranean waters.

In 1755 the hostilities between the English and French continued. The British concern about being outnumbered by the French caused them to forcibly remove six thousand French Acadians to points from Georgia to Louisiana. The poem entitled *Evangeline* by the American poet Henry Wadsworth Longfellow immortalizes this forced exodus. Many stayed in the American South, where "Acadian" became corrupted to "Cajun." Others found their way back to their Nova Scotia home. Along with the skirmishes between natives and colonists and the wars between the French and the English, there were pirates. With France and Britain almost always at war, privateering and piracy did not cease.

The list of possibilities of just who could be responsible for burying a treasure on Oak Island is not a short one. From the nineteenth century to the present, those who searched for the treasure during the summer would spend their winters rooting out leads to what they might eventually bring up from the depths of the Money Pit. Theories of who hid the treasure are as numerous as the islands in Mahone Bay: the crown jewels of the royalty of England and France, pirate banks, Viking hoards, the original manuscripts of William Shakespeare, and even the booty of a Mayan ship are said to be buried there. There are even theories that declare that the pit was not dug to hold a treasure trove at all but was used as an elaborate hydraulic lift to clean and repair ships. The tunnels and drains were employed simply to raise and lower the level of water.

This theory, not unlike Oak Island itself, has a few holes in it. The first is that most reasonable estimates of the time required to construct the Money Pit say it took more than a year as well as an immense amount of labor. Since the Bay of Fundy is within close sailing range of Mahone Bay, and this bay may have the greatest difference in sea level between high tide and low tide of any location in North America, there existed a much simpler method of what is called "careening" a ship. A ship can be beached and repaired at low tide and carried back out to sea at high tide. No elaborate structure would be necessary. Another hole in the theory is that no such complicated structure similar to the Oak Island Money Pit exists anywhere else in the world. No precedent for such a complex ship-cleaning device exists, and the area would be a very unlikely place to invent one.

There are also claims that the pit was a natural occurrence—a sinkhole that sucked in logs or one in which stones and logs were simply thrown in to close the hole. Michael Bradley, an author discussed in Fanthorpe's *Secrets of Rennos-le-Chateau*, proposed the theory of a "limestone blowhole" created by nature. These theories ignore the fact that the flagstones were brought from the mainland, that the oaken platforms were evenly spaced, that cove drains with foreign fibers were put in place, that a false beach was built, and that stones were inscribed. The theory also overlooks the fact that the island was uninhabited before the earliest digging started and that the need to fill in a sinkhole on an uninhabited island would be minimal at best. The Money Pit was clearly man-made.

In this light, it is necessary to compile a list of candidates who could be responsible for burying the treasure and to more closely examine the time frame. While official and state-sponsored voyages of exploration are often a starting point, there are also unofficial and unsponsored journeys. Our first suspects then are the Vikings.

The Vikings

The Norse travelers can be considered suspects because they are one group that we now can say with certainty crossed the Atlantic before

Columbus. Evidence in favor of the Vikings must start with their reputation as marauders of the sea. As such, it is no stretch of the imagination to believe that they might have had treasure to bury. While it was
once a matter of debate, we now know that the Vikings had reached
North America by A.D. 1001 at the latest. That this date is no longer in
question is testament to the persistent effort of the respected team of
Helge Ingstad (a former governor of East Greenland and Spitsbergen)
and Anne Stine Ingstad, an archeologist.[14] Basing their belief on an Icelandic map dated to 1590 and directions in the Norse sagas, they decided to explore Newfoundland. There they uncovered Norse ruins on
that province's northern coast. After lengthy excavations at L'Anse aux
Meadows, the Ingstads proved that a farming community had existed
there, able to sustain one to three hundred hardy souls.

The remains of the five- to six-room sod houses, a smithy, a kiln, a
bathhouse, and several boat sheds have been excavated. Numerous artifacts, including iron nails and rivets, a soapstone spinning wheel, an oil
lamp, and bronze cloak pins, were also recovered. The excavation, begun
in the 1960s, firmly established that the Vikings had at least one settlement in the New World five hundred years before Columbus. L'Anse
aux Meadows has been reconstructed to show what life was like for the
Norse settlers, and the area is now a Canadian historic park. The discovery of other Norse artifacts in New England, farther north and west in
Canada, and as far west as Minnesota in the United States (the authenticity of these artifacts remains questionable) do not merit the acceptance that the Newfoundland farm does, although there is little doubt
that the Viking ships could have reached Nova Scotia.

The Vikings, however, lacked the means and motivation to construct
the Money Pit. Those who reached the New World, by island-hopping
through the North Atlantic, were not plunderers, but farmers.[15] Unlike
their Norse cousins—the invaders who traveled and raided the Mediterranean, the Black Sea, the navigable rivers of Europe, and the coasts of
nearby Ireland—these Vikings were poor even by European standards
of their time. They did not have any treasure to hide, nor did they have
the ability to construct such complicated facilities and complex hydraulic systems.

Native North Americans

Another theory is that native North Americans may have been responsible for the Money Pit. Certainly they were capable of much more than the Europeans have given them credit for. They had complex governments, established trade, and advanced scientific knowledge that went beyond the ability of early explorers to comprehend. Only now are we able to understand the rock structures that served as solar and lunar calendars, found in the Southwest and northern Mexico. Similar structures, with grander designs, have been discovered in New England but are still dismissed since they do not fit into our understanding of the native peoples who populated most of North America before Columbus.[16] While we now accept the idea that trade took place between native tribes from Florida and those of New England and that southeastern tribes traded as far away as the Rockies, stone calendars as sophisticated as Stonehenge are dismissed because many historians are afraid of the implications. Still, there is no record of native North Americans having prized a monetary treasure enough to commit to such a great amount of labor to constructing a hiding place for their prize. Indeed, nomadic peoples would often find hoarding an inconvenience. The opposite extreme, their custom of potlatch, exhibits the belief in giving rather than receiving.[17] Despite the complicated calendars and mounds found across North America, none have shown evidence of a knowledge of advanced hydraulics. With a lack of motive and means, Native Americans can be eliminated from our list.

Spanish Marauders and Incan Defenders

The Spanish may have been the first settlers in America to amass a great deal of wealth for their efforts. Spanish treasure ships laden with gold and silver would often fall victim to shipwrecks and pirates that sought the treasure for themselves. The excavators of the Money Pit left few stones unturned in their search for answers. In their desperation they went to any lengths to further their knowledge. Psychics and dowsers were consulted along with scientists and engineers. In one of their less conventional attempts, Frederick Blair and Mel Chappell hired a psychic known as an "automatic writer," a medium who allows the dead to communicate with the living. According to this medium, the treasure hidden deep in the Money Pit was Incan gold.

The story told was that about 1524, the Spanish conquistador Francisco Pizarro reached the Incan city of Tumbes in Peru.[18] He did not yet have the authority to loot their treasure, so he left two men to guard the city. Four years later, after finally receiving authorization from King Charles V of Spain, Pizarro returned to find the city empty and in ruins. It had fallen victim to a civil war between King Atahualpa and his half-brother, Huáscar, the pretender to the throne. In the course of Huáscar's bid for victory the city had been plundered. Through the medium, John Wicks, the spirit of a priest who had been one of the men left behind by Pizarro at Tumbes told Frederick Blair and Mel Chappell that the treasure had been carried overland to Panama and put on Incan-built ships. These ships were battered by storms on their voyage north and came ashore on Nova Scotia, where the specially constructed hiding place was built.

Most would call the story preposterous; it is in fact complete fiction. History records the fact that it was Atahualpa who emerged victorious from the civil war, and he kept all of his gold and silver at Tumbes. This treasure he later turned over to Pizarro, filling a room once with gold and twice with silver in an attempt to buy his freedom. The Spaniards had him strangled. Spanish gold has always captured the romantic imagination of treasure hunters. It is possible that of all the ships that were supposed to have crossed the Atlantic with bulging holds of booty, one may have been diverted to a secret stash of some colonial governor, never to be found by its owners or by later historians. If so, it would more likely have been buried by Spanish conquistadors, rather than Incan sailors, in the cold North Atlantic. Spanish ships did sail with the currents on their return trip and would often go far north, within four hundred miles of Nova Scotia.

The ships that were lost during the Spanish conquest of Mexico and South America number in the hundreds, and not all of them went down off the coast of Florida or in the Caribbean. In fact, the North Atlantic has more than its share of individual wrecks. In Nova Scotia, tiny Sable Island has claim to 250 such shipwrecks. The odds are high that Spanish ships, blown off course, are among those that lie wrecked in the treacherous waters of Nova Scotia. Could one or more have landed on tiny Oak Island and, unable to return home, buried its treasure under such a massive structure? The Spanish did employ miners for operations in South America, and it would not have been uncommon to have a mining engineer on board.

In *The Big Dig*, D'Arcy O'Connor proposed that such an event may have happened.[19] A battered ship is forced to land for repairs and is unburdened of its weighty cargo. The agent of the king who had the responsibility of safekeeping the king's treasure orders a vault be constructed. Here the treasure will be stored until a better ship can be sent back. Once the work is done, the wounded ship, repaired as well as possible under the circumstances, sails off again, only to sink at sea. Thus there are no witnesses and no evidence—only a truly secret treasure. The idea of gold and silver looted by the Spanish conquistadors is intriguing. If the Spanish themselves did not build the elaborate Money Pit, there is the possibility that one of the many pirates and privateers who raided the Spanish Main was responsible. One of history's most well-known privateers was Sir Francis Drake.

Sir Francis Drake

In 1990 I spoke with David Tobias, the current owner of most of Oak Island and the force behind much of the excavation since 1970. His theory is that Sir Francis Drake had the pit constructed to hide a portion of his privateering spoils. Drake made his name raiding the Pacific coast of Spain's territory in the New World, where the Spanish assumed the English would not tread. That he was never hung as a pirate is testimony to his relationship with the Crown. He started his career young, capturing small ships in American waters. In 1572 he was ready for the big time and joined forces with William Le Testu, a French pirate who was later hung for his joint efforts with Drake. Drake not only survived but returned home a wealthy man.

In 1576 Drake had a private meeting with Queen Elizabeth I, presenting a secret plan within a secret plan, according to James A. Williamson, his biographer.[20] His cover story was that he was going to sail into the Pacific to discover lands to claim for his queen. This secret could safely be leaked, since it caused no embarrassment to the queen. The real secret may have been an arrangement to split the rewards of piracy with the Crown. On Drake's voyage, his ship, the *Golden Hind,* circumnavigated the globe after taking on twenty-six tons of Spanish gold. Because Spain and England were not at war at the time, his acts could not openly be sponsored by Queen Elizabeth. We know, however, that he returned home as a hero, allowed to lead an openly wealthy lifestyle. He purchased the home of a rival and spent his own funds improving the water supply of his hometown, Plymouth, England.[21]

After a few years of enjoying the good life, he returned to sea with the blessing of the queen. England was by then at war. During 1585 he raided ports and looted ships from the Caribbean to the Azores. Ten years later he set out for what became his last raid, he died of dysentery in Panama less than a year after setting sail. Tobias claims that after one of Drake's raids he employed a boatload of Cornish miners to construct the secret treasure depository on Oak Island. The idea is certainly plausible in that Drake had the ability to mount such an expedition, which would have been too costly for most other individual pirates. He also could employ the technology, which an ordinary pirate could not. I considered the theory and at first rejected it—ironically, because it fit too well. It appeared to be just another "Captain Kidd" theory, which gave this short-lived pirate credit for half of the treasure stories of the Atlantic coast. Looking further, the theory seemed more believable but still appeared to lack a motive. Drake had no reason to hide his wealth; in fact, the act of buying his rival's home was characteristic of Drake's flaunting of his wealth. He publicly spent his funds, and even though his acts of piracy were never officially condoned, they were officially rewarded. In 1580 he was even knighted by the queen.

It was wise to have friends in high places in the sixteenth century. The Inquisition had blazed across Europe starting in 1558, and Queen Elizabeth I of England had no room for its persecution of those who did not adhere to the Catholic doctrine, until she, too, was excommunicated. One reason for her expulsion from the Church was her belief that kings and queens could heal with their touch. She had even consulted her astrologer, John Dee, to fix the date for her coronation. Dee later wrote a book entitled *The Perfect Art of Navigation,* which convinced Drake of the possibility of circumnavigating the globe. While she lived her intellectual life through magicians and alchemists like Dr. Dee and Dr. Philip Sidney, Elizabeth lived a life of adventure through her privateers Sir Francis Drake and Sir Walter Raleigh. Raleigh, however, fell out of the queen's favor and was banished from her court.

Under James I, Raleigh was imprisoned for conspiracy against the Crown and languished in prison until 1616. There he wrote his own history of the world. In it he declared the sea god of the Philistines, Dagon, to be the same god as the Greek Triton. Just why this was important to him is unknown, but the god of Greek mythology has some significance to the Oak Island mystery. Triton was the god who came to the aid of the argonauts in their search for the Golden Fleece. Raleigh also wrote of his belief that the philosophers' stone, the hypothetical substance that medieval alchemists believed would convert base metals to gold, was the Golden Fleece sought by Jason and his argonauts. Both Raleigh and Drake had pushed Elizabeth to pursue her rights to land in the New World. Since the Elizabethan court included magicians and alchemists like Dr. Dee, was there a prevalent belief that the philosophers' stone, or the Golden Fleece, was in America? The Elizabethan court was a whirlwind of intrigue, and with the likes of the mysterious Dr. Dee and plotters like Sir Francis Bacon pushing Elizabeth to take her rightful place as Queen of America, we cannot rule out agents of the court as the catalyst for Oak Island's construction.[22] Another intriguing theory, however, is the belief that the original works of Shakespeare lie hidden in the Money Pit.

Shakespeare's Manuscripts

More than one hundred years after the Bard's death, a British clergyman, James Wilmot, decided in the 1770s that he would write about the man who was one of his two favorite writers.[23] He went to Stratford-upon-Avon to collect stories about his subject, only to discover that there were none to be found. He then tried to locate books that once belonged to Shakespeare, since surely a man displaying such a worldly intelligence would have had a large private stock of books. Those, too, were not to be found. What Wilmot did discover was that this respected writer was a butcher's son who took up acting, a less than respectable career in those times. He also determined that most of the stories about the butcher's son were made up by people who stood to gain by the cottage industry of Shakespeare idolatry in Stratford-upon-Avon. Finally, Wilmot came to the conclusion that the works of Shakespeare were not his works at all. Shakespeare did not even own any of the original manuscripts at his death, nor did he provide in his will for any to go to friends or relatives. In fact, Wilmot concluded, the plays written by Shakespeare were written by his other favorite author, Sir Francis Bacon.

Bacon had the worldly intelligence that Shakespeare only seemed to have. He had studied such varied topics as botany, law, government, history, and medicine, while there is no evidence that Shakespeare could even read or write. As a member of the Elizabethan court, Bacon had reason to hide the fact that he was writing for the theater. It was at best less than respectable; at worst it was mocking to the queen, who did not appreciate the works of Shakespeare.

Later, in 1857, another British writer, William Henry Smith, published *Bacon and Shakespeare*, which chronicled the lives of both men and came to the same conclusion. Bacon had the knowledge to write the works; Shakespeare did not.[24] In America, Delia Bacon (no relation to Sir Francis), a schoolteacher, author, and lecturer, came to the same conclusion. Her work led others to question Shakespeare's authorship; the list eventually grew to include John Greenleaf Whittier, Ralph Waldo Emerson, Nathaniel Hawthorne, and Oliver Wendell Holmes.[25] Ten years after Smith's book appeared, a librarian commissioned by the duke of Northumberland to seek out and preserve original manuscripts discovered manuscripts that had been in Bacon's possession and a list of other works, not in the folio, that were allegedly written by Shakespeare.[26] From then on, other books on the subject of Bacon and Shakespeare

were released. There may be as many as four hundred such books cover-
ing the debate. Among those writers supporting the Bacon-as-author
thesis were such luminaries as Walt Whitman and Benjamin Disraeli. So
far, no one has located the manuscripts.

The debate still rages today. William Shakespeare was the son of an
illiterate butcher. His own children are known to have been illiterate,
and there is evidence that he himself was at best "unlettered" and that
he was paid by a supporter of Bacon for the use of his name.[27] The
mystery of the original manuscripts of the works attributed to
Shakespeare still plagues supporters of the Bacon theory. While the
manuscripts of most important English writers have made their way
into the museums of Britain, not a single one of Shakespeare's has surfaced. Bacon alluded to the fact that his real self would not be known
until after his death. Why would his real self have to be so concealed?
The answer can be found in the climate of the Elizabethan court.

His very close friend was Henry Wriothesely, the earl of Southampton.
The earl is known in history as the early patron of Shakespeare's works.
In fact, he allowed one of the Bard's works to be performed on the estate
of another friend, the earl of Essex. The play was *Richard II*, in which
Shakespeare questioned the divine rights of kings (and queens). Essex
and the earl of Southampton were then ordered arrested by the queen
and attempted to start a rebellion to avoid their fate. The rebellion and
their attempt to avoid death both failed. Sir Walter Raleigh and Sir
Francis Bacon were forced to choose sides—they sided with the queen.

Supporters of the Bacon theory believe this event to be the motive
behind the concealment of the manuscripts by Bacon. In 1911 a certain
Dr. Orville Owen came from Detroit to England to search for Bacon's
secret manuscripts.[28] From clues he had found in one Bacon text, he led
an expedition to Wales. Underneath the silt in the Wye River in southeast Wales, he found a stone and cement vault with coded inscriptions.
The vault itself was empty. Dr. Owen and others believed the works had
been there but later were removed to an even more secure location. The
same text that took Dr. Owen to Wales contained a formula for preserving texts in mercury. The fact that Bacon had written of concealing
works in mercury, and of constructing artificial springs, was brought to

the attention of Oak Island treasure seeker Gilbert Hedden, by a student at Michigan State University, Burrell Ruth, in 1939. Hedden acknowledged that flasks of mercury had indeed been found in a dump on the island.[29]

Sir Francis Bacon believed in the ideal of a New World. His most well-known work is the utopian fable *The New Atlantis.* In it, he proposed an ideal society, as many had hoped life in the New World would be. Bacon and his circle of friends in the Elizabethan court ended up owning property in the New World, although Bacon himself never made the trip to Canada to visit his property. The theory that Oak Island could be the repository of the underground works of a very public man has certain merits. The time frame fits, in light of the fact that Nova Scotia was parceled during Bacon's time. The means were also available, since Drake had miners and engineers at his disposal. There is motive at least on the part of Bacon himself. The idea of constructing the Money Pit complete with the massive expense; the hiring and swearing to secrecy of hundreds of engineers, miners, and laborers; and the transatlantic voyages required, however, seem elaborate at the least.

The theory that the Shakespearean originals were simply added to an already massive treasure hoard begins to hold water when the collusion of those in the court of Elizabeth is factored in. Bacon certainly had one foot in the visible world as a member of both Elizabeth's court and later that of her successor, James I. He had another foot in a darker world. In addition to harboring beliefs that challenged the rights of royalty, authoring works under the pseudonym of a living person, betraying friends to save his own neck, and taking bribes of which he was later convicted, he was also reputed to be homosexual (as was the earl of Southampton).[30] If all that were not enough baggage in a time when people were regularly executed for religious beliefs, Bacon may have been a member of a secret society known as the Invisible College.

This group was composed of those who struggled for academic freedom in a world where science was decreed heresy and witchcraft. Numerous scholars, scientists, biologists, doctors, and philosophers communicated with each other, but away from the watchful eye of the Church. In 1660 the Invisible College emerged into the world as the Royal Society, but in Bacon's time it was still deserving of suspicion. Bacon was at least aware of the group through his contact with several of its members. The Bacon link to Drake, Raleigh, Dr. Dee, and others will be shown to be very significant, but other theories abound. The next in a long line of suspects is the group we call the Acadians.

The Acadians

The British constantly harassed these French settlers because they were afraid that the French outnumbered the English. One theory proposes that the Acadians, once prosperous farmers and traders, built the Money Pit in preparation for raids by the English. The Acadians, of course, would have been correct in preparing for attack by the British when they took control of Nova Scotia. As we saw, the French were, in fact, forcibly evacuated from their homes and moved to locations as far away as Louisiana. The problem with the Acadians as suspects in the Money Pit scheme is that there is no evidence to back the theory that they ever amassed enough wealth to justify spending the time and effort to construct the secret complex. Religious persecution in Europe has contributed to another theory as well.

The English Catholics, the French Crown Jewels, and Exiled Huguenots

In the seventeenth century, the rising Protestant religion banned the trappings of the Catholic Church. Statues regarded as idolatry as well as gold and silver objects were confiscated from churches all over Britain. After the execution of Charles I in 1649, a hoard of these confiscated items disappeared. Oak Island theories have suggested that these items found their way to the New World and to the bottom of the Money Pit. In the same vein, the crown jewels of the French royalty, which disappeared during the French Revolution, also may have found their way into the Oak Island complex. It is a romantic idea, without any record or substantiation.

Another, more plausible possibility adds the French Huguenots to the list of candidates. In 1685 fifty thousand Huguenots left France to avoid persecution. Many went to America. From their home port in La Rochelle, France, these settlers found their way to New York and a town they named New Rochelle. In 1928 Dunbar Hinrichs, a historian from Nova Scotia, said that he had been told a story by a man in France, the story of an underground vault built in Haiti and used to store Huguenot wealth.[31] The unnamed storyteller also said that a second vault had been built in Nova Scotia. In Haiti evidence of a secret underground repository was supposedly found in 1947. Efforts to uncover it made by those excavating its Nova Scotia counterpart met with failure.

Everybody's Favorite: Captain Kidd

The most commonly accepted candidate for just who it was that hid the treasure in the Money Pit is Captain William Kidd. Before his execution for murder and piracy in 1701, Kidd made a last-ditch effort to save his life. He told the British authorities that he would reveal the location of a treasure worth one hundred thousand pounds sterling. While he said it was buried in the South China Sea, treasure hunters took that to mean it could lie anywhere from the warm seacoasts of the Caribbean to the colder waters of the Canadian Atlantic.

Kidd's career as a pirate was relatively brief.[32] As a successful and wealthy merchant skipper based in New York City, he led raids against the French and, starting in 1689, against pirates. In 1691 the Commonwealth of Massachusetts hired him to catch a group of pirates that had fled to Nova Scotia. Receiving a tenth of the booty as his reward, he found it to be a lucrative business. And so, like Sir Francis Drake, he became a privateer. Kidd was in the employ of King William III of England, his mission to suppress piracy. His territory stretched from New England to the Caribbean. Once at sea, Kidd began to indiscriminately attack anything that moved, including one ship flying the English colors. If this were not enough, he was also accused of the on-board murder of a member of his crew. In 1699 while wintering in the Indian Ocean, Kidd discovered that he was being denounced as a pirate and could expect to be arrested.

As insurance against losing all, he decided to take precautions. He transferred most of the loot captured from the *Quedagh Merchant* to another ship, the *St. Anthony.* The *St. Anthony* stopped first in Lewes, a town in Delaware, where some of the treasure was buried. Its second stop was in Oyster Bay, on the northern coast of Long Island, where Kidd may have buried more treasure. Sailing east from Long Island Sound, the ship then went to Gardiners Island on the extreme eastern end of Long Island and buried still more treasure. Other stops included Block Island and Rhode Island. Only on Gardiners Island would treasure be found and removed by agents of the Crown. Kidd's last stop before landing in New York City was to deliver a jeweled necklace to the wife of the earl of Bellomont. Not happy with the attempted bribe, Bellomont, the governor of New York, sent Kidd to Boston where he was arrested and sent to England for trial. The earl had financed Kidd and was entitled to seventy-five percent of the booty Kidd had captured. It was Bellomont's belief not only that he was not getting his fair share but also that Kidd's exploits would bring the governor under attack. Meanwhile, the *Quedagh Merchant*, Kidd's other ship, set sail to the West Indies. There she may have been taken by the man Kidd had entrusted to protect the ship. One man claimed that she was burned in the harbor at Santo Domingo. There was never any evidence that Kidd buried treasure in Nova Scotia, but legends of his booty spread anyway.

In 1935 Gilbert Hedden read a book entitled *Captain Kidd and His Skeleton Island.*[33] The book included a map that appeared to Hedden to depict Oak Island. The author, however, claimed that the island was in the South China Sea. At great expense and after much time, Hedden finally caught up with the author in England only to be told that the map was the author's creation. Despite the fact that pirate treasure rarely stayed buried for long and was usually placed in shallow locations, the theory of a pirate "bank" was advanced by Dunbar Hinrichs, the same man who had come up with the notion of the Huguenot banks. The Money Pit, it was said, had been built as an elaborate treasure trove where wandering pirates could deposit their stolen goods in a protected vault. The construction allowed protection not only from outsiders but also from other pirates. Although such banks were supposed to be located in Haiti and Madagascar, they have never been found. After the execution of Kidd in England, treasure searching became the rage all over the world. There has never been any hard evidence that Kidd was ever in Oak Island, but that did not stop anyone from believing he had buried a treasure on the island.

Military Payrolls

The turbulent eighteenth century history of the New World provides us with a few more ideas about just what might be hidden in the Money Pit. The Louisbourg fort of the French had been the recipient of substantial funds from France to rebuild the fort and to pay France's soldiers. The fort itself had cost millions to build, and the ongoing payment of soldiers, engineers, and common laborers required that the French have a more convenient local source of funds. In 1744 Louisbourg was lost to the English after a two-month seige, only to be handed back to the French again. It was clear that the fort was not invincible and was likely to be attacked in future hostilities. One theory has it that a secret repository was built away from the fort. While this theory provides motive and means, it remains untested and unproved.

The possibility of a lost payroll ship is another theory. Several ships sank in the Saint Lawrence Seaway and off the coast of the dangerous Sable Island. Other ships simply disappeared in storms, their location unrecorded. Still others were captured. No incident, however, points to the building of the Money Pit or to its use as a repository for funds. In 1746 a fleet of sixty-five ships was struck by a storm in the Atlantic. Many of the ships were lost, including several that went down off Nova Scotia's Sable Island. Many of the survivors were killed by disease. A fortune in the form of coins must have been aboard one of the ships just to pay the three thousand soldiers who were being transported by the fleet. Speculation has it that the surviving payroll ship may have made it to Oak Island, where the pay of the French soldiers was buried to save it from English hands.

The same type of hypothesis later applied to the British in Halifax. It is said that in 1775 George Washington had discussed invading the city. The British then allegedly constructed Oak Island to hide their payroll. In *The Money Pit* Rupert Furneaux says the Royal Corps of Engineers in Halifax could have constructed the shaft, but never buried the war chests of its army.[34] The army and their pay presumably were both sent home. By that time, however, such a project would have led nearby residents of Mahone Bay to discover the construction that could have taken a year to complete. After 1775 there was little opportunity to construct the Money Pit in secrecy.

UFOs and Ancient Civilizations

If pirates and payroll ships, Huguenots and Acadians, Shakespeare and Spanish conquistadors are not enough, William Croocker, in *The Oak Island Quest*, brings us theories not found elsewhere. He ties together Easter Island, the Bermuda Triangle, ancient Egypt, and UFOs to come to the conclusion that the Money Pit is evidence of an ancient civilization.[35] Looking at the idea logically, if aliens from another planet had spent the time to construct the pit, they would have been more imaginative in their choice of materials than spruce, oak, and flagstones.

The Secret of the Money Pit

To Mel Chappell's credit, no theory, even those of the "off the wall" category, went uninvestigated. One such theory was outlined in a letter dated 1934 from Charles B. Thomas of Great Falls, Montana. Thomas, an eighty-year-old insurance salesman living at a YMCA, said the "treasure of far greater value" than a pirate treasure or payroll ship consisted of "gold and sacred things of the temple of Jerusalem." It is unknown where Mr. Thomas had gained his supposed knowledge, but his revelation to Mr. Chappell may just end up being the closest to the truth.

Many of the extant theories are plausible, but the real story of the treasure that lies in the Money Pit could be even stranger. It starts in Jerusalem, where the treasures of King Solomon were stored in an underground complex. The temple was looted by the legions of Titus during Roman domination and the booty carried back to Rome, only to be stolen again. The same treasures were then taken by the Visigoths (who raided Rome) to the south of France and again protected underground. In France a secret society was formed to guard the treasure, and when the king and Church threatened the group, the treasure was carried to Roslin, Scotland, where one family was named as permanent guardians. In Scotland an underground complex took years to build; when it was complete, the trove was threatened by the armies of the English king. The threat of an attack on newly independent Scotland required the treasure to be moved once more, this time to Nova Scotia. The Scottish guardian family supposedly built the Money Pit. Stranger still, both the secret society and the guardian family who purportedly constructed and hid the treasure within the Oak Island Money Pit still exist today. The evidence for their existence and their operation lies on both sides of the Atlantic, and their treasure is said to be still intact.

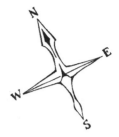

Chapter 3

PRELUDE TO EXPEDITION

*I*n June of 1398, ninety years before Cabot would reach America, a Scottish earl, Henry Sinclair, landed in Nova Scotia.[1] The natives he came across were most likely reluctant to come forward at first, but during the time he spent exploring his new land, he inevitably spoke to some of them. "What do you call this land?" was the most natural question a European in a new place might ask. This very common question, posed in a strange language, often produced comical results. The conquistadors who landed on a certain peninsula of Mexico asked this question. The Mayan to whom they made the inquiry replied with another question, "What are you saying?" In Mayan, this response sounded like "Yucatan," and thus the Spanish believed Yucatan to be the name of the peninsula of southern Mexico.

A Spanish explorer in Peru pointed to a strange animal he had never seen and said, "What is the name of that animal?" The Incan replied, "Llama?" he was repeating the Spanish word for "name" as he heard it.

The misunderstanding gave the llama its name. In Alaska an early explorer posed the typical question, "What do you call this place?" The Eskimo replied, "I don't know," which in his language was "Ka-No-Me," and so the soon-to-be city of Nome was named.

When the newly arrived Scotsman Sinclair asked the Micmac inhabitants of Nova Scotia where he was, they answered "Fertile Land." In Micmac this was "Acadie." To Europeans, "Arcadia" was nothing short of the equivalent of the "Promised Land." While this name has little significance to us in the twentieth century, to a medieval European it meant an idyllic place, an unspoiled land, an Eden. To Henry Sinclair, the significance of a promised land of Arcadia was profound. In the chapters ahead, we will meet Henry and his family, the Sinclairs, which by the time of expedition were the hereditary guardians of a religious and monetary treasure. Henry and the Sinclairs ultimately made Nova Scotia their sanctuary and the place where they could protect the secrets entrusted to them.

In our own time we are slow to recognize the ability Europeans had to sail the Atlantic. In 1992 we celebrated the five-hundred-year anniversary of the voyage of Columbus. In 1997 a full-size replica of Cabot's ship crossed the Atlantic, marking the quincentenary of his voyage to Nova Scotia.[2] Other voyages made in earlier days by numerous fishermen of Breton, Portugal, and Bristol go largely unheralded for lack of proof. The question of the presence of Europeans in America before Columbus can no longer be debated, although acceptance of the notion outside Scandinavia was slow. The fact that the Norsemen reached the North American continent began to be accepted by many in 1837, when a Danish historian, Carl Rafyn, declared the Norse sagas to be history. The sagas are collectively the recordings of the Norse people who traveled outside their country. Many of these tales had been preserved in Iceland, but they had been considered fiction. Researching the sagas, Rafyn found that he was reading about real families in Norway, Iceland, and Greenland. Some were simply tedious listings of people and their goods. Others described Atlantic voyages, the natives encountered, and the harsh life endured by the Norsemen, who were not out to conquer and loot but simply to farm and trade.

The sagas became a source of enormous controversy for more than a century because they told a history of America discovered well before Columbus.[3] To accept the ability of a Scottish earl to reach Nova Scotia in 1398, it serves to understand just how common transatlantic sailing was four hundred years earlier. The oldest of the sagas that record the journeys of the Norse to America was written in 1137 and is entitled *Islendinabok*.[4] The book calls North America "Vinland the Good" and recalls the travels of Ari Thorgilsson. Thorgilsson is mentioned again in another saga, the *Landanamabok*, as having been driven off course to Hvitramannaland, meaning "Greater Ireland."[5] Irish monks had preceded the Vikings to America (as they had to leave Iceland),[6] driven west after Viking raids off the western isles of Ireland sent them packing. Their monasteries became more and more remote and one of the farthest from Ireland, on an island off Iceland, is called Papays, the Norse name for Catholics, which referred to their obedience to the Pope. From Iceland the Irish, too, had sailed farther west.

The story of the Norse and the Irish in Atlantic waters five hundred years before Columbus seems remarkable, but the source of this history was not meant to be sensational. The *Landanamabok*, for example, includes the names of three thousand individual Norse settlers as well as the location of their farms. It was not meant to be a mythical document. Another Norseman, Gudleif Gudlaugson, was also described as having sailed to a place in Greater Ireland, Eyrbyggja, and meeting people who spoke the Irish language.[7] Gudlaugson was a trader, and Dublin was one of his ports of call, which is how he recognized the language. The most well-known Norseman, of course, is Leif Ericsson. In A.D. 1001 he had heard the tales of another trader, Bjarni Herjolfson, who had been blown off course and who actually might have been the first Norseman in America.[8] As a trader, Herjolfson regularly traveled the icy North Atlantic between Iceland and Scandinavia. One year he landed in Iceland, only to find that his father had moved to newer settlements farther west, in Greenland. On his way to Greenland a storm blew his ship farther west and south of his destination. Afraid to land, he sought only to return to Greenland to which he was traveling to see his father. For this perceived lack of adventurous spirit, Herjolfson later was rebuked by Leif Ericsson.

Ericsson was from one of the more colorful Norse families. His father, Eric (or Erik) the Red, had been exiled from his home in Iceland as a result of committing several murders. The sagas give us little detail about him, except that he settled in Greenland. Naming his new land Greenland appears to have been an advertising ploy, since it was, in fact, harsh land for farming. The name and Eric himself brought more Norse to settle there, and Greenland grew in population. While many of the Norse were farmers, those who could trade prospered and became prominent and wealthy. Both the Ericssons and the Herjolfsons were among those traders.

Ericsson decided to see the lands that Herjolfson had described. He bought Herjolfson's ship and traveled to Labrador, which the Norse called Helluland, meaning "Flat Rock Land." From there he went on to Nova Scotia, calling it Mark Land, or "Forest Land." Finally turning south, he arrived at Vinland, which may have been as far south as Virginia but more likely modern-day Massachusetts. Leif's brother, Thorvald, also made a voyage to Vinland in A.D. 1002 and most likely reached Massachusetts, where he named a cape Kiarlanes meaning "Keel-Cape" in the Old Norse language. Norse and American historians believe this to be the keel-shaped Cape Cod.[9] At another promontory Thorvald and his crew were attacked by natives; eight natives were killed along with one Norseman, Thorvald himself. He was buried under a cross, and the crew dubbed the place Krossanes in his memory.

Outside of L'Anse aux Meadows, the settlement discovered by the Ingstads in Newfoundland, we do not have proof of any permanent settlements in the New World. The Norse sagas report several trips to Vinland, but all had lasted three years or less. The long distances between New England and more established settlements in Greenland might have hindered the Norse ability to establish regular contact and trade on any long-term basis. Nova Scotia and Labrador at least were much closer. Because the Norse settlements in Greenland lacked one important commodity, lumber, trade was established between the new lands and Greenland. Just how many Norse settled in America we will never know. In Greenland, however, a modern archeologist found the remains of two large Viking settlements at Godthaab and Julianehåb, so it is possible that L'Anse aux Meadows was not the only North American community. The Norse maintained a presence in North America for three centuries, although Leif Ericsson might have stayed for only three years. During his stay, a son was born to Gudrid, Leif's sister, and her husband, Thorfinn Karlsefni. The child named Snorri is the first recorded birth of a European in America.

One of the reasons why historians have been reluctant to accept other claims of discovery such as those of several Norse voyages, is that such claims, until our present century, were followed with claims to territory. It was never simply a question of whether a particular group had the ability to cross the ocean, it was more a question of who was there first. It is then significant that besides the Norse claims made in the sagas, a neutral party also recorded their voyages to the New World. Even before the publication of the various sagas, a German historian, Adam of Bremen, writing in A.D. 1070 (*Descriptio Insularum Aquilonis*), told of a land called Vinland where wild grapes were found, as well as self-sown wheat.[10] Today we are not completely certain why the Norse settlements in America died out. Defeat by Native Americans is one strong possibility—the Norse indeed recorded skirmishes with natives they had met. A second factor might be the bubonic plague in Europe, which wiped out at least one third of the population of Europe. The reasons to sail west for new lands were no longer valid, since there was plenty of land after the plague decimated the European population. The plague also might have impaired trade. Reduced trade with the western lands would have cut off the colonies in Vinland and Greenland, and new colonists were not forthcoming. The Norse who remained, isolated from their home, may have intermarried with North American natives or the *skraelings*, as they called the Inuit peoples. They also may have been wiped out by them.[11]

Besides the sagas and Adam of Bremen's text, the Roman Catholic Church has preserved written records of their far-flung outposts in Greenland and Vinland. Thirteen bishops had served in Greenland starting in A.D. 1112. These bishops were always referred to in the Vatican as the bishops of Greenland and Vinland. And at least one, Erik Gnupsson (known as Henricus), was sent to Christianize the Norse settlers in

America.[12] In 1112, Henricus traveled three hundred miles across land from Maine to Rhode Island as a missionary. Another bishop, Olav, visited the Arctic lands to tend to the Christian flock.

Later, the pope in Rome became concerned for his missionaries in the Norse lands because of the prevalence of piracy. He instructed King Magnus to send an expedition westward and offered him half the tithes collected in Sweden and Norway for his efforts. The king sent Sir Paul Knutson to find out what had become of the western outposts. Knutson left in 1354, never to return. The next year, King Haakon, the successor to Magnus, took over the quest. He sent another expedition, which encountered piracy among the Inuit peoples in Greenland. This second expedition returned with two kayaks, which the bishop of Oslo hung in the cathedral of that city, a memorial to those who had not returned. With the Norse outposts in Greenland gone, trade ceased, and the cold barren islands toward the west were forgotten.

If the Norse sagas, published in 1837, and the earlier writings referring to Vinland did not advance what we know about the early history of North America, then the discovery of L'Anse aux Meadows by Helge and Anne Stine Ingstad in 1960 made the literary evidence all the more believable to those critics demanding more proof. Following the stories in the saga known as the *Flatey Book,* which described the settlements in Greenland, the Ingstads were led to believe that Newfoundland would yield proof of a Norse colony. They traveled from one remote village to another until a local man, George Decker, told Helge of ruins that he had seen. There, at L'Anse aux Meadows, the Ingstads uncovered the foundations of eight structures, including several of the "longhouse" style with six rooms. Nearby were cairns used by the Vikings as time markers, most likely as a primitive counting method. They also discovered a spindle whorl of Norse design, a soapstone whorl used for weaving.[13] The Newfoundland settlement was typical of the Greenland settlements, which also had houses, each with five or six rooms and a central hall in the same longhouse design.

In 1981 another archeologist, Peter Schledermann, reported on chain mail found on Ellesmere Island in the Northwest Territories and other Viking finds in Canada.[14] Such physical evidence as the artifacts found in the Arctic and in Labrador corroborated the literary evidence, and it became impossible to deny that Norse settlers and traders had traveled the new lands. Just how extensive were these wanderings of the Norsemen is still the subject of debate. While historians now accept the ability of the Norse to reach and settle Newfoundland and Labrador five hundred years before Columbus, further proof is required to accept Norse explorers in Massachusetts, Rhode Island, New York, or farther west. The camp in favor of further explorations has documentation in the recent studies of linguistics that indicate the Norse not only reached these areas but also stayed and even intermarried. In separate studies, at least two writers, Arlington Mallery and Barry Fell, have come to the conclusion that northeastern native tribes had commerce with Europeans before Columbus.

Arlington Mallery was a navigator and engineer by trade.[15] In 1951 his work *The Rediscovery of Lost America* was published, detailing the connections between Amerindian peoples and the Norse. His thesis was that the Iroquois and neighboring Huron peoples had encountered and borrowed technology and even language from the Norsemen. The Norse word for "devil," for example, is *loki*—and the Huron word is the same. In both cultures he was considered to be not the horned, tailed demon of Christianity, but the "trickster" god, evil yet comical at times. To the oceangoing Norsemen, Niord, a sea god, was of primary importance among a host of deities. In Huron, he survives as Niyoh. Barry Fell, in *America B.C.*, compiled an extensive list of Celtic and Algonquin words that he thinks rules out any coincidence of similarities between the languages.[16] He believes that even earlier crossings than those of the Norse traders and Irish monks took place. The Norsemen may even have given the Iroquois their style of dwelling. As the Norse built their communal longhouse, so did the Iroquois, separating themselves from the other tribes of the United States and Canada.

Linguistic evidence alone cannot be accepted as proof, since it is at best an inexact science. There is ample evidence to substantiate the ability of pre-Columbian Europeans to sail to America; not only could the Norse make the journey, but so could Irish sailors from even earlier dates. The primary source for this information is the Norse themselves.

In the sagas, there are several references to monks and Irish-speaking peoples who reached America first. The *Landanamabok* tells of the Icelander Ari Marson, who was driven by storm to Hvitramannaland, or Greater Ireland. The land is described as being near Vinland, and Marson found Irish Catholics there.[17]

Another written record of an Irish crossing of the Atlantic is the *Navigatio Sancti Brendani Abbatis,* or the Voyage of St. Brendan. This work is preserved in the library of the British Museum and tells the tale of Saint Brendan, dubbed the "Navigator," who crossed the Atlantic in A.D. 539. Brendan is one of Ireland's most important saints, and features of his life and his numerous travels are extensively documented.[18] Saint Brendan sailed to the Shetlands, the Faeroes, and Brittany. His greatest adventure was transatlantic. The *Navigatio* describes his leaving Ireland from County Kerry with eighteen monks. It also provides modern readers with wild descriptions of the sights seen by these medieval monks. While his descriptions seem fantastic, to monks who had never before been aware of the Arctic, its icebergs, glaciers, whales, volcanoes, and native Inuit might have been truly fantastic.

From the written description left behind by Brendan, we learn that he and his monks first landed on Saint Kilda, an island in the Outer Hebrides, and then sailed to the "Sheep Islands." These islands are now known as the Faeroes, and they are still famous for sheep raising. From there to Iceland is a short hop equal to the distance between Scotland and the Faeroes. It was a dangerous voyage, however, to sail the cold Atlantic in boats made of skin, but the Saxons had sailed to Great Britain in such vessels, and archeologists have determined that humans have used such vessels for five thousand years. From the islands north of Scotland, it is estimated that the journey required two days on the open sea. The peaks of Iceland could be seen for half the way. In Iceland, Brendan and his group were treated to their first view of a volcano. Volcanic activity in Iceland exists today, an unforgettable sight for modern travelers as well as medieval monks. From Iceland to Greenland is another equally short hop, not without danger. Whales and giant ice floes could be both fatal hazards and incredible visions for any visitor.

Where did Brendan make landfall? One intriguing site preserved on ancient maps is the island of Icaria, which since has disappeared (though there is another of the same name in Greece).[19] Although there are several theories concerning the location of Icaria, the name itself may be a clue. Kerry in Ireland was Brendan's home, I Caria, and may have been the name given to the site where Brendan and his party landed. In Brendan's time the Church in Rome became afraid that the religion of the Celtic Christian Church did not always conform to their own dogma. The Celtic priests wore their hair in an ancient style more closely resembling the pre-Christian Druids, for example, and they celebrated major feast days on days different from those set by Rome. They resented the intrusion that Rome seemed to force on their Irish ways.

Later, the Celtic priests of the Celi Dei, a monastic organization, came to believe themselves to be more closely following their God than did the bishops and pope in Rome who they often considered corrupt. They isolated themselves from the main Church and fled as other monastic groups had, to remote outposts. From the Norse descriptions of the dress of the Irish they met in Vinland, it seems that the Celi Dei might have followed Brendan across the Atlantic. Brendan's voyage might have paved the way to Iceland for other Irish Christians. The Norse recognized that the Irish had settlements there and preserved records of the Irish in Iceland. The sagas refer to Papay, an island off the southern coast of Iceland, named for the Papars. *Papar* was a term the Norse used to describe the Christians who adhered to the doctrines of the pope in Rome. The suffix "-ay" or "-ey" indicates an island. The records of the Norse add credibility to such annals of the Irish.

Iceland and the islands to the west had their own rise and fall. In 1347 the Black Death (bubonic plague) made its way to Iceland. It decimated the population, and the reports that one third of Europe had died from the plague might have sent some settlers farther west instead of east. The combined effect of the plague and the depopulation due to fear left Iceland much less populous. After a second plague in 1402, the monasteries of Iceland were abandoned. But the country was not forgotten, and Columbus visited Iceland before his voyage to America. By the time Columbus sailed to Iceland in 1477, he must have been aware of the stories of Norse voyages to western lands. That same year he had also been in Ireland, and while he was visiting in Galway, two flat-faced bodies washed ashore. They might have been Inuit or North American natives who drowned while fishing, but Columbus decided they were Asians. Columbus was a mapmaker and seller during the years he lived in Portugal, and he collected the tales of pilots and seafarers from all over the world. He even visited the Azores, islands in the mid-Atlantic that were governed by the family of his wife, and may have known about the existence of Vinland. Columbus, however, was not looking for a better fishing ground or lumber; he was searching for the riches of China, known to him as Cathay.

Others, however, did travel west looking for the better fishing grounds of the Grand Banks of Labrador and Newfoundland. In *Newfoundland*, Harold Harwood says that the Basques had fished there for whales since 1450.[20] Orkney fishermen had fished in "Estotiland," believed to be the Maritime Provinces of Canada, from 1371. British ships from Bristol had fished in Icelandic waters from the early 1400s, and despite the lack of records (fishermen have not been known to keep written records), Bristol's history tells of exploring the seas west of Ireland in 1480 for better fishing grounds. The French ships from La Have that met Jacques Cartier on his voyage of exploration had been sailing west for years. European knowledge of Iceland and points west had been unbroken from at least A.D. 1000. It was, in fact, a fisherman from the Faeroes who first told a Scottish earl and a Venetian shipowner about the place called Estotiland that lay one thousand miles west of Frislandia (northern Scottish Islands). The Scottish earl and his new friend, the shipowner from Venice, were impressed. They decided to find this new land. And they did.

Chapter 4

THE SCOTTISH
DISCOVERY OF AMERICA

*O*nce upon a time the inhabitants of the remote islands off the coasts of the North Atlantic had a particularly brutal custom toward visitors. If a storm blew them ashore, the islanders would rush from their homes, kill the survivors, and divide the booty. The practice gives a new dimension to the phrase "tourist trap." It was from these dire consequences that a chance meeting occurred that came to unite two of the greatest families of the pre-Columbian seafaring world, Sinclair and Zeno.

Henry Sinclair was the earl of the Orkneys. These windswept islands that lie off the northernmost point of Scotland had been inhabited by Scots, Picts, and—before Sinclair's day—Norse settlers.[1] His family had received these lands through inheritance and marriage. The Sinclairs already owned large stretches of land in the Scottish northlands and strategic property near Edinburgh, which had been a reward for fighting alongside William the Conqueror in A.D. 1066. In 1390 Henry Sinclair was showing his strength in his new possessions by sailing there with his fleet. His arrival came just in the nick of time for Niccolo Zeno, an Italian of royal blood who had traveled north as an adventurer. Zeno's father was a nobleman descended from one of the strongest, wealthiest families of Venice. His brother Carlo, a naval war hero, had saved Venice from a Genoese invasion. Not one to live in the shadow of his brother's glory, Niccolo was out to make a name for himself. On tiny Fer Island, however, he almost lost his life.

He had sailed from Venice north up the Atlantic along the coast of Britain and planned to explore still farther north. On this tiny island, between the Shetlands and the Orkneys, Zeno's ship ran aground on a reef just off the shore. The islanders there still have a custom called *grindadrap*, which means whale hunt, but the term does not come close to describing the gruesome scene.[2] Anywhere between a handful and a group of a hundred pilot whales will swim close to the shore, and the war cry *grint*, goes out through the island. Within minutes the entire population is on the scene carrying everything from ten-inch knives to harpoons. Men in powerboats in modern times force the whales to shore. If the event takes place at a sloping beach, many of the whales will be forced on to the beach, where groups stand ready for them. A handful of men will rush a beached whale, thrusting their knives into the whale's spinal marrow and causing the whale to thrash violently and thus break its own spinal cord. More men then descend on the whale and attack it with knives until the bay froths with its hot pink blood. Lawrence Millman describes the modern scene in *Last Places*, complete with the image of local children playing with a whale kidney and heart as their parents complete the butchery. All of the islanders eat well, since all would share in the bounty. The Lonely Planet travel guide to the Faeroes describes the scene as a "Greenpeace sympathizers' nightmare" and goes on to say that "to most Faeroese [it is] as much a part of life as Christmas."[3]

Just as the whales are considered fair game today, so were the explorers and windswept fishing boats of a few centuries ago. The islanders were ready to *grindadrap* Zeno and his crew with their ten-inch fishing knives until the earl of the Orkneys arrived at the last minute. Henry Sinclair, their nominal ruler, dispersed the crowd and spared the sailors' lives. This fortuitous meeting of Niccolo Zeno and Henry Sinclair became a momentous event for both of them. The two seafarers swapped tales of their adventures and their knowledge of modern warfare. Sinclair had heard of Niccolo's famous brother Carlo. Called the "Lion of Venice" for his role in the Genoese-Venetian War, he was famous throughout the world.[4] The Crusades also had brought the not-too-distant ancestors of Henry Sinclair in touch with the Zeno family—Scots and Britons had taken Venetian ships on the last leg of travel to the Holy Lands.

Sinclair was impressed enough by the Zeno name to appoint Niccolo as his admiral. Niccolo wrote home to another brother, Antonio, of his appointment by "Prince" Henry Sinclair and instructed Antonio to join him in Scotland.[5] Sinclair and Zeno joined forces to assert the Sinclair claim to the islands around Scotland. Niccolo, the explorer, traveled the lands that Sinclair had inherited around Scotland and even made a trip to Greenland on his patron's behalf, where he mapped the coastline.

Henry Sinclair had learned that lands existed west of Greenland from a Faeroese fisherman who had been captured during a voyage to the Grand Banks. The fisherman's story was remarkable. He described his capture by natives in this strange land and how he had met a man living with his captors who spoke Latin and had books. He traveled south in the new land with six other fishermen who had been with him when their ship was wrecked. In the south they fell victim to cannibals, who ritually murdered his companions but spared him because he taught them how to fish with a net. He was allowed to return to the north through a land called Drogio and finally found his way back to Estotiland. From there he built a vessel large enough to make the eastern crossing to Europe.

The fisherman described Estotiland as being smaller than Iceland, from where his original fleet had started. He said that this land had a great mountain in the center and four rivers. The people there had traded with "Engroueland" (Greenland), receiving goods for the furs and pitch they brought from their own country. Sinclair heard this story in 1397, and the next year he set sail west to see firsthand these lands beyond Greenland. He was no stranger to the existence of Greenland. The bishop of Orkney had been sent there by Pope Boniface IX in 1394, and it was a Sinclair ship that provided passage for the bishop. The Church in Greenland was centered in Gardar, a settlement on the western coast of that island. From western Greenland to Canada is not a longer distance than the number of miles from there to Iceland.

By the time Henry Sinclair was ready to make the voyage, Niccolo's brother Antonio had joined them. Before the journey could take place, Niccolo died, and so it was Antonio Zeno who accompanied Henry Sinclair to America and recorded the entire history of the voyage. Antonio inherited his brother's titles and wealth, although he never received the title admiral from the earl. Part of this inheritance included the maps and reports compiled by Niccolo, who had spent his last few years exploring and charting the coast on a three-ship expedition. The voyage of Henry Sinclair and Antonio Zeno was preserved for posterity in the maps and letters that Antonio sent to Venice, which were published in 1558. They recorded the first expedition since the Norse crossed the Atlantic. Zeno even sent home a map of the New World.

It is possible that Sinclair already knew of lands west of Greenland. The Sinclair family had Norse connections through marriage, and they were aware of the Norse settlements in the western isles. Sinclair may have known of lands in America even before the fisherman told him of his capture. The most intriguing part of the fisherman's tale might have been the warmer climates described in comparison to the frozen northern isles inhabited and explored by the Norse. The story of the discovery of America loses part of the drama without the tales of the sailor's fears of ships toppling off the edge of the known and flat land, but such tales are fiction. The fact that the Earth was round was understood from at least Roman times. Pliny the Elder's *Natural History,* compiled in the first century, records the controversy concerning the measurement of the circumference of the Earth. Such calculations had been debated more than a thousand years earlier. By Henry Sinclair's day the eastern coast of Canada had been reached by intrepid Norse sailors for hundreds of years. In fact, this chain of knowledge had been unbroken as evidenced by the records that became known as the Norse sagas and by the communications between Rome and the far-flung bishops of the Church. Discovery, then, becomes a relative term.

The Voyage of Sinclair and Zeno

In 1398 Henry Sinclair and Antonio Zeno were ready to sail, but their expedition was marred by the death of the fisherman just three days before they were to embark. He had given Zeno and Sinclair directions in terms that medieval seafarers understood. They measured distance from their home in terms of the height of the sun. The altitude of the sun was calculated with a tool called the astrolabe. This tool combined with a shadow board allowed the sailors to calculate latitude. The journey would go on.

The expedition started in Scotland, and as seems to have been the custom for such western voyages, it was made by hopping from one island to the next. From Scotland, through the Orkneys, past tiny Fer Island, and then farther north. The Faeroes, a group of islands two days north, were most likely the first planned stop. There is some disagreement among later historians trying to trace the voyage—the result of variations in spelling. On Antonio's map, Fer Island, where Sinclair had rescued Niccolo, was written as "FerIslanda," and later as "Frisland." Fer Island is only one day away from the Orkneys, and although sailors liked the landmarks, it was unnecessary to stop so close to the home base.

In an article on the voyage written in 1951, William Herbert Hobbs claimed that Iceland was also called Frisland.[6] Tim Severin, author of *The Brendan Voyage*, studied pre-Columbian Atlantic crossings and declared that the Faeroes were just where Zeno said they were.[7] *Faer* meant "sheep" in the Old Norse language, and "Faer-Eyjaer" was the Norse name given to the Faeroes, where, as noted earlier, sheep raising was the main industry.[8] Fishermen from the Hebrides called the Faeroes the "Faraways," which was most likely a pun in their language, a mixture of Old Norse and Old English. The "Faraway" Faeroes were really only two days' sailing.

From the sixth century onward Irish hermits had set sail with their sheep to the western islands to live in peace and freedom from Norse attacks. The Norse arrived in the ninth century. Iceland was also reached by these early Irish, and the Norse could have easily applied the Faer-Eyjaer label to Iceland as well.

North of Fer Island are the Shetlands, a more suitable place to take on stores or seek shelter from bad weather. Antonio's letter indicates that there was bad weather and that they stayed in the Shetlands for a week before pushing north. When the winds were better they took off for the Faeroes, but again a storm intervened. The plan of the Sinclair expedition was to follow the Viking route west. After passing the Faeroes, they would have reached Iceland, where food and supplies could be found. From Iceland, Sinclair's crew was adept enough to sail directly to New-foundland without first going north to Greenland. The bad weather changed the plans, and the ships passed Iceland and made one unscheduled short stop on the route to North America, which would cast doubt on the whole voyage. The island in question was called Icaria.[9] Either it does not exist anymore, or modern historians are simply unable to identify it.

The narrative of the Zeno expedition records that between Iceland and Greenland they stopped at Icaria, which was ruled by a king. They encountered the openly hostile forces of the king among whom only one man, an Icelander, could speak a language that Sinclair could understand. The Icelander told them they could not have permission to land. Through the interpreter, Sinclair learned that the "king" of Icaria refused to engage in commerce with any foreigners, and at best he would allow one of them to stay. The rest of the group could either leave Icaria without harm, which they did, or face a battle in which every inhabitant of Icaria was ready to fight to the death. Sinclair was further informed that Icaria was made up of those who had fled before religious persecution and Viking plundering, and they were not ready to flee again. The expedition had no desire to engage in warfare.

Sinclair instructed his ships to circle the island to avoid the hostile inhabitants and find a suitable landing. The islanders persisted, however, following Sinclair's ships as they circled the island. It was decided that the expedition would press on without supplies. From Icaria the expedition sailed directly past Cape Race on the coast of Greenland, where Norse ships in the past had stopped to take on supplies. Zeno reports that while they were now running low on supplies, they did not believe they had far to travel before reaching a safer landfall.

Two days later they reached the coast of Newfoundland, but because of stormy conditions they decided not to risk a landing. The weather cleared, and after two more days they reached Nova Scotia. There, according to William Hobbs, Tor Bay was their most likely stopping place.[10] He bases his conclusions on the descriptions recorded in the letters that Zeno sent home to Venice. When they entered the harbor they saw a hill in the distance (Nova Scotia is very flat and has one high hill in what is now Antigonish, in Pictou county, which is visible from afar). After making landfall they gathered food by fishing and gathering bird eggs (extensive fisheries and rookeries exist even today). Sinclair sent one hundred men to cross the "island." When they returned, they reported sighting another sea (the Northumberland Strait) and a spring where pitch ran into the sea (asphalt, very rare, is found in Stellarton, Nova Scotia).

Hobbs had been the first to show that "a spring from which issued a certain substance like pitch" was almost unique.[11] There is, in fact, only one place within a few days' march from the Atlantic Ocean where such a rare phenomenon exists besides Stellarton, and that is at Trinidad in the Caribbean. Even in Trinidad the pitch formed a lake, not a "spring." The name Stellarton is derived from Stella coal, an oil-charged coal that runs throughout the area in a very thick vein. Zeno also described a "smoking hole," which could have been caused by lightning or man-made fire that had smoldered for a long period of time.

The soldiers also reported that very short people had run from them and hid in caves. The Micmacs were a shorter race than most North American natives, and the Stellarton region was one of their main centers of population. They were known by other European traders to be timid, but they had the ability to travel great distances and had experience in trade. The large number of Sinclair's strange-looking force would undoubtedly have surprised the Micmacs and caused them to flee. The fact that they hid in caves lends further support to the theory of the geographic location, since there are very few caves in Nova Scotia and the area immediately surrounding Stellarton is where these caves are situated.

Frederick Pohl, who wrote extensively on early European discoveries in the New World, added much weight to the observations of Hobbs and pinned down even more specific locales and dates for the Sinclair-Zeno voyage. Recognizing that sailors often took place-names from the religious day celebrated on their day of discovery, Pohl was able to calculate Sinclair's landing date. The safe harbor of the Sinclair-Zeno expedition was called "Trin," and the month, according to Zeno's letters, was June. Pohl found that in earlier times the eighth Sunday after Easter is always the date of the celebration of the Holy Trinity and is called Trinity Sunday. He verified with the Vatican that this day was celebrated in the fourteenth century, and from there he narrowed down the possible dates. Since Easter can be celebrated as early as March and the records from Zeno say the expedition reached the harbor in June, there are very few feast days that match with the dates of Zeno's letters. Trinity Sunday and Sinclair's landing in Nova Scotia must have been June 2, 1398—ninety-seven years before the next European reached Nova Scotia and ninety-four years before Columbus "discovered" the New World.

Henry Sinclair liked the new lands he had discovered. The fish and game were abundant, the climate was moderate, and the harbors appeared good for shipping. He declared that he would someday build a city there and leave Scotland behind for a new home. His crew had other plans. They wanted to return home before the seasons changed and the Atlantic crossing became even more dangerous. It was agreed that Antonio would captain the expedition and all who wished to do so would return to Scotland, while Henry and a smaller group would stay on and continue their explorations. Zeno sailed to Scotland, first stopping in the Faeroes. He recorded the voyage and immediately sent his story back to his brother in Venice. Thus the journey was recorded for history.

Apart from the letters Zeno sent home, we have no other written records of this expedition or even of what happened to the crew after they reached Scotland.[12] Sinclair did explore the New World further, and one of Zeno's letters says that he built a "town in the port of the island newly discovered by him." Since Zeno had most likely not seen the town, this is only a supposition. Other evidence of Sinclair's overland travels has been preserved. If Sinclair had sailed or marched along a coastal route to explore what would come to be called New England, he would have traveled along coastal New Brunswick and soon would have reached what is now the border between Canada and the United States at Saint Stephen. Just past that point he would have entered Maine in the area of Machias Bay.

Discovery of a whale-back ledge "jutting into Machias Bay at Clark's Point, Maine," was made where a "petroglyph of a cross incised beside one of a European ship of the late fourteenth century" stood. The historian Andrew Sinclair, a distant descendant, says this stone confirms the voyage.[13]

It may, but Sinclair might not have been the first to land in Machias Bay. On my own coastal exploration of Maine, I learned of the belief that Vikings may have been there also. Near the tiny town of Cutler, Maine, is a pond complete with stone walls that no one is able to explain outside the local legend that says Vikings built them. On a very small island named Manana, which is offshore of Monhegan island in Maine, runic inscriptions are found.[14] While the Zeno expedition would have left inscriptions in their own language(s), Monhegan gives us further evidence of the pre-Columbian travels of Europeans. Farther south there is more direct evidence.

On a granite perch in the small Massachusetts town of Westford lies a carved rock memorial to a Scottish knight.[15] The rock has been known to exist since colonial times, but it had been allowed to become overgrown by brush. Frank Glynn, an amateur archeologist from Connecticut, became interested in the tale of the rock carving and set out to uncover the memorial.[16] After finding the rock ledge, which is now on Depot Street in Westford, he cleared the brush. The worn and faded rock was found complete with inscription and immediately sparked a debate. Some say the carving appears to be an Indian with a tomahawk, and not a knight. To highlight the carving, Glynn poured chalk into the punched holes and incised lines. The figure of a knight complete with chain mail and a coat of arms became visible.

Glynn sent a rubbing of the worn stone to T. C. Lethbridge, a British writer, archeologist, and curator of the University of Archeology and Ethnology at Cambridge, England. In 1954 Lethbridge researched both the coat of arms and the figure itself in Wales and Scotland. He concluded that it was a depiction of a knight and that this particular knight was important. The full size of the knight depicted in the memorial carving is six feet. The carving includes a "basinet" helmet, which came into use in the 1360s and subsequently fell out of favor in the fifteenth century, which helped establish a time frame. Lethbridge also told Glynn that such effigies in stone were often made during that time period in Ireland and the western isles of Britain. They would be carved at the place where the knight had fallen, usually a place of battle. The detailed carving included the hilt of a sword held over the breast of the knight and a shield with a coat of arms. The coat of arms depicted a buckle, a crescent, a five-pointed star, and a ship.

Personal correspondence from Lethbridge to Glynn in 1956 describes the armor and the crest as coming from the outer islands of Scotland circa 1350. A buckle (actually a brooch) on the shield was an emblem shared by only a few families; after consulting early Orkney medals, Lethbridge was able to narrow his list of families down considerably. He declared the coat of arms to be "clearly the arms of some maternal relation of the Sinclairs." Further research brought new information about the incidence of galley portrayals on Scottish coats of arms. Those bearing this heraldic emblem were either from Norse kings of the isles, or from the line of the "Norse Jarls" on Orkney—the Sinclairs. Further research honed down the list even more. In medieval Scotland families in the employ or under the protection of an important family might take their last name from the clan of their protector. The shield and coat of arms belonged to a branch of the Sinclair group, the clan of Gunn, and to a knight that was Henry Sinclair's principal lieutenant, Sir James Gunn. In 1973 Sir Ian Moncreiffe, one of heraldry's foremost experts agreed with Lethbridge's conclusions.[17]

The importance of the Gunn clan connection and the identity of the knight in the Westford stone carving is that the Gunn and Sinclair clans were closely linked in Scotland. In the north the Gunns were the "Crowners of Caithness," and tradition held that without their consent, no one could rule over their province in the Scottish northlands. This right was affirmed by the insignia of the buckle on their coat of arms. The Sinclairs gained the lands through inheritance, but still they ruled with the consent of the Gunn clan. Both families had strong Norse ties, and this alliance between the two families might have existed from the eleventh century. The history of the Gunn clan may even predate the recorded history of Sinclairs in Scotland. They are related to the first waves of Norse settlers in the Orkneys, who are collectivized as "south island men," or Sutherlands.

In addition to the carved rock at Westford, a second marker nearby the ledge emerged in the 1960s. A farmer had discovered it in his field but did not know what, if any, significance the inscribed stone had, and simply left it in his barn. The stone was of little use in solving the puzzle, but it was of the same punched carving style as the stone depicting Sir James Gunn. The depths of the holes as well as their diameter were identical to those on the first stone. A mysterious "184" and an arrow might have been meant as an instruction to the finder; the rock, however, had been moved, and any such instructions were meaningless. Another ship was portrayed on this second carved stone, again the galley design that would fit the style of a Scottish ship in the years 1350 to 1400. The second stone was moved to the lobby of the Fletcher library in Westford, not far from the Depot Road granite memorial. A twentieth-century search for a fourteenth-century camp failed to turn up any other evidence of the Sinclair expedition in this region. From the Westford area, Sinclair may have traveled even farther south.

The Taunton River of Massachusetts empties into Assonet Bay near Fall River, Massachusetts. On the east side of the bay there is a large rock with a seven foot by eleven foot face on which symbols have been inscribed. Described as runic, the "Dighton Rock" has been called a hoax. Since it was Cotton Mather, the fire and brimstone preacher of colonial America, who recorded the rock's existence in 1690, it is at least a very old hoax. The Glynn-Lethbridge correspondence describes it as being of the same "punch" style as the Westford inscription.

In Fall River in 1831 the skeleton of a man wearing heavy metal plate armor was dug up at the corner of Fifth Sreet and Harley. Could Sinclair have left behind the body of his second-in-command or another in his party after what may have been a skirmish with the locals? Henry Wadsworth Longfellow wrote a poem about the mysterious "Skeleton in

Armor," who he believed built the nearby Norse Tower for his "fair lady." A fire in the museum in 1843 deprived posterity of any further chance to examine the skeleton of the knight. Anthropologists and experts from Harvard's Peabody Museum did come up with some unusual guesses. Their best explanation was that the armor was that of a Wampanoag Indian, although they were not known for wearing such armor. A knight such as Sir James Gunn, however, would be expected to be prepared for battle, and armor was typical of the fourteenth-century knight.

The piece of architecture with the most controversial origin is a rounded tower of gray stone set above arches that stands guard in Newport, Rhode Island. The tops of these arches are ten feet above ground, with a floor built above the arches. On this floor was found the remnants of a fireplace that may have been used as a signal light for the harbor at Newport. The inner diameter of the tower is eighteen feet, but because the walls are so thick (three feet), it is twenty-four feet in diameter measured from outside the walls. Historians have attempted to explain the nature of Newport Tower for centuries. Some historians favor the notion that the early Norse explorers built it and that it is related to nearby Dighton Rock.[18] The tower, they believe, was a church dedicated to Henricus, one of the last Norse Catholics to be sent to the New World by the Church.[19] Others claim that it was used as a grain mill by Governor Benedict Arnold (not to be confused with General Benedict Arnold of the American Revolution), avoiding the fact that earlier maps had it situated there well before Arnold owned the property.

The first map on which it was marked was made by the Verranzano expedition, which recorded it as a "Norman Villa"—certainly earlier than the American Revolutionary era, a point missed by those who refuse to accept that there were earlier visitors to the New World. Verranzano's record also discusses the occupants of this area as "inclining more to whiteness" than the other New England natives. Was a settlement left behind that ended in intermarriage between Europeans and North Americans? Another theory I encountered on one visit there was that it was built by pagan Norse, who were able to calculate time thanks to the circular construction and the series of eight arches. It had ledges especially designed to hold torches at night, from which one could observe from above the ground the positions of the moon and stars. It may also have been a solstice and eclipse calculator—a Rhode Island Stonehenge?

Andrew Sinclair made the observation that it is the sign of a second Sinclair settlement in the New World.[20] Its construction is the same as the round churches of the Knights Templar, which are circular and complete with eight arches. These churches are rare; the only one in Scotland was built in Orkney, the home of Henry Sinclair. The Sinclair family acted in Scotland as the protectors of Freemasonry, an outgrowth of the outlawed Templars. Hjalmar Holand had reached a similar and more intriguing conclusion thirty years before Sinclair's work. The tower was modeled on a first-century "baptistry" constructed by followers of Jesus Christ.[21] Such baptistries did not last long, but after the Crusades, the knights brought the model home from the Holy Lands. They then started constructing a handful of such baptistries in Europe. While this could suggest that either the Sinclair expedition or a Norse expedition could have used the model and constructed the tower, Holand goes on to trace the construction to the Cistercian monastic order. It was this order that was influential in both starting the Crusades and founding the Templars. This information pushes the scale in favor of a Sinclair-initiated construction.

The Templars were an order of soldiers who were sworn to vows of poverty and chastity very much like the monks. This order, founded in the twelfth century, grew in power and wealth over a two-hundred-year period and like the Cistercian order of Saint Bernard, they were also builders. Europe is still dotted with bridges and churches from this era.

Sinclair's base of operations in North America was likely situated in Nova Scotia. It is possible that Sinclair had brought as many as three hundred men to America. His fleet, as previously mentioned, was larger than that of the Norse king of Norway. It is also possible that Sinclair made more than one journey. How long he stayed in the New World is not known. We are not even sure of the year of his death. Father Hay, an early Scottish genealogist with a reputation for hurried biographies, says that Henry died in the year 1400 as a result of an English raid. Another biographer, Raphael Holinshed, says that the fatal raid took place in 1404.[22] A more contemporary biographer of Sinclair and his voyage, the late Frederick Pohl, says that just about all of Sinclair's life can be accounted for except the years 1400 to 1404, but he believes that Sinclair stayed in North America until 1400 and came home to Scotland to be felled in a raid that same year.

There is also evidence that Antonio Zeno wished to return home in 1400 but was not given permission by his Scottish employer—this notion derives from his letters home. He finally made the trip back to Venice in 1404, which could be evidence that Sinclair's death in that year freed him from his obligations. It is also possible that Henry Sinclair came home in 1400, made a second trip to the New World, and then returned to Scotland to meet his death in 1404. Under any scenario he had little time and less motivation to publicize his travels and, as we will find out, a strong motivation to keep the secret within his family. In 1558 a descendant of Antonio Zeno's reconstructed the old maps and letters of the voyage and turned them into a narrative. At the time it was widely accepted and the maps and charts were published by some of the great mapmakers of the era. But in our own time, doubt was cast on the voyage. The greatest reason for disbelief stemmed from an island that is no longer an island.

The Problem of Icaria

The staunchest critic of the Sinclair-Zeno expedition is Samuel Eliot Morison, and his greatest criticism is for what he cynically calls the "FlyAway Islands." The confusion of identifying Frisland and Fer Island could be a result of translation or even simply misspelling. The story of Icaria and a king, however, caused Morison to brand both the Zeno maps and the entire journey as fake. Worse, he goes on to blame the future explorers' misfortunes on their use of the Zeno map.[23] If the tale of the Zeno journey was recorded correctly, then what happened to Icaria?

Arlington Mallery and other modern mapmakers finally proved that the Zeno map was correct after making a startling discovery.[24] There was once a group of islands between Greenland and Iceland that no longer exists today. These so-called FlyAway Islands are also known as

Gunnbiorn's Skerries, and they didn't actually fly away. They are named for the Norse trader Gunnbiorn, who was blown off course in A.D. 920 and reached Greenland. Gunnbiorn is given credit for discovering Greenland, and it was his description that led Eric the Red to make a settlement in that inhospitable land.[25] The islands he found off the eastern coast were given his name. There is no doubt that they existed. They are, in fact, depicted in *Description of Greenland*, which dates to 1873, and are now shown on the United States Hydrographic Office maps.[26] The only problem is that they have sunk and are now underwater. Today they form an undersea plateau that was determined to be the result of a sinking ocean floor.

By 1456 most of the main island of the Skerries was underwater, although the islands are still shown on maps until 1600. In 1456 the main island was sixty-five miles long and twenty-five miles wide and was called Gombar Skaare. William Herbert Hobbs was brought into the debate on the Sinclair-Zeno journey because of his extensive research into the coastline of Greenland. He was a professor of geology at Michigan and in charge of the university's expedition to Greenland. He served as the president of the International Glacier Commission until 1936. When he saw the Zeno map he was immediately fully convinced that it was an accurate depiction of Greenland's coastline. It was the superimposed lines of longitude and latitude that was its shortcoming. "The long axis of the island appeared rotated clockwise through about half a right angle."[27] These lines, however, had not been drawn by Zeno but were added later by a relative. In Charles Hapgood's *Maps of the Ancient Sea Kings*, the author also defended the original Zeno brothers' work and concluded that the member of the family who was responsible for publishing the map and the narratives in 1558 was the cause of the error.[28] It was this armchair explorer, the younger Zeno, who incorrectly placed longitude and latitude lines on the map of his ancestors.

Captain Arlington Mallery, a navigator and an engineer, studied differences in the coastline of Iceland on the modern map and on the Zeno map. His work led him to a book entitled *Floods and Inundations* by Cornelius Worford, written in 1879, and an account of volcanic activity in Iceland by T. Thoroldson. These accounts and other references to

Iceland discussed the submergence of "several provinces" of Iceland that occurred after a forty-year period of "terrific volcanic explosions" that took place from 1340 to 1380; the effects lasted into the next century. In his own work, *The Rediscovery of Lost America*, co-authored with Mary Roberts Harrison, he concluded:

> Scholars have been frustrated mainly because they have overlooked the tremendous changes in the natural features of the Greenland-Iceland area due to natural phenomena. Unaware of the consequent sinking of land and the forming of undersea shelves as the surface of the earth shifted under the weight of glacial ice, they have not realized that some landmarks on the Viking trail have even vanished under ice and water.[29]

Mallery and Hobbs were not the only ones to document the activity of the restless floor of the Atlantic. History records the eighteenth-century earthquake that devastated Lisbon, Portugal. In six minutes, sixty thousand people perished, and the harbor fell six hundred feet to the Atlantic floor. In 1811 a large volcanic island rose from the sea into the island chain known as the Azores. Named Sabrina, the island was put on the maps, only to be reclaimed by the sea again. In 1963 an island grew from a volcano off the coast of Iceland. Named after the Norse god of fire, this one did not "fly away" but instead reportedly grew at an incredible rate of one acre per day. There are literally scores of coastal towns, harbors, and islands that have been lost to a changing ocean floor, from Martinique to the Mediterranean.

The damage to the credibility of the Zeno charts and the expedition had been done before the works of more modern cartographers and scientists. Morison blamed Zeno's map for the errors of Mercator and Ortelius, who worked from the Zeno charts in the late sixteenth century, and the problems of Frobisher, who carried a Zeno map in his 1576 expedition.[30] Frobisher reached the eastern coast of Greenland and decided he was in Frisland. Whose fault was it? When Frobisher was sixteen days out of the Shetlands he also mistook an island off the coast of Baffin Island for Labrador through no fault of the Zenos. He then sailed north, where he first mistook Inuit natives in kayaks for seals and later called them Tartars. Failing to find the sea route to Cathay, he returned home with iron pyrites he believed were gold and a kidnapped Inuit native who later died from pneumonia. Morison's decision to blame Frobisher's inadequacies on Zeno seems thin at best and is certainly misplaced.

Explorer John Davis, for whom the Davis Strait is named, did not recognize a certain inlet of Baffin Island in 1586, thinking it was Greenland. Morison again put the blame on later mapmakers for using the Zeno map.[31] The French cartographer Alexandre Lapie, however, had also depicted a wide strait cutting through southern Greenland on a map that dates to 1841. Lapie was not referring to a Zeno map. The letters that were sent by Antonio Zeno to his brother in Venice told of the landfall at Icaria and the people encountered on this island. Because the island no longer exists, Morison brands the entire journey as fictitious. From evidence cited by more modern writers, such as Hapgood and Mallery, who have determined the Gombar Skaare to be a very large landmass once existing just where Zeno placed it, it is very possible that this island was Icaria. Brendan, too, had a description of Icaria and admitted even his journey was not a first made by Irish Christian monks who fled the mainland to practice their religion and remain free from the pirates and Vikings who plagued coastal settlements.

The most recent biographer of Sinclair and his voyage to America is a distantly related descendant, Andrew Sinclair. For this modern historian, the story of the voyage is interesting in a personal sense, and he was able to add much to the knowledge about the Scotland Sinclairs. He, too, had a problem with Icaria, which he attempts to explain away as an out-of-sequence part of the tale. His argument is that the expedition must have stopped in Kerry or Saint Kilda and that somehow the order of the Zeno letters was confused. The problem, however, is that neither Kerry nor Saint Kilda matches the physical description of "Icaria" or the description of the denizens of this remote isle.

Morison believed that there would not be a "king" on such a "Fly Away island." Zeno had already dubbed Sinclair a "prince," and in this light incorrectly calling a religious leader a "king" would not discredit the entire expedition. The Zeno narratives record great shoals that threatened the ship as it was leaving Icaria. No such shoals threaten the seafarers at Kerry. Since Gombar Skaare was the main island of a sinking chain, there should be no surprise that such dangerous shoals existed, and this description adds credibility to the travelogue. The inhabitants of Gombar Skaare (I Caria) eventually left their isolated outpost but would not be the last inhabitants of Gunnbiorn's Skerries. Mallery states: "In 1476, Didrik Pining, sent by the King of Norway to put an end to pirate raids in Greenland waters, made his headquarters on this mountainous island, which he named Hvitserk."[32] Pining later became a pirate himself. Amsterdam maps continued to show the islands until A.D. 1600 and the United States Hydrographic Office put Gombar Skaare on its chart in 1932, noting that it was 120 yards below sea level.

Historians who are critical of the Sinclair voyage claim there should be more evidence than the letters and charts sent home by Antonio Zeno. They also question just why the discovery set off no shock waves in Europe. One hundred years later Columbus's voyage would start a frenzy among gold- and glory-seeking Spanish adventurers. There are several answers. The first is that the expedition was not "sent." It was not sponsored by the Spanish Crown or the king of France or of any country. The Sinclair expedition was made simply because Henry Sinclair could mount such an expedition. The second reason is that these were lands that northern sailors had known about for almost four hundred years. They were not on a "sea route to Cathay" or even likely to turn up the gold and silver sought by the Spanish. They were simply new lands, possibly rich in fishing and good forests but too far north to be promising farmland. Irish and Norse sea travelers knew that beyond the western isles lay Greenland, and farther west there was more of the same. The lands had some positive attributes but were not likely to start a land rush of immigrants or gold seekers. Instead of firing the imaginations of wealth-hungry Spaniards, the new lands were kept secret by the dour Scotsmen. A third reason is that the printing press had not yet been invented when Henry returned from the New World. But the most important reason is that Henry Sinclair wanted his discovery kept secret. For Henry Sinclair and his family, the land so far from the English king and the Roman Church offered a refuge. It was best kept secret.

The North American Evidence

In Nova Scotia there is evidence of another sort. The native population encountered by Sinclair was the Micmac tribe. Micmac legends tell of a "Great Prince" who brought his people to their world "on the backs of whales."[33] This prince stayed with them for half a year, only to leave. Legend records that he returned to their land a second time. The Micmacs claim he lived in a wigwam he called "Winter." The word *wigwam* is one of the most significant words in the pre-Columbian history of the North Atlantic. While we have no problem believing that ancient mariners of Scotland and Ireland and even the Saxons could cross large expanses of water in flimsy skin boats, we give the natives of North America no such credit. It is very possible that Inuit, Pictish, and Micmac peoples and a horde of unnamed residents of the north had been sailing both west and east well before Columbus, Leif Ericsson, or even Brendan. The word *wigwam* might be part of the evidence.

Inuit natives in subarctic Greenland built their homes by digging into the ground, as a defense against the weather. Picts, the "tribe" of people found in the north of Scotland by the Romans, did the same. The Inuit people called their homes *gammes;* the Picts, who later used such earthen structures just for storage, called them *weems* (*wee* as in "little"). From the two words, we can derive "wigwams," or "little houses." The American Indian tribes of the frozen north built their houses in the same manner and also had less permanent tent structures for homes. Both found their way into our language as "wigwams." American Indian tribes and the neighboring Inuit peoples may have had direct contact with each other, and perhaps contact between the Micmacs and the Picts was made only through the Inuit, who lived between these two groups.

The Picts and Inuit peoples shared the same "*ulo* blade" tool—a stone knife—and both made boats from various materials. Skin boats had been in use from prehistoric times and were still in use during the fourteenth century. As a part of their Orkney heritage, the Gunn clan would be no strangers to hunting whales (orcas) from these tiny craft. These "sea pigs," as whales were called, and those other "sea pigs," dolphins, gave their name to the Orkney Islands in antiquity. Just how far back in time the Picts, the Orkney sailors, the Celts, and the pre-Viking Scandinavians had been launching these frail craft in the choppy frigid seas of the North Atlantic may never be known. It is almost a certainty, however, that their seagoing ability led them to communication and commerce with each other well before any historian would record such trade. The rulers of the Orkneys, the sea kings of the western and northern isles, are recorded from early times as using wicker craft, hide-covered boats, and, later, wooden ships manned by as many as sixteen rowers. It is likely that such Orkney fishermen reached America, either by intention or as a result of storms that blew them off course.

And there are other points of connection. The Celtic, Norse, and North Amerind languages have several words in common. One of the most interesting word similarities between the Celtic and North American languages suggests their early communication. The word is *mac*. The Micmac tribe of Nova Scotia shared matriarchal customs with the Picts of Scotland. Every member of the tribe was a *maqq*, a "child of the tribe." Wealth was passed to the children through the mother. *Maqq* took on the meaning of "friend," as in "one of us." The Picts used the same prefix for the same reason. For the Picts, too, wealth passed from the mother to the children. Women were equal to men and were even allowed to rule. On both sides of the Atlantic the practice of fosterage was an outgrowth of matriarchal custom. Sons were given to the mother's brother to be raised. The natural father did not have any social importance to his children. *Maqq* may have become *mac* in Scotland, where the same matriarchal customs prevailed as a result of transatlantic communication. From Scotland, *mac* traveled to Ireland as *mc* when the Scots settled there in early times. The shared prefix, which denoted "belonging to" a tribe, a clan, or the smallest subset, the family, attained the meaning "child of" when patriarchal customs and more Roman Christian practices reached the Celts.

"Kin" is another concept shared by Norse and Celtic peoples in Europe and the American Indian peoples on the northeastern Atlantic coast of North America. The word *kin* referred to a related person and meant loosely that this person was a member of the extended family. A variant on the word sounded almost the same but meant "head"— either the head of the kin or literally the head attached to the neck. An old custom of the Celtic and Norse peoples in war was to take the head of the enemy. The skull was removed and would be made into a drinking vessel. It was a show of pride, a trophy of war; in a spiritual sense it was an act signifying that the owner took the strength of the person killed. Skulls would be used as drinking and cooking vessels.

While few of us have ever taken our meals from a skull, the word for a skull used as a cooking vessel survives. In Old Norse the term for cooking pot and skull was the same—*canna*; our modern equivalent is "can."[34] A much bigger pot was used for cooking but also for religious and magical practices. Animals were sacrificed and put into this big pot, which in Norse was called the *ketill*, and in Norse its meaning is "sacred cauldron." Christianity and civilization reached the more primitive northern Europeans later and changed the word for this utensil and its use. *Ketill* became *kettle*, and no more eye of newt concoctions were ritually prepared, just meals.

Just how early North American Indians and Celtic Europeans made contact is unknown, but the North Atlantic Indian word for kettle is *kannaken*, which might have meant "big skull" on European soil. In the British Celtic language, *kenn* (spelled *ceann* in Ireland) meant "head." When the Celtic languages split, *penn* took the same meaning among the P-Celtic–speaking groups (those using the "P" sound) as *kenn* had to the Q-Celtic–speaking groups (those using the "Q" sound). Our own former President John Kennedy's surname literally means "ugly head." *Canmore* (alternately spelled *Kenmore*) means "big head," which could refer to a chief or may simply be a descriptive term.

The pelican, a bird with a distinctively long beak, was named by the Greeks for its *pele* (meaning axelike) *can* (meaning head). The pelican was literally the "axhead." In the language of the Welsh, which was P-Celtic, an example of *penn* referring to an important person, a chief, is "Penndragon," the name of King Arthur's father. He is the "chief dragon," or "head dragon," a term with the connotation of a practitioner of magic. It was the sailors of Sir Francis Drake's most celebrated voyage, which passed by the Antarctic coast, who named the strange birds they saw there on the ice floes. For lack of a better term, these Welsh and Cornish sailors called the white (*gwynn* in Welsh) headed (*penn*) birds "penguins." These funny-looking denizens of the ice were lierally "whiteheads."

In the Scottish language, the name MacCan took on the meaning "son of the chief" as the father's role and patriarchal custom emerged from more ancient Pictish customs. The name Duncan came to mean brown (*dun*) chief (*can*). The Celtic spelling was *Donnacaidh*, and everyone with the name Duncan is supposed to have descended from the original brown chief. In 1534 when Cartier met with the American Indians along the Saint Lawrence Seaway, he was introduced to a certain Donnacana. This individual had the role of "chief of the chiefs." The relationship of *Donnacaidh* and *Donnacana* may be considered coincidental, but it is one of many shared words whose meaning is similar to or exactly the same as its meaning on the opposite shore.

When white Europeans traveled across the Atlantic they may have impressed the Micmacs with the trappings of a higher civilization. Because he had been told by the Faeroese fisherman that his life was spared when he taught the natives how to fish with a net, Sinclair always brought them trinkets, as would later explorers. The trappings of civilization were regarded very highly. As mentioned earlier, the Micmacs have a legend of a prince who came to their world on the backs of whales. He brought with him many men and taught them how to fish with nets. The prince also gave them a magical instrument that made music, a flute. And he showed to them his "sword of sharpness."[35]

Silas Tertius Rand was a missionary and a student of languages who lived among the Micmac people in the mid-1800s. He could speak Greek, Latin, and Hebrew as well as his own English language, and eventually he learned Micmac, Mohawk, and Maliseet. He is responsible for recording most of what we know about the Micmac language. He translates the name of the prince who brought civilization to the Micmac as "Glooskap." Frederick Pohl identifies Glooskap as Sinclair and also points out that Rand's recordings of Micmac songs were actually very similar to Scottish sailing songs.

Glooskap literally means "deceiver," but this was in fact a title that conveyed respect among northern Atlantic peoples on both sides of the ocean. The Norse god Loki was the trickster god who, like the Greek Prometheus, stole the fire from the gods and gave it to ordinary people. This legend of fire-stealing is shared by many and points to the contact between Stone Age people and more civilized people. Glooskap had the knowledge to make fire. When ancient peoples started a fire, they would keep it lit for as long as possible, since they might not be able to start another one. The Micmac regarded Sinclair as "wasteful" because he put his fire out at night.

According to the Micmacs, Glooskap built a town, which Sinclair told Zeno that he intended to do. This settlement may have been in a place the Micmacs called Piktook, now Pictou. This was a center for the Micmac people, and when the Europeans came to stay, it was a center for them as well. From his first meeting, Sinclair-Glooskap was welcomed as an important chief by the natives. Legend painted him in mythical proportions, but more down-to-earth tales have the chief eating, drinking, and sleeping among his Micmac friends. He taught them games that are similar to existing Scottish children's games. He also taught them new words and learned a few of theirs.

From his camp in Piktook he went exploring. His travels are recorded by the Micmacs as having started in the Minas Basin area and then crossing a narrow point of the Bay of Fundy to the Parrsboro area and heading west to Cape d'Or. In this area, in a small harbor now known as Advocate Bay, Sinclair may have built additional ships to replace those that sailed back to Europe with Zeno. In 1957 Pohl explored the region closely for clues but found that most of the area had been mined and bulldozed for roads. According to the Micmac tale, Sinclair-Glooskap then left this promontory and headed due west to the ocean. The real Sinclair, if he had sailed west from this point, would have reached New Brunswick, Maine, and then Massachusetts and Rhode Island. From Rhode Island or Massachusetts, the current would take him to Nova Scotia again, and later that current would take him back across the Atlantic and home to Scotland.

The longer Sinclair stayed, the more likely it is that his men might have married among the native peoples he visited. Children born to such a marriage may have been prized and honored if the first European–North American contact was friendly. The Micmacs belong to the Wabanaki tribe. The Wabanaki, in turn, are a branch of the Algonquin group, a confederation of languages more than an alliance of tribes. *Wabanaki* means "People of the Dawn"—the word *dawn* signifying "east," the place from which the sun rises every morning. A closely related tribe is the Wampanoag, their tribal name refers to them literally as the "white people." Being a descendant of the white people who landed in their world may have been considered an honor, and a person of the "white people" therefore might have been of partly European extraction. The presence of the "skeleton in armor" of Fall River, Massachusetts, might indicate that a Sinclair soldier stayed among the "white people" tribe and married into their clan.

The Gaelic word for woman is *ban,* and in certain dialects of the Algonquin language the word for woman is *bhanem*.[36] It is interesting to note that a type of baked bread was called *bannock* by both the Scottish and the Abenaki branch of the Micmac. Algonquin women had a special name for their babies who were still being breast-fed—*papoose* or *papisse.* Our own English *pap* refers to breast, and a woman's breast provides pablum for her baby's nourishment.

The Micmac did not regard Glooskap as their most supreme god; this god was Mn'tu, pronounced and often spelled *Manitou.* Celtic sailors brought their gods with them, the most important of whom was their god of the seas, Manannan. The Celtic sailors navigated by the constellations, including the Great Bear, which we know alternately as Ursa Major. Silas Rand and Cotton Mather found that the Micmac and Natick (of Massachusetts) both called the same constellation by the same name. The Milky Way of the European sailors was called the Milky Road by the Micmacs.

Places on Earth, too, had names with similar meanings. A sacred waterfall in Maine is Penobscot, and the tribe that took its name from this waterfall called their village *Pennacook,* meaning "down the hill." The British and Scottish surname Pennycook similarly describes people who lived "down the hill." The "oc," "ock," and "ook" word endings in Native

American dialects often mean "hill" or "place." In Scotland hill is *uck* in the highland and *ook* in the lowland dialects. In Ireland *knock* and *cnoc* also means "hill." Gaelic *Mor-riomach* means "from the deep place." In Algonquin, the river still remembered as the Merrimack in New Hampshire means "deep fishing place." The Scottish clan of Morrison debates the origin of their name. Both sides of the debate acknowledge it means "Sons of the Deep," and both sides agree it signifies people who arrived in Scotland because of a shipwreck. They disagree only about whether they had originally sailed from Ireland or Scandinavia.

The New Hampshire river that remains on our map under its Algonquin name of Merrimack has a second name at the place where its width is the greatest—*Kaskaashadi*, or "slow moving waters." In Gaelic, *G-uisge-siadi* has the same meaning. Another river in New Hampshire is called the Quechee, meaning "gorge" in the native language; the word resembles *cuithe* the Gaelic term for "gorge." Similarly, the rivers Piscataqua, Seminenal, Amoskeag, and Cabassauk as well as the brook named Cohas have related meanings in Gaelic.

The Iroquois were a very powerful confederation of tribes that lived west and south of the Algonquin. Was their organization, which brought them power, the result of early contact with those other European visitors, the Norse? As previously mentioned, the long halls that were favored by the fierce Vikings were similar to the longhouses of the Iroquois, which made them unique among native tribes.[37] The Iroquois word for "stones" is *ariesta*, which is also their word for "testicles." The Norse, too, called both stones and testicles by the same name—*eista*. The Norse word for "eat" is *eta*, and the Iroquois word is *ate*. The Norse word for "ice" is *iss*, the Iroquois word is *oise*. The Norse word for "woman" is *kvenna* (which later gave us our word for the female ruler, queen), also known as *kona*. In the Iroquois language *wakonnyh*, *akonkwa*, and *iskwe* are all words for "woman."

The multitude of shared terminology on both sides of the Atlantic is certainly a significant clue that points to early commnication between these groups. How much of that interaction was a result of Gaelic seafarers, Norse Vikings, or Sinclair's hardy Scots is not as important as the fact that such communication existed in the first place. What is also important is that it is very likely that contact was relatively constant for a period of time that may stretch back one thousand years before Columbus. The steadfast refusal by some to accept that Faeroese whalers, Basque fishermen, Norse farmers, and Irish monks reached the western shores of the Atlantic before Columbus paints them into a corner. The North Atlantic was crossed by sailors well before Columbus. The Sinclair-Zeno voyage was just one more of those many pre-Columbian crossings. It is also the first step in the construction of the Money Pit at Oak Island. Future Sinclairs would be back in the years to come. The newfound Arcadia held a greater significance for them than simply new lands. It became a sanctuary and a hiding place for a family with the need for such a refuge.

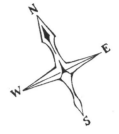

Chapter 5

"... IF TWO OF THEM ARE DEAD"

There is a saying that "three can keep a secret if two of them are dead." If Henry Sinclair felt that he had discovered a New World, he decided to keep his world a secret. He had just enough time to pass on the knowledge of his new lands to his family before conflict with England took the life of the "prince" of the New World. He never had had a chance to see his settlements grow, since he died defending his lands in the north. His son, Henry, the second earl of Orkney, was chief attendant to Prince James, who later became James I of Scotland.[1] On a mission to France he was captured at sea and sent to the Tower in London. He was later released and spent his last days on the family estates in Scotland. Henry had time to pass on the knowledge of the New World to his own son, William, the grandson of the first earl, who was singularly responsible for preserving and defending the sacred treasures that were to come to Oak Island.

There were two other principals in the 1398 expedition—Sir James

Gunn and Antonio Zeno. Sir James Gunn was left in a shallow grave in Massachusetts and shared the secrets of the new lands with no one. His Orkney crew may have already included sailors who were as well traveled as the Faeroese fisherman, but for such commoners the new lands held no riches beyond those of good fishing. There is reason to believe that the Zeno family did not see the value in lands to the west of Iceland. New lands were not needed at the time. The year in which Zeno returned to Venice was the tail end of the plague. This plague hit Italy even harder than it hit remote Iceland, possibly killing two-thirds of the population. New lands in the icy waters of the North Atlantic held little value. Antonio himself died in 1405, just months after returning to his home in Venice.[2]

Andrew Sinclair's family biography, *The Sword and the Grail*, takes the stance that the Sinclair-Zeno expedition had been a "secret mission" all along, but there is no evidence to support this claim.[3] The expedition was mostly simply an adventure, embarked upon for the thrills and possibilities, in the spirit of all adventures. Evidence that the two families had known of each other three hundred years earlier, when the crusaders traveled to Jerusalem on Venetian ships, is circumstantial, but it does not mean that they had any more than a shared event in their respective family histories.

The Zeno family did not keep the voyage secret; they simply had no reason to publicize it in light of the fact that there is evidence that these lands were not "new" at all. Visits to Iceland were not uncommon in Zeno's day. As we have seen, the pope in Rome had sent bishops to Iceland and Greenland, and Columbus had sailed to Iceland in 1477. And two thousand years before Zeno or Columbus, the intrepid Greek sailor and astronomer Pytheas had sailed to "Thule."[4] Discovery of the Zeno voyage was not considered significant until much later, when European countries began to fight over the lands discovered by accident while trying to find a sea route to China. By the time Zeno's letters and charts emerged, the Old World was squabbling over the territory in the New World.

In 1558, a descendant of the two seafaring Zeno brothers who had sailed with Sinclair compiled the letters the brothers had sent home—

Niccolo's letters to Antonio asking him to come to Scotland and those that both brothers wrote to Carlo in Venice. A great-great-great grandson, who was also named Niccolo, is responsible for compiling the letters. As a youth, this younger Niccolo Zeno had been playing in a storage area in the palace of the Zeno family when he came across the letters and maps. The five-year-old child destroyed much of what was there. Later, when he discovered that his father had shown the letters to a relative who was planning to include them in his publication *Discendenza Patrizie,* he realized his folly.[5] As an adult he came across the papers again and preserved the remainder.

The letters and charts that had survived Niccolo's childhood were in poor condition, and in many cases Niccolo copied the letters and maps in his own hand. What was not understood he updated, and anything that translated poorly from century-old language was edited. When details appeared to be missing, he added his own. And he superimposed the lines of longitude and latitude to the map.[6] It is no surprise that some of the detail, including place-names and names of individuals, suffered in the translation. As a result, we will never know just who is responsible for the inaccuracies of the maps and manuscripts.

In 1558 the claim of the authenticity of the letters might have been debated at a time when the question of just who first landed where started to take on monumental significance. Before lands were colonized, conflicting claims led to continuing challenges. Resolution by the authority of the pope resulted in the "Papal line of Demarkation," which so inaccurately divided the world between Spain and Portugal that it failed as a solution to the growing conflict.[7] The English, French, and Swedes were soon to start pressing their claims to every square mile of North America, barren or otherwise.

During Antonio Zeno's lifetime, new lands were not needed in a depopulated Europe. Once the plague ended, however, open space, farmlands, and the ever present possibility of gold and silver drew great attention to America. The same farflung outposts of eastern Canada that had been abandoned a hundred years earlier became the reason for life and death struggles between European nations. A claim from any Giovanni-come-lately would be ridiculed as just a counterfeit effort to take lands that one had no realistic reason to claim. Because the tiny city-state of Venice would never make any such claim, sixteenth-century mapmakers put much greater stock in the Zeno voyage than historians of the nineteenth and twentieth centuries. Mariners and cartographers snapped up copies of the Zeno map, which soon circulated widely throughout Europe.

Gerardus Mercator, whose Mercator projection is familiar to every student of modern mapmaking, was a German who Latinized his name, as was the custom for scholars of the day. He studied cartography at university, but took his science into the commercial arena immediately upon graduation. His career was launched selling maps of the Holy Lands to the religious minded. Upon inventing his technique, which is still used today, he redrew the map of the world, again employing both his genius for science and his talent for commerce. He called his new world map a "New and Improved . . . Description of the World," creating a marketing slogan that would be employed by advertisers four hundred years later.[8]

His map showed a gigantic Australia, originally extrapolated from Greek maps. It also increased the size of all lands that lie near the poles, which could create confusion for less-educated seafarers. His maps depicted "St. Brendan's Isle" and a "Brazil" situated in the North Atlantic, directly west from Ireland. Mapmakers of his day seemingly would rather add an island that wasn't there rather than miss an island that was. Abraham Ortelius was a friend of Mercator's from Antwerp and also used the Zeno map along with more ancient sources for his own maps.[9] With Mercator, Ortelius is given the credit for creating the first atlas.

That there may have been inaccuracies, either in the original or in the copied version of the Zeno charts, does not discredit the Zeno voyage any more than the fact that Cabot labeled North America as Cipangu (Japan) discredits his voyage.[10] Much of what earlier was considered inaccurate has been confirmed by modern experts, including Hapgood and Mallery, especially the detailed description of the Greenland coastline and points farther west.

The Zenos are well-known to history both for their wealth and their long-term prominence in their home city-state of Venice. During the sixteenth century Venice was possibly the wealthiest city in the world because all commerce with Asia was overland on a route that passed through the city. Such trade produced great wealth, and the palace of Zeno was a center of Venice's power. The history of the Zeno family stretched back into European history one thousand years.[11] They started in Padua and became one of the first twenty-four families who built Venice in the eighth century. They were among the greatest fleet owners of Venice, a center for seabound commerce. Their ships traveled from the cities of Europe to Constantinople, to the Levant. The Roman Church and the Catholic kings were required to pay the Zeno fleets for passage to Constantinople and eventually to Jerusalem. The Zeno family was represented on the Council of Ten, which had run Venice since the fourteenth century.

Twice the family received credit for the survival of their city-state— first in 1253, when Renier Zeno brought financial life back to a Venice wracked by revolts that had hurt trade. His diplomacy put an end to the struggles and reestablished the commercial primacy of Venice. His fleet defeated the Genoese fleet in their trade war for the Levant, and he was rewarded with the title of doge. While being the doge of Venice might be compared to being mayor of a great city, Venice was the richest city and the doge was entitled to make the rules governing world trade and to benefit from them. When this first Zeno saved his city, the real reward was riches, and when he died the fortune he left behind was vast.

The second rescue of Venice by the Zeno family was in 1380. At that time Venice was still the strongest principality in a divided Italy as well as the heart of the world's trade linking the East and West. Everything that came overland passed through Venice, where a fee, sometimes one-third of the entire value of the goods, would be charged. Such a monopoly on world trade attracted the jealousy of other states that lived in the shadow of Venice. Two of Venice's enemies, Padua and Genoa, teamed up with Hungary against Venice. The early conflict started badly for the outmanned city, and the Genoese fleet captured and occupied Chioggia on the lagoon of Venice and prepared to take the entire city. There were two fleets of importance in Venice at the time. The fleet commanded by Vittor Pisani was defeated by Genoa. The second fleet was under the command of Carlo Zeno.

The Zeno fleet had been away in the east when the conflict started. Messengers had been sent out from the city, to find the fleet and to tell of the dire threat hanging over Venice, but there was no confirmation the message had even gotten through to Zeno. The city was starving under the Genoese blockade, and the question on everyone's mind was "Where is Zeno?" A vote was taken, and it was decided that Venice would surrender on New Year's Day in 1381. Just as it appeared the war was over for Venice, the Zeno fleet appeared. The Genoese fleet was immediately attacked and defeated by "Carlo the Lion," as he was called. Younger brother Niccolo commanded one of the ships. Although the war continued until the next June, the Genoese were soundly beaten.

While their financial acumen and military prowess made the Zenos one of the most important families in Venetian history, their critics charge them with one failing so great as to cast doubt on the entire voyage to America: poor spelling. The blame should not lie entirely with the Zenos, since they were forced not only to translate the Norman-English language into their own Italian dialect but also to convey their message through writing. The text and charts of the narrative were in some cases destroyed and often were illegible; then they were resurrected by the Zenos' sixteenth-century descendant, who translated freely.

One example of just what distance, time, and language can do to alter a text is the name of the starting point of the journey. The Shetland Islands had originally received their name from the Norse word for "basalt," *Het-Land.*[12] Through time the name became Shetland. The younger Niccolo was familiar with neither, and so he substituted "Este-Land," a name derived from the town of Este near his own home in the northern Italian peninsula. A family of that name had a pedigree as long and as noble as the Zenos'.

The home of Henry Sinclair, whom Niccolo's ancestor called "Prince," was Roslin, a name that has been spelled several different ways; the Scottish "Sinclairs" were originally Norman "St. Clairs," and spelling in different translations was more an art than a science. This text will refer to the Norman family as "St. Clair" and to the Scottish branch as "Sinclair," although exceptions do exist. *Ros,* means "red," and *lin,* or more often *lynn,* means "stream." Again, young Niccolo may have inverted "ros" to spell "sor" and come up with "Sorano" as the home of the prince. Another important family of Venice, who shared the leadership of the city with the Zeno family, was that of Soranza. At the time of Niccolo's writings, Soranza was the doge, the supreme head of Venice. Like Niccolo's ancestor, Soranza was an admiral of the Venetian fleet and had also been victorious against the Genoese. In Italian, *Sorano* would mean "of Sor." If Niccolo translated "Ros" as "Sor," Sorano would be the natural result. In his work on the Sinclair family Andrew Sinclair stated that Niccolo took this name from Caithness, the lands that the Sinclairs had inherited in the north; translating Caithness into Sorano, however, would be even more difficult.

Henry Sinclair's base of operations was often an island named Bressay. The younger Niccolo abbreviated the name of the island as Bres, but for once this was actually more accurate. The "-ay" suffix denotes "island" in the Norse language that was prevalent throughout the north—calling the place the "island of Bressay" would be redundant. An important island situated halfway between the Orkneys and the Shetlands was Fer Island. This island, previously mentioned, was translated on maps by various spellings that included Ferisland and later Frislandia. When the Zeno narrative speaks of Porlanda, an island south of the Hebrides, which is much more populated, it is no stretch to guess that the island of Skye with its large town of Portree is the perfect candidate. Skye was south of the Hebrides, and more populous, and Portree was the largest settlement. Such spelling and translation problems plague modern historians. Pohl says Porlanda was simply Pentland, a large area of Scotland; other writers supply Portland, which is no longer on any map. History records Portland as having had a duke who also wrote of the earls of Roslin. The Zeno narrative speaks of captured fishing boats in "Sanestol," which could be Stenscholl, also in Skye.

While such strained translations do little to enhance Niccolo's credibility, we should remember other historic translations. London is a name that was translated differently under different masters. It was originally called Lug, for a powerful Celtic god of the same name. When Roman legionnaires reached the town of Lug, they translated it as *Luguvalium*, "the town of Lug," or *Lugdunum*, "the stronghold of

Lug."[13] When Vikings left behind their city of Jarvik in Norway, it remained in their hearts. They named a place where they settled in England for their hometown. This new Jarvik was translated by the English language as "York," and it has remained so.[14] English settlers in America, again keeping a fondness for their own city, named their new settlement "New York." Very few New Yorkers would recognize their city's name as having descended from a relatively small Norwegian seaport. With London and New York in mind, it is not difficult to see how time, distance, translation, and modernization can alter an original spelling. The added hindrance to continuity in the case of Zeno's narrative is the fact that the original letters were in a mutilated condition when they were finally compiled.

If the damage done to place-names were not bad enough, it was the younger Niccolo's rendering of Henry Sinclair's name that stirred the greatest debate. Niccolo compounded his ancestors' mistake in calling Henry a prince by naming him Prince Zichmni. This title defied explanation until Johann Reinhold Forster came along.[15] This eighteenth-century writer and historian started with the declaration that while there were no "princes" in the Orkneys, there was an earl—Henry Sinclair. There were no earls in Venice, so Niccolo needed a word that translated into a title that could be understood in the Italian language. Henry's title was Earl of the Orkneys and Caithness. Forster also pointed out that the title of prince was never followed by a surname but rather by the municipality that the prince called his domain. He believed "Prince of the Orkneys" was what the older Niccolo had attempted to convey to his brother in his letters.

Translation, however, was a problem. There was no equivalent to an "ey" ending in Italian; an "I" would have to be substituted. And the "D'O" beginning of "D'Orkney" (of Orkney) appearing as a "Z" was simply poor handwriting. While Forster's work as a historian had merit, this explanation is not easy to accept. A look at the Sinclair history might be helpful. In 1392 King Richard II of England granted safe conduct for Henry Sinclair (then St. Clair) to come into his country. In this letter he described Sinclair as "Comes Orchadie, et Dominus de Roslyne." He spelled the family name as "Seintcler." It was not just the unlearned who rendered the written language of the fourteenth century less than simple to understand.

The Sinclairs themselves seemingly provide further evidence as to just how badly a name can be distorted. In 1658 one of the first direct descendants of the Sinclair family went to America.[16] Once in his new home in New Hampshire, he changed the spelling of the name to "Sinkler." A once proud and respected family name that could be traced back a thousand years to a saint was rendered in terms that might be freely associated with an implement for fishing. In America, other direct descendants did even more damage. New spellings included "Sain Clair," "Cinclair," "Sinklee," "Sinklir," and "Synkler," among numerous other versions. It was in *The History of the Sinclair Family in Europe and America,* published in 1896, that I found facsimiles of signatures that came to confuse the family name further. The signature of the son of the original immigrant, "Sinkler," appears as "Sink Por." An eighteenth-century Joseph Sinkler distorted his surname, making the "S" in the first part of the name a "Z" separate from the last letters. It was not until 1800 that most variations started to disappear and the descendants adopted the more correct "Sinclair" or "St. Clair."

While a prince in the north of Europe may have been more inclined to use his country or province in his title, a prince in any of the states that make up modern Italy certainly would have used his name. It is likely that Prince Sinclair, as Niccolo might have called his employer, translated to Prince Zichmni, if the "S" became a "Z" and a more common vowel ending was substituted in Italian. The most relevant fact is that there was only one man who ruled the Orkneys at the turn of the fifteenth century and there was only one fleet big enough to fit the description. That ruler and that fleet owner was one person, and no one else fit the bill. The earl of the Orkneys was Henry Sinclair.

Another translation of the Zeno narratives was put together by Richard Henry Major. His version, published in 1873, also said that Zichmni and Sinclair were the same person, and at that point the discussion and debate were considered resolved. The staid *Dictionary of National Biography* agreed that it was Henry Sinclair who led the Zeno expedition. Soon after the Major's publication, a new critic, Fred Lucas, came along to confuse the matter once again. Declaring that Zichmni was actually a Baltic pirate instead of the earl of the Orkneys, he threw the Zeno narratives into doubt once more. The Baltic pirate was actually named "Wichmann," but fifteenth-century spelling being what it was, that did not resolve the dispute.[17] The main flaw in Lucas's theory is that he failed to explain why two rich shipowners from an incredibly wealthy and powerful family would ever enlist in a pirate fleet in the Baltic Sea or why they would be proud to report to their brother Carlo, a war hero, that they had allowed a pirate to "knight" them.

Before the 1960 discovery of L'Anse aux Meadows and Norse settlers in Canada, any tale of an expedition, planned or otherwise, to the New World was fair game to criticism. Once the discovery became public knowledge, the old school's position began to lose ground. Much damage, however, had already been done to discredit the Zeno narratives and charts. And it would not be until later years that historians and cartographers would again validate both the story and the maps of the Zenos. The Sinclairs themselves were of no help in the recognition of Zeno's charts, considering that they may have wished their new lands to remain secret. By the time the younger Zeno brought his compilation of maps and letters to the attention of the world in 1558, the Sinclairs had already made at least one more trip, and most likely several, to their new lands.

The Clan Sinclair

In the sixteenth century the Sinclair family became embroiled in a life-and-death struggle for their own lands and the lands of the countrymen to whom they were allied. The nation of Scotland was only a concept, and most of the greatest families had loyalty to their own. A united England as aggressor, however, began to unite the Scots in retaliation to their overlords. The Sinclairs soon found themselves the targets of the English, and they needed a refuge to fall back to if they were overwhelmed. They had allied themselves by their actions to Scottish history's strongest leader and the family that would lead the revolution in Scotland. They had also allied themselves to another, stronger secret society outlawed in Europe, but called upon by Scotland to join the fight against the English. Thanks to Sinclair protection, this secret society has survived to modern times.

To understand how this secret alliance came to be, and just how the Sinclairs became both the protectors of the society and guardian to a treasure so important that it needed to be hidden from England, it is necessary to trace the Sinclair history even further back in time. The man who sailed to America before the Cabots and Cartiers of later years came from a family at least as ancient and important as that of the Zenos. Henry Sinclair and the Sinclair family are prominent indeed in the history of Scotland, but they trace their origin back to much earlier days—to a Norse migration to France and then north to the British Isles.[18]

In the ninth and tenth centuries, the Scandinavian Norse grew restless. From Norway, Sweden, and Denmark, the Vikings raided, colonized, and settled wherever they could. In the north of France, one of the earliest of the clan was Rollo, who led Norse invaders on a quest for new lands. His son Rognwald met the French king Charles, whom history calls Charles the Simple. He demanded land from Charles as well as Charles's daughter in marriage. At the place of the meeting, the Norsemen built a castle. These Norse who settled in France became the Normans.

The St. Clairs (the French version of their name) were the single most important Norman family. This family owned the castle that was built at the treaty site in A.D. 912. They, in fact, had taken their name from that of a saintly martyr who lived as a hermit near what was considered a holy well near the River Epte, north of Paris.[19] The holy man was murdered by the order of a "cruel woman" whom he had rebuked. Today his statue depicts him holding his severed head in his outstretched hands. The "severed head" came to be another significant symbol among those privy to an "underground stream" of sacred knowledge.

After the murder of this holy man, the area surrounding the well became known as St. Clair, and the people who resided in the castle took the name as their own surname. The family that had descended from a Norse invader, Rollo, became the St. Clairs. It was the Normans who, for purposes of taxation and administration, introduced surnames into Europe by such censuslike recordings as the Domesday Survey.[20]

Europe had had no use for surnames since the days of Roman supremacy. The St. Clairs were related through marriage to William the Conqueror and were present in numbers at the Battle of Hastings, where William's Norsemen took over England. William, too, had descended from a Norse family that had settled in France.

The nine Sinclairs, as they spelled the family name once they were established in England, were rewarded for their valor at Hastings with grants of land. One of the Sinclairs, Walderne, married well. His wife was Margaret, daughter of Richard, duke of Normandy. Walderne was given the title earl of Sinclair, and his son William founded what became the Roslin branch of the family, to which "Prince" Henry would later be born. Another Sinclair, Agnes, married the head of the Bruce clan, who would come to challenge England. The Bruce clan had changed their name from the French "De Brus" upon reaching England.[21]

For unknown reasons, the Bruce clan and the William Sinclair family had a falling out with their king and headed north to Scotland, where they allied themselves with Malcolm III. At the time, "kingship" had a different meaning than it does today. Scotland and England were made up of several important and powerful families who ruled alongside the king. Often these clans held more power and wealth than the king. Malcolm's first wife was the widow of a Norse ruler in northern Scotland, and the marriage had been mostly a political alliance that Malcolm used to consolidate his own strength. The Normans were regarded as conquering imperialists around the world but never as a nation. After Malcolm's death, his sons, Alexander and David, ruled by the power of their widespread loyalties in the north. They turned away from the Celtic ways to become feudal lords in the Norman style. This meant a new social structure, much more complex than that of the Celtic peoples. The social structure included taxation, which meant that the more lands the king could lay claim to through his lords, the more taxes he brought in to his own kingdom. Imported Normans were just what the king needed to keep this process growing. The distinction between Norman and Scot became blurred after two centuries.

In March of 1286 Alexander III, the reigning king of Scotland, attended a wild drinking bout with his knights.[22] Although they pleaded with him to stay and sleep off the effects of too much drink, he rode home in the dark and, in his intoxicated state, soon became lost. Somewhere along his ride, he fell from his horse and died of a broken neck, leaving no heir. For Scotland it was a fateful night, bringing about problems that would take centuries to heal.

The immediate result was a complicated battle for succession. The king of England was as eager as anyone to impose his will on the north. Norman families found themselves on different sides of the battlefield as a result of the alliances that normally kept the country together. Bishop Wishart of Glasgow and Bishop Fraser of Saint Andrews summoned a council of bishops, abbots, earls, and barons, and from this group a regency of six "guardians" was appointed, of which one would be picked as king. This did not stop friction between the guardian families, and in the process churches, schools, nunneries, and entire villages were burned. Military excursions from England led to a rise in nationalistic feeling for the first time among the amalgamation of peoples that were the Scots. With the French and the pope backing John Balliol, the Scots found their own interests were taking a backseat to foreign interests. Robert the Bruce of Carrick soon emerged as a symbol of the will of this newly inspired nationalism.

Robert the Bruce was of the French De Brus family, of Norman extraction. He opposed the choice of Balliol and in turn made enemies of many of the other Norman families, including that of John of the Red Comyn. Because Scotland was not a nation, some families allied themselves with either England or France. Most, though, were loyal only to their own families. Another very fateful night in Scotland's early history resulted from a plan to get Robert the Bruce and John Red Comyn together to settle their differences. It was in February of 1306 that the two met at the church of the Minorite friars in Dumfries.[23] This church was chosen because both sides felt that violence could be avoided in such surroundings. The Grey Friars church, however, would have no such calming effect on either opponent.

Only Bruce and Comyn entered the church; their men were instructed to wait outside. Robert the Bruce was the younger man, and early in his life Comyn had roughed him up in front of other Scottish leaders, an insult not forgotten. History does not record just what went on in the darkened church, but soon Bruce rushed out saying that he had stabbed Comyn with his dirk, a short Scottish dagger, and thought he was dead. Roger de Kirkpatrick, a trusted friend of Bruce's replied, "You think? Then I'll make sure." He rushed into the church to see the friars dragging the body closer to the altar. Other Bruce loyalists chased the holy men away while Kirkpatrick finished the job with his own dagger. The body was dripping blood on the altar of the church. Comyn's uncle rushed into the fray only to be killed by Christopher Seton, a Bruce supporter.

Bruce now had two choices—retreat and live as an outlaw as a result of the excommunication that would surely follow or seize the moment, and the power that might be his, even if only for a brief time. He decided he had only one choice, to finish what he had started. His men were instructed to seize Dumfries Castle while he rode to Bishop Wishart for absolution. Five weeks later this bishop crowned Robert the Bruce king at the ancient Stone of Scone, a sacred unifying symbol of Scotland. The approval of the bishop was a calculated move on Bruce's part to divide the Scottish Church and the Church in Rome, as well as draw a line separating the English in the south and the Scots in the north. The murder at Grey Friars served to make the cause of Bruce the cause of Scotland.

His problems were far from over despite the nationalistic feeling he mounted in his support. Edward of England marched against Bruce and Scotland, and Bruce and his close family were forced into hiding. As his wife had commented, Bruce was "king" in name only, and the early days after his crowning would support her prediction. Bruce traveled from island to island in the west, often going hungry, and dressing in peasant clothes. One fateful night he was trying to sleep in a cave. The war against England was going badly; Bruce had seen friends and family captured and killed. Lying awake in the dark cave was for Bruce a dark moment. He was not sure whether he could go on.

Looking up, he watched a spider swinging from his web. The spider kept trying to make it to the wall, but each time his momentum brought him close, only to stop him short of his goal. As the king of Scotland lay underneath, the spider went on trying. Eventually the spider swung wide enough to grab on to the wall. Robert the Bruce decided at that moment that he, too, would keep trying. He emerged from hiding only to encounter the English in small skirmishes that he usually won, but an open battle would be fatal. Frustrated by his inability to draw Bruce into open combat, the king himself actually came to Scotland to fight beside his men. The aging Edward did not survive the hard traveling and died en route to meet the Scots. This gave the forces of Bruce and Scottish nationalism breathing room, and he capitalized on the time.

Bruce used the next few years to avenge his enemies in Scotland and to seize their estates and castles. In 1314 the English returned under the son of King Edward II to reclaim Scotland. Their army has been estimated to have been one hundred thousand men strong. Although their numbers could have been an exaggeration, they were better armed. The Scots were outmanned at least three to one and were believed to be outgunned.[24] The English army was made up of powerfully armed and trained knights and experienced infantry. The Scottish forces were poorly financed and poorly armed. They were forced to rely on Gallgaels from the west, who carried only spears; Picts from the far north, who had barely emerged from the Stone Age; and hardy island warriors from the Orkneys, who often used homemade weapons. The best that they brought to the field were lightly armed horsemen.

When the English arrived it was in a column that stretched for two miles. Fearing such a show of power would cause his own forces to flee the battlefield, Bruce took a famous calculated risk. He accepted the taunting challenge made to the Scots by one heavily armed knight to send their best man into battle alone, to face the knight. Against the pleas of his horrified brother, Robert the Bruce rode out into the field. Described as a small figure on a small horse, he appeared to be no challenge to the opposing knight, who immediately charged him. To Bruce's men, watching the larger knight on a larger horse, fully armored and wielding a battle lance, the fight appeared to be lost before it even began. Bruce, however, understood that he could use his size to his advantage. As the knight charged, Bruce stood his ground, only to make a quick sidestep as the English knight reached him. He deftly avoided the weapon thrust at him and turned to swing his own ax into the skull of his challenger. The knight, Henri de Bohun, fell to the ground dead.

To see the heavily outfitted knight fall so quickly before their lightly armored leader inspired the men, as Bruce had hoped it would. Bruce had counted on much more than inspiration. Once the battle started in earnest, their cunning plans were put into action. First the mounted knights were steered onto a field prepared with booby traps such as potholes and spiked balls. As the knights' horses fell to the ground, primitive Highlanders were there to finish the job with their spears. Still the English had forces to spare and several attacking at the same time. At one point all the Scottish forces were engaged when a new flank of English knights appeared on the scene. Just as this fresh force appeared, one that could turn the tide against the Scots, their own secret weapon rode out. The English were opposed and then beaten by three hundred knights who had been previously held off the field. This superior force was commanded by Thomas Randolph. Legend says Randolph lost only one man in his attack that sent the English running and saved Scotland.[25]

The tide had truly turned in favor of the Scots. The next day, the Feast of John the Baptist, Bruce's force caught up to the retreating army of Edward II. Bruce had been against chasing the English, since he felt his soldiers were not strong enough to engage the enemy again, but one of his knights, Alexander Seton, whom history describes as a deserter but who was more likely a spy, told Bruce that the English would surrender. Some did surrender, others fought and were defeated. The result of the defeat for the English was that Scotland had achieved its independence.

After the Battle of Bannockburn, many Scottish families allied themselves to Bruce and to each other. Setons, Grahams, and the Sinclairs were the most prominent. They united under the banner of nationalism. The same nationalism served to divide the bishops of Scotland, who were forced to stand on the side of the papacy or the side of their countrymen. Bishop Wishart, who crowned Bruce at the Stone of Scone, and Bishop William Sinclair were two who stood fast despite their resulting separation from the Church.

The cause of Scotland became the cause of the Sinclairs, and the history of the Sinclair family would now be tied firmly to the unfolding history of a revolutionary Scotland. The Sinclair and Bruce families were related through various marriages that furthered their alliance. The alliance would also bring Sinclair more wealth. William Sinclair was rewarded for his stand with Robert the Bruce with additional lands near Edinburgh and in Pentland. His son William married Isabel, the daughter of Malise, the earl of Orkney, bringing even more land to this powerful family. William's second son was Henry, who became the first Sinclair to bear the title earl of Orkney and the Sinclair who would sail with Zeno to Nova Scotia. It was the inaccurate genealogist Father Hay who later called Henry's grandson a prince, although there is no recorded reason for this designation outside Zeno's letters.[26] Did the rushed Father Hay genealogy have another source to which Zeno was also privy?

The revolution in Scotland gave the Sinclair family little time to enjoy their new prosperity, since conflict with England, opposing Norman families, and Highland clans were a constant threat. After Bannockburn, England did not launch a major attack on Scotland but did harass the Norman families in the border lands. This harassment led several families to change alliances. The Norman clans were normally allied only to the cause of their clan, much in the way that Highland clans recognized only their own clan as the proper object of their allegiance. It was not an act of treason to switch from one side to another—as the family and clan always came before any nation. In Italy, the Norman sons of Tancred repeated this same pattern, with brother fighting brother on occasion in the attempt to gain control of that divided land.[27] Only when faced with an outside force did the Normans unite. In the British Isles, where allegiance to the king of England and allegiance to Robert the Bruce divided the isle, the confrontation would place Sinclairs on opposing sides, even at Bannockburn. The Roslin branch had no problem fighting their English cousins.

The war for independence took its toll on the Sinclair family, but it also brought the family wealth. For the standards of Scotland in their day, the early knights of the Roslin Sinclairs lived in a splendor not typical of their country. William, grandson of Henry the seafaring explorer, as earl of Orkney and Caithness, lived in unheard wealth.[28] Among the members of his court were Lord Dirleton, Lord Borthwick, Lord

Fleming, and other prominent landowners. William had married into the Douglas clan, and his wife, Elizabeth (whom biographer Hay called a princess), had seventy-five servants—fifty-three "of noble birth"—and two hundred "riding women" attending to her needs. Vessels of gold, clothes of silk, and an entourage more suitable to an Oriental khan hardly seemed possible in a land that visiting Pope Pius II described as a wild place where people ate the bark of trees.

Since the wealth of William Sinclair was not just made up of his lands near Edinburgh, but encompassed lands in the north of Scotland and in the islands off the mainland, he was often traveling with his fleet. When Sinclair was not at sea, he lived at his castle at Roslin, surrounded by his lands outside Edinburgh. He is given credit for designing and at least starting the construction of the Roslin chapel. The complex underground tunnel and vault system that is part of William's design has, like Oak Island, stubbornly clung to its secrets. In this century tombs that were rumored to be below ground were finally uncovered, but excavators are still baffled by such features as a stairway descending to nowhere.[29]

William was appointed grand admiral of Scotland by the king in 1436, following the tradition of his grandfather. In inheriting the traditional role of earl of Orkney, William likely also inherited the charts of his grandfather's exploits in America. The Sinclairs wanted to keep these lands secret, since they would serve a very important purpose. And they did preserve their secrets. What happened to their records in the form of maps and charts is unknown. In the eighteenth century the Sinclair estate suffered a massive fire, and records could have been lost at that time. In the fifteenth century, however, scarcely forty years after Henry's voyage, the records were probably available to the admiral.

By the time that Grand Admiral William Sinclair became the head of the family, the Sinclairs were protecting a treasure vastly more valuable than their own wealth. Sinclair had constructed the chapel of Roslin in such a way that its hidden tunnels could secure an important treasure and William's private army from their ever present enemies. The impending English invasion, however, led William to believe even his underground warren of passageways and vaults was not secure enough. The sacred treasure entrusted to the Sinclairs needed an even more complex hiding place and in a much more secure location. William Sinclair, admiral of Scotland and sea king of the Orkneys, had the means and the motive to construct the most massive treasure vault since King Solomon's temple. And he was one of very few Europeans who had accurate knowledge of the location of the new world.

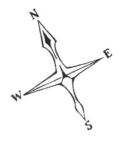

Chapter 6

The Knights Templar and Scotland

*H*istory's greatest and oldest author on the subject of war is Sun Tzu. His classic work, *The Art of War,* was written two thousand five hundred years ago in his native Chinese dialect, but it is still published and widely read today. It has one general principle, that the battle is won well before it is fought, by superior intelligence and planning. The decisive battle of Bannockburn is one powerful example of such superior intelligence and planning enabling a smaller outnumbered, outgunned force to become victorious over a superior force. Throughout the history of Scotland, the Scottish forces have been defeated by the English. Images of spear-hurling Highlanders and naked Welshmen facing legions of well-armed, uniform-clad English are not simply images. Even in the eighteenth century a desperate, hungry army of Scots was reduced to throwing stones against sixteen battalions of foot soldiers, three regiments of cavalry, and an armored division of the British at Culloden.[1]

Bannockburn, however, had been different. As usual, the Scots forces were inferior, but through superior planning and intelligence they won the battle. One deciding factor was the fresh force that had appeared seemingly from nowhere to save the day. The Scots had always thrown everything into desperate battle, but at Bannockburn, Robert the Bruce had saved this force in a gamble that paid off well for Scotland.[2] Had knowledge of this army held in the wings kept the Scots from deserting the battlefield when first greeted with the massive ranks of the enemy?

In the last chapter, the story of Robert the Bruce's personal courage in facing and defeating the heavily armed Norman knight is retold as the impetus for the courage of the Scots. Before the famous David and Goliath battle, were his own spear-carrying Highlanders aware that they were backed by a modern European force every bit as able and trained as the English and mercenary Normans? More than one modern historian claims that it was knowledge of this hidden ally that acted as the glue that held the smaller Scottish force intact in the face of the enemy.[3] That it was on Saint John the Baptist's feast day that this secret force turned the tide for Scotland was also a key factor. Where had the Scottish force found such a well-trained ally that it was able to win a decisive victory against the English? The secret weapon of the Scottish was the Knights Templar. And June 24 was a date considered sacred to these knights.

The Knights Templar

The Templars were an order of warrior-monks who once fought coura-geously for the Church against the Saracen enemy that had occupied the Holy Lands. As a group they were regarded as arrogant, as individuals, haughty. Their wealth attracted criticism, but as long as they held the Holy Lands they were considered heroes wih a mission. After being forced to abandon the Holy Lands to the Saracens, they lost their raison d'être. They had been betrayed both by the French king and the leader of the Christian Church, the pope. In 1307 they had been ordered ar-rested by King Philip of France. Over the course of the next few years they were imprisoned, tortured, and often put to the stake. Their order was disbanded and their lands and estates confiscated. Three months before the famous battle at Bannockburn, the grand master of the Templars, Jacques de Molay, the order's highest ranking leader, was roasted alive on the orders of the French king.[4] It was the final chapter in his decade-long campaign to break the power of the Templars and to seize their wealth. It wasn't the final chapter for the Templars themselves.

The history of the Templars begins with the Crusades. The Muslim rulers whom Europe called the Saracens had captured Jerusalem, and the Church aroused the populace of Europe to fight to regain the Holy Lands. When Jerusalem was recaptured, the Templars were organized. On the surface, the mission of the first Knights Templar was to protect pilgrims to the Holy Land.[5] It was a journey replete with danger from pickpockets, pirates, con artists, and highwaymen. Once Jerusalem had been rescued from the Saracens, all of Europe wanted to make this most sacred pilgrimage, but few were ready for the difficulties that lay ahead. Often, dishonest shipowners sold their entire cargo of Christian pilgrims into slavery in northern Africa. If pilgrims were fortunate enough to be aboard the ship of an honest man, they still had to contend with disease, seasickness, and Mediterranean pirates.

It appeared that the Knights Templar had created for themselves a truly noble undertaking. They styled themselves as warrior-monks, dedicating their lives to self-sacrifice. They cropped their hair and let their beards grow. They vowed personal poverty and chastity. Pledged to a celibate state and a sinless life, they slept clothed to avoid temptation. They gave away their own goods, and many had come from wealthy families and had much wealth to turn over to their order.

Their founder was Hugues de Payens.[6] Historians of the Templars and the Crusades always point out that de Payens was the son of a minor nobleman, from Champagne in France, indicating a less-than-powerful origin. The founder of the Templars, even though he had been born from a "minor" noble family, rose in status in his lifetime. He was related by marriage to the Norman St. Clair family.[7] He christened his order of warrior-monks the Order of the Poor Knights of Christ and the Temple of Solomon. In 1118 when he reached Jerusalem for the first time, his order was at its full force of eight men strong, besides de Payens himself. He presented his force to Baldwin I, the crusader who held the title king of Jerusalem. Hugues de Payens told the crusader of his mission, although it is not recorded just how these knights intended to defend Christians along thousands of miles of highway with a force of nine. And he made the request that they be allowed to house their small force in the ruins of the Temple of Solomon. It was granted. The knights took up residence in the Temple of Solomon.[8] For nine years they stayed there, admitting no new knights to their order.

After this lengthy stay the knights returned home to France to receive praise from the abbot of Clairvaux, who came to be known to history as the crusading Saint Bernard. Bernard convened the Council of Troyes in 1128 to recognize their merit and to make their order "official." Later, Pope Innocent II declared the order autonomous, answerable to no one except to the pope himself. In effect, a military order without borders was created.

Bernard was the spokesman for the Crusades.[9] His oratory was said to enflame anyone present. His speeches would cause husbands and sons to flock to join both the Crusades and the Templar organization. It is said that when he came into a town, wives would hide their husbands or lose them to the war. Bernard's backing of the Knights Templar was no small endorsement.

Bernard's concept of just what it meant to be a Christian soldier was radical even in his own time. He declared that the soldier of Christ serves "his own interests in dying, Christ's interests in killing." He said such a Christian soldier must serve as "Christ's legal executioner." Bernard had formed a military order out of the Templars, Christian soldiers willing to kill for peace. Young nobles from all over Europe rushed to join in the adventure. Along with the size of the order, its wealth grew as a result of monies and lands pledged by the knights. When the order returned to Jerusalem it held lands all over Europe and was a noble fighting army of three hundred knights. The Templars became a superior fighting force in terms of strength and courage and a superior moral force in a holy war that was very often unholy.

History plays down the fact that the Crusades were more often cruel adventures planned by manipulative and greedy rulers and carried out by peasants more intent on looting and rape. Christian soldiers were told that nothing they did in God's army was a sin because their cause was noble.[10] The first battle pitted western European Christians against Hungarian Christians as the entourage of the Crusades began to blaze through eastern Europe in the late eleventh century. The original mission was distorted the moment the crusaders left their own land. An army under Peter the Hermit, which started out in Cologne in April of 1096, burned the Christian city of Belgrade in May. German crusaders torched the houses of peasants after stealing their goods. One governor ordered a counterattack against the crusaders and killed ten thousand men—all before the army ever came near the Saracens in Jerusalem whom they were supposed to fight. Peter the Hermit finally lost control of the thirty thousand men who had survived fighting eastern Christians. The fighting force continued to attack Christian villages. When they finally reached an opposing Turkish force, they were exhausted from killing and looting fellow Christians. Their weakened force was so badly beaten that only three thousand escaped death or capture. These survivors fled to a castle by the sea where still another attack ended what is called the "People's Crusade."

In Italy the unified states were controlled by another Norman whose roots went back to France and further back to Norway, although the family was not allied with the Sinclairs. The Norman Tancred launched his own crusade. When his force reached Jerusalem in June 1099, they killed fifty thousand Saracens and Jews alike, taking no prisoners.[11] Tancred's men went through every house, one by one, in the holy city, killing, raping, and looting the unfortunate denizens until the streets flowed with blood. Coptic Christians believed that they were safe by the fact of their religion. Tancred ordered them expelled from the city but not before many were tortured in an effort to steal their wealth, real or imagined. Tancred's competition was the knight Baldwin, whose goal was to loot as many great cities of the east as he could. Baldwin took Edessa, while Tancred took Bethlehem in 1099. It was Baldwin, however, who declared himself the king of Jerusalem in 1100.

Into this immoral war marched the original nine Knights Templar in 1118. As we have seen, they were granted permission to use the royal palace built over Solomon's temple to serve as their headquarters. Before their return trip to Europe nine years later they may have done more excavating than fighting. Robert Payne, in his work *The Dream and the Tomb*, states, "From the beginning, Hugh of Payen appears to have had a larger aim."[12] Their only recorded accomplishment over the course of those nine years is such excavation work, though, ostensibly they also protected the highways for pilgrims. Finding a wall to the stables of the ancient king, they broke through it and returned to France.

Were the Templars more interested in looting than protecting the pilgrims of the highway? The original force appears to be guilty of that charge. Both the impossibility of the task and their strange actions indicate that Robert Payne was correct in assessing that they had very different goals. Later Templar armies would distinguish themselves in battle against Saracens, often taking the role of fighting last-ditch efforts so that others might escape and leading suicidal charges against an enemy much greater in size.[13] One grand master of the Templars led 130 men against a Saracen force of seven thousand. The rank and file may have taken their mission seriously and seen dying for Christ as a sure route to heaven.

With few exceptions, however, the leaders of the Crusades distinguished themselves only for being corrupt, cruel, and self-serving. The doge of Venice, the home base of the Zenos' power, backed one crusade only after forcing it to attack Zara in modern-day Yugoslavia first, to settle a score for the doge. The Venetian crusade fought against another crusader force and finally burned Constantinople, the most important Christian city in the east.

The Children's Crusade (A.D. 1212) was the result of the vision of a European teenager, Stephen of Cloyes. An army of children was recruited to fight the Saracens in the Middle East. However ridiculous that crusade seemed in the first place, the entire army of children was sold into slavery in Africa by an unscrupulous fleet owner. Frederick II, the grandson of Frederick Barbarossa, found the Saracens to be much more civilized than his fellow Europeans, and he surrounded himself with the enemy. His love for his sworn opponents led him to attack a Templar force in Acre, an act that ended in his excommunication by the pope.

Such infighting and greed among the Europeans contributed to their downfall. No act would compare, however, with the brutality and horror the Church and France unleashed on its own people. It is often left out of of the history of the Crusades that Rome launched a crusade into the Languedoc region of France. Before the Church and its minions were done killing Jews, Coptic Christians, Saracens, and anyone else who stood in their path to the Holy City, it committed possibly the worst act of genocide Europe would see until the time of Hitler. The south of France was occupied by people called Cathari.[14] Named for their purist beliefs, this faith regarded everything on Earth as evil. God had created a planet, yet the devil's work was evident everywhere. Their religion restricted their diet and their view of sex (also considered evil, since it created more humans on an evil Earth). For the most part the Cathari were a gentle, religious people whom even the warmongering Saint Bernard believed posed no threat. His investigation of them led him to say, "No sermons are more Christian than theirs."

While the religious beliefs of the Cathari are possibly very closely related to the Essene faith and the beliefs of early Christianity, they were not in tune with the new Roman political entity. They believed no one should stand between man and God and that priests could not save sinners. Their life was based on imitation of the apostles. This earned them Rome's enmity, especially after they pointed out that *Roma*, the Italian name for Rome, was the exact opposite of the message of Christ, in French, *Amor*. The Church set out to prove it.

First they condemned the Cathari, but did little. Then the rabid Dominic Guzman and his Dominicans brought the Inquisition to Europe. The misguided madness that lasted up to modern times at first allowed that anyone instigating prosecution of a heretic could then take his property. Greed in the name of religion had the Church prosecuting even the dead. In 1209 an army of thirty thousand descended on the south of France. One by one, Beziers, Perpignan, Narbonne, Carcassone, and Toulouse were attacked and their populations slaughtered by the forces of Rome. For the next twenty-five years the slaughter continued unabated. It culminated in the siege of Montsegur. There the Cathari who had survived the extermination campaign against them sought refuge in a castle atop a limestone mountain. For ten months, four hundred people—some Cathari, and some Christian Templar knights defending the Cathari—held out against the papal forces. It had seemed like an unequal struggle, with thousands of trained soldiers blockading a few hundred, but the countryside was replete with Cathar sympathizers who helped the besieged get food and water despite the standing army. Finally, the fortress surrendered but asked for a brief period to make a truce. The knights would be allowed to leave simply for their act of surrender. The devout, too, would be allowed safe passage only if they renounced their faith. If not, they would be burned alive.

In the brief period of truce, legend has it that a treasure sacred to the Cathari was smuggled out of Montsegur by three of the faithful and a guide, climbing down the thousand-foot cliff walls of Montsegur on ropes in the dark cover of night.[15] Their mission was to take the Cathar treasure, some already hidden in the forests below, to the caves of the Sabarthes. This treasure has never been found. Then the truce ended. Some of the knights had actually accepted the Cathar faith during the truce. The others were allowed to depart as promised. The faithful, including the new members, said they could not renounce their faith. They were put into a stockade and burned alive.

Just what the treasure of the Cathari is remains unknown. How much gold and silver could have been the property of a people hunted and starved out by their oppressors is in question. The south of France had once flourished, and the landowners at least were very wealthy. Legends of the treasure say that something of far greater value was being protected. Many believe that treasure is the Holy Grail.[16] The Holy Grail is often regarded as the cup from which Jesus Christ drank at the Last Supper. It figures deeply in the Arthurian cycle of mythology and in legends in France and Great Britain. Modern-day treasure hunters still search the nearby caves for whatever treasures might be found. In one is the gigantic grotto of the Lombrives, one of the largest in Europe. Deeply inscribed into a large wall in the cave is a five-pointed star, the pentagram. The cave also holds a huge dolmen, a tablelike rock structure with a large slab on three stone legs. The Celts left such structures all along the Atlantic coast of western Europe, but this may be the only one erected in a cave. The treasure has never emerged.

The Church defeated her enemies in southern France and in the east, but success in the Holy Land was not to last. The Saracens retook Jerusalem in 1188, and the war for Europe was lost. The Templars and another rival order, the Knights Hospitalers (also known as the Knights of Saint John) were among the Europeans who returned home. By the end of the Crusades, the Templars were a very strong order indeed, rivaled only by governments of Europe. In the course of executing their duties as guardians to the pilgrims that traveled to the Holy Lands, they created and established the practices that would lead to modern banking. A noble in Paris could deposit funds in Paris with the Templar "bank" and withdraw them from a Templar "bank" in Venice or Jerusalem. This protected the noble's funds while he was on the road, and it enabled the Templars to use deposited funds by making loans to kings and nobles alike. The deposits earned the Templars income, and the Templar lands earned them rents. Their growing strength, however, gained them the enmity of those jealous of such wealth and power.

Their greatest enemy was Philip IV of France. He had been denied entrance to the order, and he owed them great sums of money that he was unable to repay. Because he was broke, he levied even higher taxes against his own people, the result of which had him fleeing mobs and hiding for a time in the Paris temple. And he blamed much of his debt on his inability to tax the lands of the Templars, which were not subject to the king. In 1306 this king had ordered all the lands of the Jews in France confiscated so that he could shore up his own finances. Now he needed a new scapegoat. In 1307 he turned on his friends. Jacques de Molay had been godfather to one of the sons of Philip and pallbearer for the king's brother-in-law, Charles of Valois. Such loyalty had no merit with Philip.

While he could not simply confiscate the lands of the Templars and their rightfully owned properties, he was forced to use another strategy. The tried and true means for attacking and stealing property from Christians and Jews alike would work again. He accused them of heresy and devil worship, with sexual perversion thrown in for good measure. The

French king needed an ally to accomplish the feat of getting rid of the Templars and keeping their wealth. He turned to the only man on Earth to whom the Templars answered, the pope. He persuaded the pope to ban the Order of the Knights Templar, which was done by a papal decree in 1312. Why would the pope allow his own force to be attacked?

Historians have debated the role of Pope Clement V. His defenders say he was cornered into such ignominious action by the French king and his charges of heresy. The French King had supported one military action against Clement's predecessor, Boniface VIII, who had excommunicated him. The next pope had been poisoned. Clement V very likely had much to fear from Philip.[17]

Detractors say that the pope also had his own agenda, which included such minor sins as selling everything from indulgences to passports, and other, more serious needs, including the protection of Rome and the papal powers against a much stronger France. Whatever motivation caused the pope to allow Philip to proceed, he did. On Friday the thirteenth, 1307, he ordered all the Templars arrested.[18] In total there may have been two thousand surviving Templars at the time. They offered little resistance, because their grand master assumed that he could clear them against any charges put by a mere king. Philip's plan, however, called for more than their arrest. The Templars were subjected to the worst the Inquisition had to offer. Many died or even committed suicide as a result of the torture.

Under hideous torture, only four of one hundred and thirty-eight captured French Templars failed to confess to the crimes their torturers invented. The crimes they would confess to included devil worship; teaching women to abort; infanticide; spitting on, repudiating, and trampling on the Christian cross; homosexuality; and the worship of a skull (or bearded head) named Baphomet. Some of the crimes had a basis in what the Roman Church believed was heresy. Devil worship was an obvious charge to lay on a heretic. The crime of spitting on the cross could have been based on the Cathar belief that the cross, the murderous object of Jesus' torture, is an evil symbol. Homosexuality could be charged against any group of men who had been separated from women for so long.

Philip's plan would not be effective if the Templars were banned only in France; he needed to push the pope to carry the banner of his own anti-Templar crusade. England reacted against the Templars only after the papal decree, and even then without the same vigor as the French. Edward II, the king of England, waited until a second order came, on the fifteenth of December, 1307. After this order he waited another three weeks before ordering the Templars arrested. By this time only two Templars were to be found. They were not subjected to the Inquisition-style tortures that the French Templars received.

In England, where torture had been outlawed, there would be no confessions of worshiping a severed head, defiling the sacred cross, or homosexuality. The pope kept pushing Edward for both more arrests and more confessions, but Edward held firm against torture. To counter this stance, in 1310 the pope ordered Edward II to allow his own tortur-ers access to the imprisoned Templars. He signed the order to torture in the name of God on Christmas Eve. Despite the acts of the pope, few English Templars suffered the fate of their French brother knights.

Outside France, reaction to the pope was mixed. Arrests and torture did take place in the kingdoms of Naples and Sicily, but most of the Templars survived. In German lands (there was no united Germany, only an ever changing network of principalities), the knights walked boldly into court armed with their weapons. They were determined to go to war with this anti-pope and their accusers. No one challenged them. The German Templars would find a haven in the Teutonic Knights when the Templar order itself was disbanded.

Only in Scotland and Portugal were the claims of the French king and the orders of the pope completely ignored. The Templars lucky enough to escape France and flee to such safe havens would survive. Scotland, at odds with England, was one of the safest refuges to the escaping Templars, and many fled there to the open arms of Robert the Bruce and the Sinclair family, which had been instrumental in organiz-ing them centuries earlier.[19]

The pope would get his way in banning the Templars, but many survived and took much of their wealth underground. The properties of the Templars, their lands, and some of their monies were seized by Philip, and he decided, of course, that these confiscated lands all belonged to him. Most of the Templar wealth, however, was not to be found. As agents of the French king searched the cities and the countryside for Templars and their wealth, the resistance grew more well organized. In the course of fighting a war, the Templars had built up a fleet so substantial that some ports banned it because the citizens were afraid it would rival the trading ability of their own fleets. The principal ports of La Rochelle and nearby Le Havre, which would later become significant in the Atlantic trade, were the last of France that many of the escaping knights saw.

When the agents of the French king reached the Templar precept in Paris, they expected to find massive hoards of gold, the backbone of the Templar bank. Instead they found very little. The Templars had been tipped off, and a wagon train laden with whatever had been stored in Paris was secreted and quickly made its way to La Rochelle. In the port city it was loaded on Templar ships and disappeared from the clutches of the greedy king and from history. Only legend tells us where the treasure fleet of the Parisian Knights Templar might have gone. These legends, in fact, do not agree with each other, variously saying that the treasure reached Mediterranean seaports, Portugal, Ireland, Scotland, and possibly even Scandinavia. All were possible. While the only Templars arrested in Scotland admitted they had escaped by sea, they refused to reveal any of the ports that had granted the Templars safe passage or landing. Nor does history record any such official guarantee of safe conduct granted by any nation.

The only ports where the Templar fleet and the escaping Templar knights might be considered welcome would be places that were hostile to the pope. Scotland at the time was reeling from the murder of John Red Comyn in the church of the Grey Friars, and Bruce and others had earned excommunication for the sacrilegious act. But the larger ports of Scotland, Edinburgh, Glasgow, and even Aberdeen were being watched by English spies. In fact, these ports were blockaded part of the time by the English king, who was trying to find and capture Robert the Bruce. In England the enemies of the Templars were disappointed as well. The treasury of the London temple simply disappeared. How much of this wealth made it safely to Scotland and the guardianship of the Sinclair family is unknown, but part of it was used to buy weapons for Robert the Bruce.

Where could a fleet of treasure-laden ships and hundreds of knights seek safety? Very likely it was in the same places that Robert the Bruce was hiding. While legends of a king in hiding would equal those of Robin Hood in their re-creation, there were some very likely candidates for the sanctuary of Bruce. The most likely places were in Kintyre, a peninsula extending from Argyll, and some of the islands off the Scottish coast, including Jura and Islay. These were in the hands of the MacDonald clan, loyal to Bruce and openly hostile to invaders. Michael Baigent and Richard Leigh, authors of *The Temple and the Lodge*, had searched the western Highlands looking for both the hiding place of the Bruce supporters and the Templars.[20] One tale of "an island in a lake" brought them to Loch Awe and modern graves, but in nearby Kilmartin they found a concealed churchyard full of ancient stones decorated in Templar fashion.

Farther north, the Hebrides and the Orkney Islands would be even more suitable for hiding an entire fleet. Scapa Flow in the Orkneys was where the Germans scuttled a fleet of seventy of their own ships at the end of World War I, rather than surrender them to the British.[21] In World War II, the British fleet itself hid there, six hundred years after the Templar fleet might have enjoyed the isolated harbors of these remote islands as a sanctuary. Across from Scapa Flow is a landmark called Saint John's Head, where a distinctive rock structure rises 1,141 feet from the sea, one of the highest cliffs in the British Isles. Saint John, the beheaded prophet, featured very prominently in the Templar legends. The feast day of the holy prophet is their sacred date and remained sacred among the Freemasons and Masons that succeeded the Templars. Hundreds of years later, when English and Scottish lodges finally went public, their charter dates were set on Saint John's feast day, June 24.

Because Saint John the Baptist played such an important role in Templar iconography, it is interesting to note that this predecessor of Jesus, the voice crying out in the desert, was beheaded for his religion. Templars were charged with worshiping an idol of a skull named Baphomet.[22] Some historians have claimed that this is Muhammad, the prophet of Islam. Others suggest that Baphomet might have been a corruption of *abufihamet*, Arabic for "Father of Wisdom," or the person or deity represented on the Shroud of Turin.[23] After the publication of *Holy Blood, Holy Grail*, Dr. Hugh Schonfield discovered a very complicated form of cryptography that he called the Atbash cipher.[24] Using that method, he translated the word *Baphomet* into "Sophia." This form of cryptography may indicate that the Nazarenes, the followers of the earthly Jesus, and the Templars were in touch with each other. The decapitated head came to play a role in Templar mythology.

We will later see that Jesus of Nazareth may actually be a misnomer for Jesus the Nazarene, the Nazarenes being a group connected with the Essenes who yearned for a more strict observance of their religion. John the Baptist may have actually become more revered than Jesus himself among the remnant members of this group. There are those who believe that because John was decapitated the Templars took to revering him even more highly than Jesus. The Feast of Saint John, June 24, is the most sacred day in the Templar year.

The Orkney Islands were not yet the property of the Sinclair clan in 1307. They belonged to the Norse chief Malise, whose daughter William Sinclair later married. The Norse had been raiding the islands around Scotland and Ireland well before they are known to have attacked the coast of Ireland in the eighth century. Norse raiders gave way to Norse settlers; one group of settlers was the Mores, a powerful Norse family that settled the isles and sent a branch to France in the tenth century. The French branch of the More clan became the St. Clairs and later the Scottish Sinclairs. At the time that the Templars were being hunted by church and state, Scotland's first families were being hunted by the English. It was at this time that the clan of Sinclair chose to obtain the support of another of the sea kings, the Gunn clan.

The Clan Gunn and the Sinclairs

Geoffrey of Monmouth, writing in 1136, is one of the first historians to have compiled a history of the British Isles. He names a certain King Gunhpar (latinized as Gunuasius) as the regent of Orcadum in his list of six kings who fought alongside Arthur against the Saxons.[25] Geoffrey latinized the name of his kings, as was the European practice of the time. "Gunuasius" might have become "Gunn" in such early times. Perhaps this Gunn was the ancestor of the knight Sir James Gunn. The realm of this ancient sea king would certainly include a navy adept at crossing the choppy North Atlantic seas that surround Scotland in an icy band.

In the study of names and heraldry, the prevalent belief is that all families descend from one famous ancestor. Robert Bain says members of the Gunn clan were all descended from Olave the Black. This Norse Olave would have sailed to the "Sutherlands" (southlands), in Norse terminology, after the fifth century. In *Clans and Tartans of Scotland*, Bain declares that it was a son of Olave, named Gunnar, who became the first of the Gunn clan.[26] The name Gunnar derives from the word *gunn*, meaning "a long, strong reed." A gunn, interestingly enough, was a "spear."

A third historical text agrees with Geoffrey. In *Scottish Clans and Tartans*, Ian Grimble says the Gunn name was already ancient when the Norse arrived in the Orkneys.[27] In fact, the name was Pictish. The Pict language still remains for the most part undecipherable and essentially lost to the world. The origin of the Picts is uncertain, and history does not even document them by that name until A.D. 279, when Eumenius records them in the context of Caesar and Rome's attempt to take Scotland. In A.D. 305, a certain Constantius Chlorus campaigned against the "Caledonians and other Picts," and the son of Constantius tried his hand against them in A.D. 343.[28] The blue-painted diminutive warriors chased the Roman legions away.

When the Romans were leaving Britain, the "Scotti," actually an Irish people, were colonizing Scotland. Picts and Scots then coexisted with other tribes lost to history, including the Attacotti and Verturiones. While Rome regarded all the forces it encountered as primitive, in the same way as American settlers regarded the natives they warred against as primitive, this view discounts much. The Picts were renowned for their silverwork and adopted chariots after meeting Roman legions in battle. It was their ability to assimilate that deprives history of a correct understanding. They were also capable sailors, skilled in the ability to build skin boats and travel great distances in them. It is very likely that the Picts and the Norse had contact with each other from very early times. Whether the Gunn clan was Pictish or Norse, they were a sea power to contend with in the north.

In a very well researched body of work on King Arthur and the personages of the Holy Grail romances, Norma Lorre Goodrich makes the case that Guinevere was a Pictish queen.[29] At the time, the matriarchal Picts gave women the prerogative of picking and discarding a husband at will. Her lack of faithfulness to her husband was viewed in Grail literature as immoral, but Goodrich sees it simply as custom. Queens as well as kings of the Picts rode into battle. And kings as well as queens married to cement political alliances. A Queen Guinevere of Pictish Orkney allied with Arthur against the Britons would fit closely with a Pictish King Gunn, Geoffrey's Gunuasias of Orcadum, in granting their ancestors, the Gunn clan, the title crowners of Caithness.

Centuries later, when the Norman Sinclairs made Scotland and the northern isles their property, the Norse chieftain Malise might have already been related to the clan Gunn. Through a Sinclair-Norse marriage, this alliance was further strengthened. When William Sinclair took over as earl of Caithness and added the Orkneys to the Sinclair domain, he did so only with the consent of the Pictish-Norse clans in the north. It was this powerful seagoing alliance that admitted the Templars to their realm.

The Templars and Scotland

The Templar fleet, under agreement with Sinclair, sailed directly from France to the Orkneys. The Orkney sea king alliance was hostile to the ever growing power of France and the papal authority that claimed more than its share of Europe's wealth. Moreover, an independent Scotland was in need of an ally as badly as the Templars were in need of safe haven.

Shortly after Bruce had himself crowned as King Robert (weeks after the murder of John Red Comyn and six years before the victory at

Bannockburn), the army of King Robert and Scotland suffered a serious loss to the English at the Battle of Methuen in June of 1306. Bruce was forced into hiding, which would last throughout the winter.[30] A rival Balliol earl captured Robert the Bruce's wife, fulfilling the prediction she had made upon seeing her husband crowned earlier that year: "It seems to me that we are but a summer king and queen, whom the children crown in their sport." The prediction would have worse consequences than she had imagined. Robert the Bruce's daughter, Marjorie, was captured as was his brother Nigel, on the run with Robert—he was beheaded.[31]

When Robert came out of hiding, his string of personal disasters was still not over. Brothers Thomas and Alexander were also captured. The Bruce supporters were reduced to the status of a band of outlaws. With ragged clothes and shoes of rawhide, they would go hungry except when thievery or the kindness of strangers and friends provided. In 1307 it was simply the remnants of the Bruce clan and a few supporting clans that made up the entire nationalistic movement of Scotland.

The rest of the movement shared the disasters that Bruce suffered. The earl of Atholl was hanged for his support of Bruce. Simon Fraser, who had joined with Sir William Wallace in revolt against the king, was impaled on London Bridge. Bishop Wishart and Bishop Lamberton, who gave moral support for the cause, were put in chains. Isabel of Buchan and a sister of Robert the Bruce were exposed in lattice cages and hung out in the city of Berwick for everyone to ridicule.[32] For the cause of an independent Scotland, this winter was comparable to the winter that Geroge Washington and his ragtag band spent at Valley Forge. For Bruce, however, it was forces beyond his control that would save him.

In France in the same year, the Templars knew their relationship with the French king was deteriorating. The writing was on the wall, but only the resistance of the pope to Philip's orders delayed the arrests. Finally, when the secret orders were issued, many Templars were already prepared. Negotiations between the Sinclairs, who had already been allied in spirit with their St. Clair relatives and who had had an instrumental role in founding the Templars, paved the way. The Templar fleet sailed to the isles surrounding Scotland. Just as fortuitous as the arrest of the Templars was the death of the English King Edward on his way to Scotland. The king's death provided temporary relief for Bruce; the money and arms that the Templars brought to Scotland would save the day.

Templar legend says that the fleet sailed to the support of Scotland, but some historians have their doubts.[33] The most compelling evidence outside Templar legend is the fact that the English king complained that the Templars were at least funding weapons purchases for Scotland through a neutral Ireland. In any case, Bruce was again commander of his country's army and no longer an outlaw. After losing family members, friends, most of his wealth, and many of the fighting men that supported him, the leader of the Scottish independence movement made an amazing comeback. Suddenly Bruce could march through Scotland, consolidating his support and punishing his enemies. He seized their lands and captured their forts, executing his worst enemies. Halfhearted English incursions under the new king were either avoided or defeated. By 1313 Bruce was raiding England and had captured the Isle of Man as the result of a seaborne attack. It had been a remarkable five years.

The next year Bannockburn decided the issue of Scottish independence as well as the issue of the Knights Templar, who fought for the cause of Scotland and its leading families, Bruce and Sinclair. Outside Scotland the persecution of the Templars proceeded under the direction of Philip and the pope. It climaxed with the burning to death of the grand master Jacques Molay, which followed the mass executions of individual Templars. When the grand master finally reached the stake, he brought a curse to the pope and the king of France, saying that neither would survive for one year after his death. Neither did.

The order did not die with Molay. In Spain the orders of Calatrava and Montesa allowed the Templars to continue their work as a force for their country and religion. In Portugal, Templars were admitted to the newly formed Knights of Christ, from whose ranks came the intrepid Prince Henry the Navigator. Vasco da Gama was also a member of the same order. England alone came to the aid of the persecution because King Edward understood that the Templars were supporting the Scots against him. He ordered that Scotland arrest all the Templars within her realm; this decree would have been received as a joke, of course, as the Templars were the saving force behind Scottish independence.

Scotland lived in relative peace after the decisive battle of Bannockburn. The Templars were given homes, lands, and a "cover" as mason guilds. After all, they had been essential in constructing forts from Europe to Jerusalem. Younger Templars had an occupation, and older Templars were allowed to retire and derive income from modest grants. There were two succeeding orders that the Templars could join. One was the hidden Royal Order of Scotland, of which the king was grand master. The second order, according to Andrew Sinclair, was the Order of Heredom, meaning "sanctuary." The Sinclair family presided as protectors over this second order.

War against the Islamic Moors in the west and the Saracens in the east diverted Europe's attention from making war on itself. In 1329 Bruce died. His last request was that his heart be buried in Jerusalem. On crusade against the Moors, Sir William Sinclair, Sir James Douglas of the Black Douglas clan, and Sir William Keith rode together into battle. Sir James, believing all was lost, threw Bruce's heart into the fray, asking the heart to lead them, as always. The Moors beat the Scottish Christian contingent badly. Keith, who was the only knight of the three to survive, recovered the heart and brought it back home to Scotland, where it was buried at Melrose Abbey. It might have been chivalry's greatest moment.

Descendants of these knights continued to lead the fight to preserve Scotland's independence in a war that never ended. They also continued to fortify their own power and wealth, by conquest or alliance. The Douglas clan amassed great tracts of land for themselves in the course of these constant wars. Walter, high steward of Scotland, married Marjorie, Bruce's daughter, to continue the new royal line. Marjorie, who'd been first imprisoned in the tower and later pardoned to a nunnery, remanied a captive for eight years before she returned home at the age of twenty. Bruce's brother Edward survived and later became king of Ireland. Nigel, Alexander, and Thomas were all beheaded. Four years after the marriage of Walter and Marjorie the Scots were badly defeated at Halidon Hill, but the Douglas clan never ended its war against its neighbors, nor did clan cease fighting against clan.

After the death of King Philip, France entered into alliance with Scotland, which came to hurt Scotland's ability to preserve her independence. The alliance meant that France's continuing wars with England forced Scotland to be at war. The barons that ruled Scotland fought with each other over property and over their need to support or ignore France. James I of Scotland was a Stewart (actually a Douglas who took on the new family name as a result of his family's "stewardship" of Scotland). He started a new dynasty of kings that temporarily persuaded the clans to settle their differences. His methods, however, made enemies. Sir Robert Graham and eight men killed their king the Scottish way, with daggers. James's child, James II, inherited the throne. The child, of course, ruled in name only. It was the Celtic Douglas clans, at that point divided into "Red" and "Black" factions, that were the most powerful lords outside the Sinclairs, who traditionally chose not to take a visible leadership role.

The curse of Scotland was that the hard-earned decisive victories on the battlefield were always quickly lost by betrayal, infighting, and assassination. MacDonalds and MacLeans of the north fought on the side of Bruce, but once war was over they turned against their own king, a member of the divided Douglas clan. Douglas power was finally broken when William Crichton, the leader of one faction, killed the young Douglas children, stabbing the fourteen-year-old earl and his younger brother. In 1449 James II pretended that he wanted to reconcile with his former Douglas clan. He invited the head of the clan to Stirling castle, where he killed him. James himself became a victim of treachery. After being thrown from his horse in a battle of the Wars of the Roses, he called for a priest. The hooded figure arrived to give him the last rites, with a dagger.

While newly independent Scotland was seemingly self-destructing under the selfish agenda of rival Douglas clans, Sinclair and the Templars consolidated their power in the north. Orders such as the Templars were spurred on by the romantic notion of chivalry that captivated Europe. Romantic texts of King Arthur and the Knights of the Round Table had been written and rewritten during the time of the Crusades, and the military religious orders needed to live up to the heroic visions of their orders.

Officially, the holdings of the Templars were acquired in 1312 by their rival order, the Knights Hospitalers. Unofficially, the holdings were kept separate. Thirty years after the decree that the Templars be disbanded, the rival order did not possess the property of the Templars. When they finally took possession, they were still kept separate. The order would find itself at odds with local lords. In 1324 and 1334 they were forced to appeal to parliament to obtain title. In Scotland it was even more of a mess. By 1338 the knights of Saint John had not received title to even a single property. Over five hundred properties were listed in Scottish records as "terrae Templariae" and administered by local lords. In different form, the remnants of the Templar organization held together under the few knights who led in the Scottish war for independence. A handful of families inherited the mantle of leading and preserving the Templars.

One family was the Setons. It was a Seton who held the title of master of the Hospitalers in 1346. Another had married Robert the Bruce's sister after his role in the murder of John Red Comyn in the church of the Grey Friars. In the sixteenth century, when the Masonic order that had inherited the Templar order was again threatened by treachery, it was a Seton who led the action to preserve them.[34] The treachery that came to threaten the surviving Masons was the result of religious warfare burning through Europe in the wake of the Reformation. France was trying to remain Catholic as England had gone Protestant. Scotland again became the battlefield. The Setons tried to keep the French and Scottish unity intact, their country Catholic, and the Masonic-Templar organization in the background. It was a big job.

Mary, Queen of Scots, was the daughter of Mary of Guise of France and James V of Scotland. Their marriage had been supported by those who wanted to preserve Scotland from falling back into the clutches of the English. The other two children of James V were poisoned to eliminate their ascension to the throne. The new queen of Scotland (she became queen six days after she was born, in 1542, on the death of her father) was moved to France for safekeeping in 1548 because of the wars being fought. Protestant British excursions were met and resisted by forces that included German and Italian mercenaries who fought along-side Catholic France.

The Seton role was to protect Mary, while she was in France, against the treachery of her enemies, who often included her own family. When Mary married the French king Francis II in 1558, a daughter of George Seton and his French wife was the maid of honor. Two months after the wedding, Francis died as the result of a joust. Remarkably, Nostradamus had predicted the death of young Francis, describing his wounds exactly.

The mother of Francis was Catherine de Medici, who did not favor Mary as the queen of France. Instead, she ordered that Mary return the family jewels and go home to her estate in Scotland. England did not look kindly on Mary either. She was a foreigner and, even worse, a Guise. The Guise family was very Catholic and infamous in their defense against Protestants. Later, in 1562, the duke of Guise fired upon a Protestant prayer meeting, igniting open warfare between the two Christian religions. While the royal family and the leading houses of Guise and Lorraine wished for France to remain Catholic, Protestant ministers stirred the populace away from the Church.

The connecting thread between the prominent families of Scotland was what later came to be called the Scots Guard, an openly military establishment, no doubt united through Masonry as well as country, that included Setons, Sinclairs, Stewarts, Lindsays, Hamiltons, Douglases, and Montgomerys. This force had been fighting together since Bannockburn, both for Scotland and France but possibly more for itself. It was a Montgomery whose lance had pierced the eye of young Francis as Nostradamus had predicted and caused, in turn, the Guise-Lorraine alliance to be at odds with the Valois dynasty for the French throne. France was still not ruled by an all-powerful monarchy. The king was forced to rely on the cooperation of leading families who were more than minor powers. The struggle between the Guise and Valois families to control France weakened both and brought the Bourbon dynasty to the throne.

The Sinclairs had always had a strong connection to the Guise family through their own French relations, the St. Clairs. But the fate of Mary, Queen of Scots, was determined by her enemies and not by her family. The Sinclairs had fought for the kings of Scotland, but it was a descendant of the first kings who abandoned both Scotland and his own mother. Upon learning of the Sinclair plot to enlist France in the cause of Mary, the forces that be ordered her execution. Neither the queen of England, Elizabeth I, nor Mary's son, James, claimed to be aware of the execution, but it would not have taken place without their consent. Elizabeth had signed Mary's death warrant, and at first held off from ordering her execution. It was claimed that her jailors at Fotheringhay Castle proceeded with the execution on their own.

The Sinclairs and the Templar Treasure

Despite the constant warring and struggle, and possibly because of it, the Sinclairs in Scotland grew, prospered, and undertook remarkable actions to preserve the Templars and the guardianship of the organization. The wealth of the Templars had not been depleted by the war against England, and the guardianship of Templar relics was the responsibility of the Sinclairs.

The castle and chapel complex at Roslin is one of the wonders of the medieval world, built by Sir William Sinclair in the mid–fifteenth century. Besides being the world's high temple of Masonry, it served as a hiding place for the treasures of the Templars brought from their London and Paris temples.[35] In modern times secret vaults have been found, as have stairways that lead to nowhere and even cave entrances behind waterfalls—but no treasure.

It is said that when Sir William Sinclair decided to build the chapel, he imported stonemasons for the work. More likely, these "masons" were Templars already under his protection. The very unusual building was much more than a temple, and it was much later that anyone became aware of just how complicated the construction was. It could hide a treasure and an army, and probably did. Sinclair designed and planned the work himself, unusual in light of his rank and obligations.

The connection between Templars who built forts around the world and Freemasons whose guilds were first formed near Edinburgh in 1475 is obvious. This "trade" organization's members included those knights who fought in the Crusades and the knights who fought for Bruce: Sinclairs, Setons, Stewarts, Hamiltons, and Montgomerys, not an ordinary "stonemason" among them. Under the guise of a trade guild the Templars survived intact, and the Sinclairs, once among the founders of the Templars, became the hereditary protectors of that guild. With the enterprise of both were secrets that had been kept for a thousand years and an immense treasure protected from the greedy hands of the enemy.

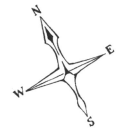

Chapter 7

THE SECRET OF THE TEMPLARS

$\mathcal{T}$he Sinclair clan inherited the role of guardians of the Free-masons, which concealed the remnants of the Knights Templar. They also inherited the role of guardian of the treasures of that organization, which had once been held in the vaults of the temples in Paris and London. The wagon trains laden with the coin of the realm entrusted to the Templars was now hidden in Scotland in the secret passageways built into the chapel of Roslin. The treasure itself was monumental—more significant than what would be gained if one of the largest banks in the world today were looted completely. It was the only bank in Europe, and it disappeared.

The Templar organization could be used as a means of depositing money for safekeeping in one city and withdrawing it in another. It also could provide loans. Earning interest was still considered usury, so the Templar bank would earn the proceeds of an estate that served as collateral until a loan was repaid.[1] There was no script or checks or bonds. It was gold and silver, bullion and coinage, and even the crown jewels of some of Europe's wealthiest families that were entrusted to the temple bank. This wealth was portable and huge enough to require wagon trains.

If the disappearance of this treasure were not enough, the temple also held greater treasures in its care—treasures that could not be allowed to sink into the hands of the French king. Legend has it that one of the treasures being safeguarded was that secreted from Montsegur by the Cathari.[2] There, at the last stronghold of the Cathari, Templars fought for the persecuted and against the Church they were sworn to obey. Montsegur held much gold and silver coin but also gold and silver objects, many that were sacred. The chalice that held the blood of Jesus Christ at the Last Supper was there, the miraculous Holy Grail. Legends of other treasures, significant in monetary terms and important in religious and historical value, are said to include the Visigoth's loot from Rome and the Oracle of Delphi in Greece. The objects taken from Rome by the Visigoths in the fifth century included what the legions of Titus had looted from the Temple of Solomon in the first century.[3]

Possibly the most important of the treasures held by the French temple, which was taken from the Temple of Solomon, had originated through a secret mission accomplished by an order within an order. A small, elite group of the most powerful families, which had banded together years before, was still intact, at least in part As the feudal era was ending, families still held sway over their local lands. This group vied with the king for power. The treasure that they owned was of greater than simply monetary value. The nature of it was a history of the family of Jesus, the Messiah. The genealogy of Jesus, which started in the priestly families of Aaron and David, did not end at the Crucifixion. One thesis of *Holy Blood, Holy Grail* is that the lineage of the priest-king who was Jesus continued.[4] An elite order within the Templars uncovered this secret. And it was up to the Sinclairs to guard it.

The Sinclair Family and Scotland

This treasure given to the Sinclairs to guard was possibly one source of their wealth in the fifteenth and sixteenth centuries, but it was not the source of their power. They had always been prominent and always close to the ruler of whichever land they chose to make their home. From their ancestral home in Norway to their lands in Norman France to their estates in Scotland, they were always a most powerful clan. They understood that the king was ruler in name but also the target of those displeased with his role. The real power would always be with those close to the king but never in the forefront.

In France, the Treaty of St. Clair, signed at their castle, gave the Norse families their land in France but allowed the king, Charles the Simple, to remain king.[5] In England, after the Battle of Hastings, William the Conqueror could take the credit for the victory, but Sinclairs received their spoils. In Scotland the Bruce family hid in caves and were imprisoned in lattice cages, while Sinclair power grew in the background. It was a role created for them, and one they would live up to. They were the puppeteers behind the scenes.

From Bannockburn forward the Sinclairs had two hundred years to consolidate their wealth and power, and they met their responsibility as guardians. They were the patrons of the Freemason trade guilds into which the inheritors of the Knights Templar survived. They would be named by James II of Scotland as the guardian family of Freemasonry, a role through which they kept the secrets and the wealth of the Templars. As the hereditary grand masters of Scottish Freemasonry, they may have furthered the exploration that their ancestor Henry had started in 1398—and all from behind the scenes.[6]

By 1545, however, the Sinclairs were pushed into the limelight. Oliver Sinclair was the military might behind King James IV. But the death of James at the Battle of Flodden forced Sinclair to the front. The new king, James V, was only two years old when he was made king. Sinclair became his guardian and guardian to the country of Scotland. James V later married Mary of Guise, of the Catholic French family, to whom the Sinclairs were allied both by marriage and the politics of their secretive elite group.[7]

While the marriage united France and Scotland, it threatened the English and was one of the catalysts of the battle at Solway. The Scots were beaten badly, and Oliver Sinclair was taken captive.[8] James V had depended on Oliver Sinclair since childhood. Without his guardian he believed all would truly be lost. He died within days of hearing of Oliver's capture. Six days earlier, his daughter Mary had been born, while her father was suffering the breakdown that led to his death. He predicted that Mary's birth signified the end of the Stewart line.

Oliver Sinclair, too, might have felt a touch of despair after Solway, with his king dead and an infant female on the throne. The French relations had possibly been richer than the Scottish Sinclairs, but they did not have their resolve. They failed to come to his aid in battling the English. In Oliver Sinclair's care was much more than the Sinclair lands. He was entrusted with the guardianship of a treasure much greater. Granted a short respite from prison, Oliver Sinclair took action. He disappeared from Scotland and history.

The true power of the Sinclairs had remained hidden in the earliest days of the Knights Templar as well. In 1982 *Holy Blood, Holy Grail* was published in England. Michael Baigent, Richard Leigh, and Henry Lincoln had done extensive research into a mystery and treasure search in the south of France. It led them to the earliest days of the Templars and a secret order within the order.[9] Sometime between 1090 and 1099, the Ordre de Sion was founded by Godfrey of Bouillon. This order coexisted with the Templars but lay far beneath the surface. Its aim was different from the external mission of the Templars, which would serve as a cover organization for as long as needed. The plan of a secret order within another secret order has allowed the Templars and their elite creators, the Ordre de Sion, to survive even today. Godfrey of Bouillon later became the conqueror of Jerusalem. In a history clouded by secrecy and shrouded in the mists of time, the lands owned by Godfrey's aunt served as sanctuary to a group of Calabrian monks. On her land they built an abbey. *Holy Blood, Holy Grail* suggests that they also built a bridge to the future Templars at that time. When they left, Godfrey led them in the crusade that devastated the holy city of Jerusalem in 1099. Once he conquered the city, another Calabrian monk crowned him king. He then built an abbey on the site of a ruined church, which would come to be called the Abbey of Notre Dame de Sion.

The original Templar order, the group of nine knights under the minor noble Hugues de Payens, arrived in Jerusalem in 1118. As we have seen, their nine-year stay produced little except some knocked-out walls in the stables of the Temple of Solomon. Yet on their return to France, the small band received a hero's welcome by de Payen's lord and Bernard of Clairvaux.[10] Bernard held a council to recognize and promote the organization of the Poor Knights, and his Cistercian order created their code of conduct. Bernard might be compared today to a televangelist, promoting the fight against the Saracens, raising funds from both rich and poor alike. For his role, he was given the abbey at Orval, built by the Calabrian monks on Godfrey of Bouillon's family property, which was made into a Cistercian house. The order received greater benefits as well.

Saint Bernard's order had gone from nearly destitute to very wealthy in a short period of time. The theory that the nine knights had been on a treasure hunt in Solomon's temple is not the source for the new wealth of Bernard's order. The basis for the sudden wealth of the Cistercian order was a combination of Bernard's ability to rouse a crowd and the support of several of France's wealthiest families. The Knights Templar, however, did not make the roads safe for pilgrims. The secret mission was, in fact, to unearth the secrets and treasures of the Temple of Solomon.

King Solomon and Jerusalem

There is no question that the Temple of Solomon once held great treasure. It was King David whose collaboration with the Philistines enabled him to take the throne of a divided Israel. He made Jerusalem the center of his kingdom. It was already a center of wealth as a city of the Jebusites, who called it Yerushalayim, meaning the "Foundation of the god Salem." Salem was their god of prosperity.[11] And it was already sacred. A tablelike rock behind the city, named Moriah, was considered sacred in times before the Israelites. This table rock was renamed Zion after Israel took it over. A Jebusite priest, Zadok, anointed Solomon king. And a Jebusite farmer, Araunah, owned the Rock of Sion (Zion) until Solomon's time.

Solomon built the city and its temple to be the center of a victorious Israel. The workforce needed to construct the temple was numbered at one hundred and eighty thousand, which included thirty thousand workers imported from Phoenicia. The Phoenician architects and masons had much more experience in building cities than the pastoral nomads who were the Israelis. The city of Jerusalem was already in existence when the construction started. Underneath the city was the tunnel of Gihon—a large shaft that went down into a tunnel that led from the spring of Gihon. There was no significance to the tunnel except that it served as a source of water to Jerusalem when the city was besieged by an enemy. But it was the water tunnel that had allowed the Hebrews to capture Jerusalem. Springs always had a religious significance of a sort to pagan peoples, since they represented fertility. Water, especially in a desert area, was a source of life.

The massive temple complex that King Solomon ordered to be built included an annex that would serve as the treasury. This was not the only place where treasures would be hidden. Throughout the turbulent history of Jerusalem, the temple was looted several times, yet mysteriously always had more treasure to be found. The Jerusalem of the Hebrews became an even greater center of wealth as the peace with the Philistines brought increased trade.[12] Ships from faraway places like Sheba (in Arabia) brought goods that originated in the Orient. Ships of the Dan, a sea people of the Mediterranean who traded with the Phoenicians, sailed far west to Spain and a mysterious kingdom near Spain, called Tartessus. Solomon even had his own fleet.

After Solomon's days, however, the wealth of Jerusalem also attracted enemies. Sheshonk, a Libyan pharaoh, forced Jerusalem to ransom itself when the Hebrews were ruled by Reheboam. His grandson Asa used the treasury to fight off a contender to the throne. Joas found the treasury entirely depleted when he took over. But as long as Jerusalem remained powerful, the treasury could always be replenished. In 716 B.C., Hezeliah added to the tunnel system underneath the city and was later able to resist siege by the Assyrians. The Babylonian captivity that followed these times (starting in 586 B.C.) put an end to the rule of the Davidic kings, and the history of Israel became a list of outside conquerors.

The temple destroyed and rebuilt served almost constantly as a source of revenue for Herod.[13] Herod regularly plundered the structures around the temple looking for caches of wealth. When he finally penetrated the tomb where the coffins of Solomon and David reposed, legend has it that one of his bodyguards was struck by a flame that incinerated him. Herod's reckless arrogance eventually caused the Jews to revolt against pagan rule. Rome had decided to erect an eagle over the entrance to the temple, symbolizing both the power of the great city and their pagan god Zeus (Jupiter). Two zealots took it upon themselves to tear it down— Herod had them executed.

An angry Jesus decried the use of the sacred temple as a place for the stands of merchants and currency changers, overturning their tables and expelling them from the holy ground.[14] The action, to some, was the most politically charged threat made by Jesus and may have contributed to his execution. Roman invaders continued to loot the temple and carry as much of the treasure back to Rome as they could. The greatest defilement by Rome came in their effort to quell the Jewish rebellions in A.D. 66, leading to the mass murders and expulsion of the Hebrew citizens of Jerusalem. Today there is not a single trace of the original temple, the location of which is marked by the Islamic Dome of the Rock.[15]

A theory presented in *Holy Blood, Holy Grail* is that there was an actual treasure sought by the secret Ordre de Sion (also called the Prieuré de Sion), the order that remained hidden under the guise of the Templars. The treasure itself may be much more significant that the monetary wealth of Jerusalem. The authors are not the only ones to have studied the mysterious order behind the founding of the Templars. Graham Hancock, in *The Sign and the Seal*, says it was the Ark of the Covenant that brought this small group of men to the Temple of Solomon. In a most fascinating work, Hancock tells of the remarkable Ark and its powers. Moses was instructed by God to build the Ark to exact specifications. In chapter 25 of Exodus the precise instructions are found including shafts of acacia wood, rings of gold, and a slab of pure gold as a cover. After Moses initiated Joshua in its powers, the Ark was used to win battles, kill people, and cause sickness. Its source of power came from two stones that fell from heaven. These are alternately the stones on which the Ten

Commandments were inscribed, or even stones of a more mysterious origin that were reputedly brought to Earth from heaven. Only those who were mystically trained and knowledgeable in its secrets were safe from its destructive ability. A special priesthood grew up around the Ark, and only Levites, a religious caste among the ancient Hebrews, were allowed to possess it.

The Ark soon disappeared from history recorded in the Bible. Josiah (circa 609 B.C.) instructed the Levites to return it, but it never reappeared.[16] Hancock believes this magical object was taken to Ethiopia for safekeeping and is still there today. In his research he discovered that the Ethiopian Jewish community has claimed to have possession of the Ark, which is called the "tabot." In many of their round, Templar-like churches there are tabot replicas, but there is only one Tabota Zion, the Ark of the Covenant.

Hancock claims that the early Templars, the representatives of nine families from the north of France, were in search of the ark. Both works agree that the original Templars could be better compared to archeologists than to an army. The actual "foundation" of Salem on the tablelike rock is called Shetiyyah in the Hebrew language. This foundation was in place before the construction of the temple in 950 B.C. Legends from medieval times told a story of the Ark being hidden in a cavern within this foundation before the Babylonian captivity. It was such legends that brought the Templars, who tunneled their way through the foundation in search of it. But the Ark was never located.

Hancock compares the Grail to the Ark.[17] Like the Ethiopian protectors of their tabot, who believe the living guardian must find a new guardian, the Templars appointed themselves guardians of the Grail. The Ethiopian guardian's other job was to protect the laity from the Ark, which the Bible states can cause much damage to the uninitiated. In 1 Chronicles 15:2 it is said that "none ought to carry the Ark of God but the Levites" and in Deuteronomy 10:8, "At that time he separated the tribe of Levi, to carry the Ark of the Covenant." The warnings are clear.

There is no evidence that the guardian families in Scotland ever had the Ark of the Covenant. In fact, there is evidence to the contrary. In 1768

James Bruce, who claimed to be a direct descendant of Robert the Bruce the king, made his own search. His expedition to find the Ark took him to Ethiopia. Also a Freemason and steeped in the speculative (read "religio-mystical") side of Masonry, Bruce returned home with the Book of Enoch. This book was sacred to the Masons because Enoch is identified as Thoth, the Egyptian god who originated the art of building.

Holy Blood, Holy Grail hypothesizes that the treasure that was sought by the early Templars was not the Ark. They sought a record of the continuation of a line of kings that extends from Solomon and David through Jesus and then to the descendants of Jesus. *Holy Blood, Holy Grail* says the Grail represents the sacred bloodline.[18] The treasure may be the evidence that this bloodline survived the Crucifixion and is somehow alive and intact in France. This theory, if substantiated, might be damaging to a church structured on rigid truths. It would be seen as evidence that the Arian concept of Jesus-as-man is more correct than the Roman Church's concept. Arius was a religious man from Alexandria who preached from A.D. 318–355. He preached that Jesus was a mortal, not a son of God, or divine. While he had no conflict with a Supreme God, he regarded Jesus only as a messenger from that God. The theory fit well with the Judaic concept and also was seen as more acceptable to monarchies and military who had no room fo a weak or meek god. But just why such a "truth" would be rewarding to a Catholic order, like Bernard's Cistercians, remains unexplained. And a monetary value, possibly derived from blackmailing the Church, was also unlikely, since the Church had more forceful ways of protecting its dogma.

In those times, few could read and write, and thanks to the Inquisition, knowledge of such "arts" could have a person branded a heretic.[19] Owning a Bible, too, was not allowed by the Church, who kept their monopoly on the word of God. The populace knew of their religion only what they were told by priests at Mass. We know from the Gospels that Jesus descended from the Davidic line. It was a bloodline that did not die out; it simply lost the kingship during the captivity in Babylon. Like the English looking for the return of King Arthur, the Hebrews sought a day when a Hebrew king would again free them from the yoke of foreign oppression. The prophets had said the king who would be their savior would be from both the line of the house of David and the line of the house of Aaron.[20] Matthew claims that Jesus was aristocratic in bloodline and that this bloodline had been recognized by the leaders among the Jews. His Gospel shows the birth of Jesus being attended by three kings. The final entrance of Jesus into the city of Jerusalem is greeted by the multitudes shouting, "Hosanna to the son of David."

The other Gospels played down the lineage of this prince of David's house and his claims to an earthly throne. Jesus, instead, was depicted as the son of a carpenter. But the term "carpenter" did not refer to a common laborer, just as the term "mason" implies more than its surface meaning.[21] God himself was referred to as the "fashioner" and the "architect" in the Gnostic texts. That Jesus was the son of the "Architect of the Universe," the carpenter, may have been intentionally laden with double meaning. Medieval and modern-day masons have created a folklore that sees them as descending from a line of builders responsible for the Temple of Solomon.

Builders in the ancient world had to have skills far above the average education of their fellows. In a day and age when writing was the skill of an elite few, a builder, who needed command of such higher mathematics as geometry, had to be very well trained. The architect would have had to be well versed in what many believed to be a field as mysterious as magic. That magic today is nothing more mysterious than science. Most of the construction of the ancient world, including the prehistoric slab construction of monuments like Stonehenge and medieval churches, was oriented to some type of celestial activity. Up until very modern times, sites of churches were always carefully chosen and carefully oriented. The architect knew the workings of the visible universe as well as any shaman or Druid. He had to. Distance was measured in the same way as time—by the sun and shadows. This is the "sacred geometry" that would be considered a mystery to those who were not initiated into the craft.[22]

The role of Jesus as "architect" or "carpenter" allegorically would be to restore the temple that Solomon had built. Jesus as king would restore the glory of the Hebrew people as an earthly power. The carpenter, the architect, the mason would build their church on a rock. While the common Jew did look for a savior, the Saduccees and the Pharisees, the aristocratic class and the middle class, respectively, did not want a savior who would disturb the established order. Jesus was considered a Nazarene from Galilee, an area known for its rebels and highwaymen.[23] He studied at an Essene community, where radical zealots sought to overthrow both the regime of the invader and the complacent and willing Jews who were their hosts. Qumran, (known today as Khirbat Qumran), the community where Jesus studied and lived, was far from the mainstream. The Qumran community attracted mystics and rebels alike, and while the historic Jesus was touched by the highly moral world of the Essenes, he did not adhere to their rigid discipline.

John the Baptist also visited the community of Qumran. It is likely there that John was first introduced to the Essene custom of baptism.[24] The Essenes made baptism a daily practice, unlike the one-time sacrament accorded to John. John then "baptized" Jesus, in the custom of the Essenes. Or did he anoint him as "king"? In the later Gospels this anointing is said to be the basis for his title "Christos" in Greek: the "anointed one." The Greeks molded the religion of Jesus into something different from the religion that the original followers of Jesus might have conceived. Luke, as a Greek physician, and Paul, as the "apostle" to the non-Jewish pagans, saw Jesus more in the role of a god than did his own family and the other apostles.[25] The title that Jesus was given by his own people was "messiah," which denoted a king in the royal bloodline of David, rather than simply any king or religious leader. A messiah had the distinction of being a priest-king.

The distinctions of the titles of Jesus are lost to the modern reader, just as we do not understand that calling Jesus the "man from Galilee" was another way of saying he was a rebel. The hills of Galilee in Herod's time were a hotbed for dissent and even a widespread guerrilla movement, as the iron rule of the dictator drove the antiestablishment Jews away. Reading the Bible leaves us wondering whether Jesus was from Bethlehem, Galilee, or Nazareth. The claim of Bethlehem as the birthplace of Jesus was important in that it fulfilled the prophecy of the Bible that the Savior King, the Messiah would come from the city of David.

While Jesus could have come from Bethlehem, it is unlikely that he came from Nazareth—that town was not yet in existence in his day. Jesus was called the Nazarene only because it was a designation that alluded to a political affiliation. The Nazarenes were a sect that believed in guiding their own Hebrew faith properly through corrupt times. They also preserved a body of knowledge that was sacred to them and that was overlooked by both recorded history and conventional religion.

"Nazarene" derives from the Aramaic word Natzar, which means both "to guard" and "to watch." The Nazarenes were more than the guardians of their own faith, they were guardians of a science that understood the relationship between the stars, the calculation of time and distance, and humankind's relative place in the universe.[26] They were both the custodians of the secrets of the universe and the guardians of their enlightened science. Their guardianship extends back in time to the Sumerians, whose civilization emerged suddenly in the fertile crescent known as Mesopotamia. In their language the gods themselves were the "watchers," the overseers of the universe.

This guardianship was passed down through history—the Essene sect living in the desert lands of the Middle East had inherited the task. They believed that they were in the last generation, the time before the ultimate battle between the forces of light—the good—and the forces of darkness—the evil.[27] Religious historians think that they had been directly influenced by the Persian religion of Zoroaster. Historians of the Masonic organization similarly trace certain traits of this group to the same Persian faith. Both the Essenes and the Masons included in their religious paraphernalia an apron and a small hatchet, the significance of which may have more to do with an inherited body of knowledge of the building arts than anything more magical.

Jesus himself may have rejected the Essene doctrine, at least in part. The life of Jesus, as preserved in the Gospels, does not appear to have the same emphasis on fanatical purity as history has colored the dogma of the Essenes. Jesus ate with the publicans, prostitutes, and sinners. At the same time, he was considered both pacifist and militant, as were those with whom he associated. Peter, the right-hand man of Jesus, was not actually named Peter. "Peter" meant "rock," a nickname for his strength, his resolve. His historical name is given as Simon bar Jona, which signified a member of the Baryonim, a rebel force also called the Angry Men.[28] Today he might be called a terrorist, although the label might not correctly apply.

"Judas Iscariot" is a mistranslation of Judas Sicari. Like the Baryonim, this name signified a rebel group, its literal translation is "dagger man," a killer or assassin. John and James were two apostles called *boanerges* by Jesus, which in his native Aramaic meant "sons of the storm wind." The other Simon in the original group was called the "zealot," a name for those who were steadfast against the corruption of their Jewish faith by the Sadducees and Pharisees. The band that Jesus had recruited went beyond the original twelve apostles. Although the Greek influence in composing and preserving the history of Jesus played it down, the role of women was significant. Women like Mary Magdalene were a strong presence in the early group and traveled with the apostle, which also violated Jewish custom.

Jesus truly appeared to be creating a religion different from what the established religious custom had become. It is possible that he was more educated than most, having studied in a rabbinical school. It is also likely that he was unique and that while the Sadducees and Pharisees could not accept his message, neither could the political zealots and the Essenes. This may be why the fanatical John the Baptist sought out Jesus to address him for his violation of convention. A mutual baptism may have been significant in reconciling them and cementing the common bond they shared in fighting the establishment, which both believed to be corrupt.

John the Baptist was steeped in the Essene tradition and was a member of a very exclusive Nazarene sect. Michael Grant interprets *Nazoraios* as the word for "guardian," but at the same time he considers *netser* to mean "shoot" or "branch." The importance of this connection is that both Jesus and John belonged to a sect into which one had to be born. The "shoots" of the bloodline of David had preserved this unbroken line from one thousand years earlier. Both John and Jesus were members not only of the exclusive bloodline of David but that of Aaron the "magician," the priest, as well. Grant says the Egyptian word *NTR* had the same meaning—"one who watches." The language comes to us with no vowels. N(e)T(sa)R "netsar" might have been the pronunciation, as in Nazarean (with z as a ts sound). When Jesus is described as a Nazarean, we cannot assume it was of Nazareth as that town might not have existed at the time. It was a designation of a caste of priest-kings steeped in an ancient wisdom (Sophia). Jesus was a "watcher," an observer of the ancient custom, a guardian of secret knowledge. It is Hebrew tradition that awaits a messiah from the houses of David and Aaron. Early Christian teachings and the Gospels place an emphasis on the genealogy of the Son of God, although in teaching the divine nature of Jesus, a human genealogy would seem insignificant.

There is further circumstantial evidence that Jesus and John were members of an elite group. They are both remembered as having untrimmed hair. This, Grant says, is characteristic of the guardians; there was power in the hair, as the legend of Samson records. Belief in the power held in the hair is not confined to this sect. The word *kaisear* means "a crown of hair," which is preserved also as "caesar" and in Russian as "czar." The early Church writer Eusebius, in explaining that James, the brother of Jesus, was a very holy man, says, "no razor touched his head."[29]

Characteristic of the guardians was the concept of purification through water. The Essenes practiced this ritual daily, and the early Christians practiced it as a rite of initiation. John the Baptist was truly a voice crying out in the desert, the voice of a rabble-rouser who was so incensed by the second marriage of Herod that he called the very act illegal and the participants worse. He constantly plagued Herod, and the family of Herod. Such radical criticism led to his decapitation. As has been pointed out, his feast day of June 24 and the relic of the severed head came to play an important role in later Freemasonry.

In the year after the execution of John, Jesus, too, was martyred in a style reserved for those who sought to overthrow the government. He had declared himself "King of the Jews," or so his accusers said. Roman law dictated that no one could be a god unless the senate decreed it.[30]

The followers of Jesus were forced into hiding, which took a great toll on the unity of the group and on the message Jesus had sought to teach. His own family, who had doubted him while he was alive, came to revere him, but only in the light of their own Hebrew religion. He was a messenger of the purity of the people of Israel, contaminated by the Roman and Greek presence. The message of James and the family of Jesus was that his teaching was only for the "chosen" people, who were Jews. Paul, once known as Saul, who had been a persecutor of Jesus and his early followers, became a convert. He believed that the message of the Messiah was intended for Jews and Gentiles alike. He had followed Jesus from the beginning and understood the radical concept of love being above the law, but the message was being altered by the family of Jesus to a more conservative concept of the purity of the law. Torn between James and Paul, Peter eventually went on the road to preach the message of Jesus.

Some of Jesus' original followers and apostles literally headed for the hills and the safety of the Essene sects, which they might have considered more pure. Peter and Paul spread the word through the Mediterranean. But the concept of Jesus as king, the heir to the throne of Solomon, died on the cross. Or did it? The Gospels indicate that Jesus had brothers and sisters who also may have been in the same bloodline. In Mark, four brothers are listed: Jacob (also known as James), Joseph, Judas, and Simon.[31] The most important was James, who inherited, or took over, the leadership of the small group. His goal was to preserve the kingship of a Jewish priest-king in the David-Aaron bloodline. He fought with Paul over the rite of circumcision, which Paul felt was a major stumbling block in converting Gentiles. James didn't care to convert Gentiles. James eventually became an embarrassment to Paul, who would find converts whom James would refuse to admit. James and the family of Jesus, who had once denied Jesus' role, seem to have capitalized on their status after his death, although more likely in a political rather than a religious sense.

Paul influenced the Church greatly, but three hundred years later the Church sought to remove James from the historical records and raise the status of Mary to a virgin. One explanation of the concept of Mary as virgin is that it was done to answer the needs of converts from the Mediterranean, to whom the Greek mystery religions had appealed. Jesus was not the first god to be born of a virgin. The Greeks had Jason, Perseus, Miletus, Tammuz, and Adonis. Another explanation of Mary as virgin was that it was simply an error in translating. A word that meant "maiden," it more correctly referred to a woman of marriageable age, but in translation it ended up as "virgin." This explanation is less likely.

A third explanation is that it was a political compromise. The brothers and sisters of Jesus are referred to both in the Gospel of Matthew and in Paul's letters to the Galatians. In the early history of the Christian Church, the descendants of the family of Jesus are said to have lived well into the second century A.D.[32] Why, then, deny their existence? To the Pauline Church, not intent on crowning an earthly king and wishing to avoid what Rome might misconstrue as a threat, the family and descendants of Jesus were a topic to be avoided, and soon denied. Jesus was the Son of God and not a son of man, who might have heirs.

It would have been very unusual for a Jew in the time of Jesus to be unmarried. There is even circumstantial evidence in the surviving Gospels that Jesus had a wife. Jesus was addressed as "rabbi," which implied that he was a teacher who had been taught by the elders—a suggestion confirmed in the Gospels. A rabbi would begin his ministry at age thirty, which is also substantiated by the Gospels. This title also implies that he took a wife; being married was a necessary condition to becoming a rabbi. A teacher had to be a married man.

As further evidence, proponents of this theory say that the marriage at Cana was actually the wedding of Jesus.[33] If, they ask, it was not the wedding of Jesus, why would his mother be so concerned that their host was running out of wine? She was concerned enough to induce Jesus, her son, to work a miracle. The responsibility for providing food and drink was that of the host of the wedding, who would be the bridegroom. But such evidence is circumstantial. It may have been a sister or brother of Jesus whose wedding took place at Cana, and in the absence of their father, Joseph, the responsibility would fall to the older brother, who may have been Jesus. Similarly, being addressed as "rabbi" may have been a show of respect for the man who was his group's teacher, ordained or unordained.

The debate over the possible marriage of Jesus and the question of potential heirs has strong advocates on both sides. Those who deny the possibility of marriage consider the suggestion tantamount to heresy. At the same time, priests and laypersons alike have commented that being married not only would not detract from Jesus' message but would strengthen it, since as a husband, and possibly a father, he bore more human responsibilities. When the marriage of Jesus was left out of the Gospels, it was not because the Church was against marriage or women; that stance would come later. Two thousand years ago the marriage was not being debated as a religious issue—it was a political question. The Christian Church had to make itself acceptable to a militant Rome, which needed no new rivals. A wedding of Jesus, or even a brother of Jesus, implied potential heirs, and heirs would be a threat to Rome's earthly kingdom.

Holy Blood, Holy Grail expands further the theory of Jesus being married to encompass the likelihood that his bride was Mary Magdalene.[34] There is little evidence for this claim. Mary did travel with Jesus and was present at his execution; she was also the first to see his empty tomb. None of this, however, proves such a claim. She was simply a devoted follower. On the other side of the debate there are stories of a relationship between Jesus and Mary in the Gnostic texts. The strongest argument in favor of Mary Magdalene as the wife of Jesus is the Church's campaign against her. Her story seems to have grown over the years—she has been said to have had "devils" and been exorcised and to have been a prostitute. In the Gospels, Mary was not the same woman mentioned as the prostitute in the passage where Jesus saves her by instructing the one without sin to throw the first stone. In Church lore, however, she somehow took on that mantle.

Without the political overtones, the issue of a married Jesus might also have been affected by the way Paul preached. The Pauline Christian doctrine was filtered through a Hellenistic screen. Jesus was represented as a shepherd, like the Greek god Tammuz, whose job was to tend his flock. The Greek mystery religions had some taboos, but sexuality was not a sin because fertility was important. The religion, however, had originated from an area where sex was taboo, or at least considered unclean, and was reserved only for the necessity of procreation. Paul tried to preserve the moral tone of the Jews who followed Jesus while making the message acceptable to his fellow non-Jews.

Celibacy, however, was not a requirement of the followers of Jesus or of those he appointed as his apostles and guardians of his Church. Peter was most definitely married, and his wife's martyrdom is recorded. For reasons of its own, the Church forced priests to give up their wives one thousand years later; it had never been a requirement of the founder. The Church soon lost its roots entirely in its assimilation into the Roman world. Constantine, the emperor of Rome, was an adherent of the cult of Sol Invictus, the victorious sun—a male-dominated warrior cult, decidedly pagan, that celebrated the "birthday" of the sun on December 25 (on or near the solstice).[35] At the First Council of Nicaea in A.D. 325, the Church, in its new role as state religion of Rome, had to make modifications. December 25 was taken as the birthday of the Son of God as well as the sun itself. The day of rest, the Sabbath, which had always been a Saturday, was changed to Sunday (the day of the sun). In the new and improved Roman version of the religion, women were given less of a role, and the pope took a much greater role. The message of Jesus had been love; the message of the Roman Church was power.

If Roman Christianity altered the message of God, what became of the followers of Jesus the man? Jesus had not wanted a revolution and a crown for himself, but many of his followers searched for a more earthly kingdom. These followers went into the hills as the Roman persecution and ensuing warfare led to more war. Thirty years after the execution of Jesus, hostility between the occupied Jews and the Roman overlord came to a head. The Jewish revolts in A.D. 65–67 and in A.D. 133 started a reaction that led to the destruction and mass deaths at the Essene fortress at Masada on the shore of the Dead Sea. Many surviving sects traveled in four directions, and some survived under different names. Medieval texts tell another story.[36]

Joseph of Arimathea, a wealthy supporter of Jesus, was a merchant whose fleet sailed as far away as England to trade for such commodities as tin. He was single-handedly responsible for procuring the body of Jesus from the Roman Jewish authorities. He wanted Jesus to be buried in a worthy tomb, and in this single act, he exposed himself to the authorities as a supporter. Knowing that this revelation could easily cost him his wealth if not his life, he gathered those closest to Jesus and sailed away on his own ship. Medieval texts may be novel in the telling of this story, but the Bible fails to provide an alternative. Outside the medieval texts and Grail romances, we have no record of the death of Mary Magdalene or of Joseph of Arimathea.

Tradition and these texts say that Joseph of Arimathea took the family of Jesus to Marseilles in France and then traveled alone to England. It is said that Joseph came to Glastonbury and founded the first Christian church in England. Calling Joseph a "secret disciple," even a renowned historian such as Barbara Tuchman, in asking about the connection between the abbey at Glastonbury in England and Joseph of Arimathea, says, "Perhaps the answer is that he actually did make his way from Palestine to Britain."[37] Historians who scoff at finding any truth in literary tradition often find themselves being proved wrong. Heinrich Schliemann, the "amateur" German archaeologist who found Troy, disproved the claims of establishment historians that Troy was just a story. In his lifetime he was criticized for his belief, and he is still criticized today for his methods. Historians of the establishment do not like to be proved wrong.

Today we accept that Troy and the Trojan War were real, but we still deny the accounts of those who returned home from that long conflict. If Homer's first tale, the *Iliad*, is now accepted, why is his second tale, the *Odyssey*, considered fiction? Medieval stories of wandering refugees from the leveled cities of Trojan shores are regarded as total fabrications. Trojans reputedly settled in Italy, France, and other parts of Europe. In France, it is claimed that the city named Troyes was founded by Trojans, and a certain Priam is reported to have taken twelve thousand settlers there. We accept that Phoenician trade reached northern Europe and Britain. Why is it unthinkable that people from the Mediterranean traveled to western Europe? And why should it be difficult to believe that Joseph, a merchant, could have sailed there?

Eusebius, one of the earliest writers on the history of the Christian Church, tells of the official persecution of the direct descendants of the family of Jesus and others in the Davidic bloodline before such history was censored.[38] Rome had reason to take seriously the threat of a king emerging from the bloodline of David—the hostilities were real. James himself was executed by the Sanhedrin in the year A.D. 62. After his death, Clopas, brother of Jesus' earthly father Joseph, may have taken over the leadership of the group. Certainly the son of Clopas, Simeon, who was a cousin of Jesus, became the first bishop of Jerusalem. Other surviving members and family would surely have sought safe refuge from the Roman suppression that is unrecorded by the Gospels but documented in both Church and non-Church histories.

In A.D. 65 Simeon led his followers, who called themselves Nazoreans, away from Jerusalem. They may have founded the town of Nazareth. In the year A.D. 66, we know they were forced into hiding. In another town called Nazara, and in Cochaba, the family of Jesus, known as the "Heirs," lived and survived persecution. The Nazarean Church became completely separate from the Pauline Christian Church. Later, the emperor Vespasian sought to ferret out the descendants of Jesus and his followers, although the threat against them appeared to diminish as Jewish Christianity slowly died out. Eusebius was scornful of this group of Jewish followers of Jesus because they had never accepted Jesus as a god, only as a man inspired by God, a prophet. Even after Vespasian there were further references to the descendants of the family of Jesus. Jude, another brother, had two grandsons who were brought before the emperor Domitian. They were leaders in the Church and had borne witness to the life of Jesus, but Domitian dismissed them as not being a threat to Rome.

Despite the writings of Eusebius and other early texts, which included the Gnostic Gospels, the Church ignored the descendants and treated much of the writings at best as unimportant and at worst as hoaxes. When the Christian Church decided two hundred years later at the Council of Nicaea just which texts would be admitted into what became the New Testament, they allowed much that had been adopted from Essene teachings to remain. Activities such as the communal feast, baptism, the celebration of the Pentacost, and the exorcism of devils remained from the early days of the Church. The term "New Covenant," proclaimed by the Essene teachings, came to be applied to the teachings of Jesus. Another Essene doctrine, that the poor would inherit the Earth, also was adopted, but the Church was by that time attracting a better class of followers. A doctrine applying just to the poor was no longer acceptable. The church that Jesus founded had appealed to the underclasses. Now the Roman-sanctioned Church had to take on a new character to accommodate the ruling class as well.

Nazoreans and Ebionites, known as "Poor Christians" were by then just small sects hiding in southern Lebanon and near the Euphrates River. The Church itself no longer recognized the Essene community, nor did that community recognize the Church. The lives of the people who had played a part in the life of Jesus were recorded by Eusebius. Herod was deprived of his throne and exiled to France, where he made his home in Vienne. Jewish merchants and traders gave passage to both Jews and Christians, and both were found in France in the early days of the Church. (Eusebius refers to "the servants of Christ at Vienne and Lyons in Gaul.") The family of Jesus survived in Roman Gaul, and they would have been forced to maintain a low profile, since they had been the hunted heirs to the Davidic kingship. They were the "sprouts" of the vine of David, the "scions" in his priestly line.

The Hebrew name *Levi* literally means "scions" and, in its agricultural context (levy) "sprouts." It became a code word surviving among the Templars and later among high-ranking Freemasons. It would be very important to those who believed in a Davidic line of kingship, specifically in a secret society—the Prieuré de Sion—that lay behind the Templars and Masons. The stated reason for their existence was to preserve and advance the bloodline of Jesus and Mary Magdalene.[39]

Holy Blood, Holy Grail was written using documents that this secret group (the Prieuré de Sion) provided for much of the source material. Some of these documents were unable to be verified; others were obviously historically incorrect. But other researchers have corroborated that the society exists and that it may have taken different forms at different times. Robert Anton Wilson believes that the group had been active from the nineteenth century but that their early history is not what they have suggested it to be.[40] There is compelling evidence that an "underground stream" of knowledge has indeed been preserved by a group taking one name or another over the past thousand years. Some of this knowledge was to be held secret for only a chosen elite. The secrets of the Prieuré de Sion and their treasure was to be protected by those who inherited the task of keeping the sacred knowledge intact and the secret society alive. The Sinclairs in Scotland became its guardians.

Chapter 8

THE FRENCH CONNECTION

$\mathcal{A}$t about the time that the authors of *Holy Blood, Holy Grail* started their research, a series of bodies, murders, and attempted murders surfaced in France. One publication, called *Secret Dossiers*, that provided information for the book was written by Leo Schidlof. It is possible that Schidlof was connected with espionage or some other clandestine activity because he was refused entry into the United States.[1] What does twentieth-century espionage have to do with documents over two hundred years old? *Holy Blood, Holy Grail* does not answer this question, but soon after Schidlof's death his briefcase, reputedly containing documents relating to the Rennes-le-Chateau area of France, was in turn taken by Fakhar ul Islam, who was trying to reach East Germany but instead was hurled from a train outside Paris and killed. Three weeks later a privately published work entitled the *The Red Serpent* turned up at the National Library of Paris. It, too, contained information on the Rennes-le-Chateau area. The three authors of the work were all found

DESTINY BOOKS

DESTINY RECORDINGS

DESTINY AUDIO EDITIONS

Park Street Press

En Español

INNER TRADITIONS INTERNATIONAL

If you wish to receive a copy of the latest INNER TRADITIONS INTERNATIONAL catalog and to be placed on our mailing list, please send us this card. It is important to print your name and address clearly.

Name _____ Phone _____

Address _____

City _____ State _____ Zip _____

Country _____ Email address _____

Order at 1-800-246-8648 • Fax (802) 767-3726
E-mail: orders@InnerTraditions.com • Web site: www.InnerTraditions.com

Inner Traditions International, Ltd.
P.O. Box 388
Rochester, VT 05767
U.S.A.

hanged, at different times, between March 6 and March 7, 1967, two weeks after the death of Fakhar ul Islam. Obviously, someone wasn't happy about researchers digging into the secret of Rennes-le-Chateau.

The publication of *Holy Blood, Holy Grail* ignited a storm of controversy in 1982 at a time when the Catholic Church was already under siege. The backlash from the Church was expected, in light of the fact that the book suggested several controversial scenarios—Jesus as husband and Mary Magdalene as mother of his child, for example. Worse still to many, the book made the case that Jesus may have survived his execution. The concept that Jesus both plotted his own execution and survived the Crucifixion had already been reviewed in print, although the popularity, especially in Europe, of *Holy Blood, Holy Grail* brought the topic a great deal more attention.[2] Could Jesus have orchestrated his own execution? Could the family of Jesus have escaped Jerusalem?

The activities of Jesus the man were at the least able to incite a carefully planned stage in a revolt if not a complete revolt. He threw the bankers and money changers out of the temple not too long after two zealots had been executed for removing the Roman eagle. He challenged the Jewish puppets of the Roman state, the Sadducees, at every turn. He rode into Jerusalem on a donkey, fulfilling the prophecy in the Bible that declared that the scion of David would enter the city in this manner. He denied being a king, but the cheering crowds left no doubt that they wanted him to be their king.[3] These actions resulted in his death, an execution that history records and few challenge. Of the four accepted Gospels, the Gnostic Gospels, and one secular history, *The Jewish War*, by Josephus, all written in the first century, none hint that Christ survived his execution.

The Gospels and the Acts of the Apostles do record that the followers of Jesus fled Jerusalem. If Mary Magdalene had been married to Jesus and pregnant with his child, she would have had a very strong reason to escape Roman Jerusalem. History does not document the fate of others surrounding Jesus—the following scenario, corroborated only by legend, is possible. Under the leadership of Joseph of Arimathea, Mary Magdalene, her companions, and possibly her unborn child might have fled by sea to France.[4] The entrance of Jesus' family into France could have been at or near the port city of Marseilles.

Marseilles is recognized as the oldest city in the country of the Celtic Gauls.[5] Its ports were visited by Greek and Phoenician sailors at least six hundred years before Christ was born. The Phoenicians had founded nearby Monaco three hundred years before Marseilles, but the port city grew faster in prominence. For twenty-six hundred years, Marseilles has been considered France's most important seaport. The first recorded journey to Iceland, mentioned in the second chapter, was made by the writer and explorer Pytheas, who sailed from Marseilles in 330 B.C. The south of France soon became a crossroads for maritime and overland trade and, as a result, figured prominently in political and religious history.

In A.D. 117 Rome built a highway called the Via Aurelia from Rome to Marseilles along trade routes already established from Celtic times.[6] The highway attested to the position of Marseilles as a trade center. It was not a remote outpost by any means, but a very populated city and the gateway to a populated region. The Roman historian Strabo, writing on Palestine's growing status as a world trader during the Hellenistic period, before it was conquered by Rome, states that there was not a city in the world where the Jews were not to be found. They were accomplished merchants and traders from Solomon's day onward, as is recorded in the Bible. If Solomon's fleets traded with Tarshish, which we now identify as Spain, Marseilles was on the route.[7]

As a result of the Marseilles sea trade, the overland route grew as well, and along the trade routes from Rome to Marseilles to Spain sprang up many cities, including several that hold legends of the Jesus family and their landing, traveling through, or residing in these towns. Near Marseilles is the smaller city of Aix, now called Aix-en-Provence.[8] Then, as now, it was considered a center of healing—its hot springs attracted people from Rome and even farther east. Such centers were found along the trade route in France and in the Spanish Pyrennees. These springs were regarded as representations of Earth's fertility and were often considered sacred.

Toulon, also a short distance from Marseilles, was a Phoenician source of purple dyes well before Greece and Rome began to plant settlements there. Farther along the coast are Cannes, which possibly derives its name from sailors and settlers from Canaan, and Nice, founded and named by the Greeks for their goddess of victory, Nike.[9] Understanding just how active trade was between the Levant and the southern coast of France makes it easier to understand the accessibility of France to the followers of Jesus. Joseph of Arimathea had the means, owning ships and being wealthy, as well as the motive, his own safety as well as the safety of his fellow believers, to escape and travel there. In one Gnostic text it was recorded that he was set adrift in a ship as part of his expulsion from Jerusalem; other texts say he simply sailed away in his own ship. In both cases there is the common denominator in the evidence of his sea passage from Palestine.

There is other evidence that very early Christians traveled to France. The bishop of Lyons in the second century was Irenaeus.[10] This Church father wrote that Christianity was established in southern Gaul by followers of Jesus who had known him when he was alive. While he doesn't narrow down the date, he implies that these were people who were alive in A.D. 30 and most likely were in France before A.D. 60. Joseph of Arimathea, under a death threat from the same Sanhedrin who had wanted Jesus executed, could have been one of those early Christians. History records more migrations to France and other countries from the Levant as a result of the same Roman repression that was the catalyst for the execution of Jesus. Further rebellions resulted in the flight of large groups of Jews to Tunis, Morocco, Spain, and France. After the Bar Kochba struggle and the siege of Masada, the refugees numbered in the tens of thousands.[11]

Jews in Marseilles were so numerous that it was regarded as the "Jewish City." Many were wealthy traders and shipowners like Joseph. Despite widespread persecution during the early history of France, Jews were still numerous in Charlemagne's day. A document from his time refers to "Jewish and other merchants," attesting to their entrenchment among the middle classes.[12]

Besides the Gnostic texts that mention Joseph and early Jewish-Christian immigrants, there are other accounts held in higher regard. The Roman theologian Tertullian declared that this new religion,

Christianity, could reach areas that were not accessible even to Rome. From Marseilles comes the legend of the landing of Jesus' party in their seaport. The group is said to have included Joseph of Arimathea, the protector of Jesus and his family; Lazarus, a close friend; Martha; and the "three Marys."[13] Saint Lazarus, as he is now called, and Mary Magdalene immediately began to preach in the Temple of Diana, which caused no small commotion among her Celtic devotees. A cathedral dedicated to Mary Magdalene is now built over the site of this former pagan temple, but the victory of the Christian religion over the pagan rite was far from easy to win.[14]

Lyons was the scene of early persecutions against Christians who had arrived at the same time as Joseph and his group. Viennes, to which Herod had been deported, was also the site of Christian persecution. Saint-Tropez, that glamour spot for French vacationers, was named for Torpes, a Christian officer in one of Nero's legions who was executed for his belief in A.D. 68. Nearby, in Aix-en-Provence, is another church dedicated to Mary Magdalene. There, Saint Maximin, who had accompanied Mary, was martyred. Once an important site for pilgrimage, it still features an abbey called Saint Maximin la Sainte Baume. *Baume* is from the Provençal word *baoumo*, which means "grotto."[15] There, Mary and Maximin hid in a cave in the wooded hills that surround the coast. The church preserves a skull venerated as that of Mary Magdalene.

Aix-en-Provence was a favorite place of René d'Anjou (1408–1480), who features prominently among a medieval group that preserved the history of the Jesus family in France. The man given credit for the Renaissance was conversant in Latin, Greek, and Hebrew; a student of religion and history; and adept in the more mystical arts as well. During his reign, Aix had its golden age. René's wealth enabled him to commission great art, usually of religious themes. One painting at Aix shows the Virgin and child sitting in a "burning bush." The child is holding a mirror reflecting himself and his mother. In the background are the castles of Beaucaire and Tarascon as they once were. We can only guess at the significance, but René and others propagated the myth of the presence of the Holy Family in his lands in

France. Another of the commissioned works depicts the archangel Gabriel giving Mary the news of her conception. His wings are of owl feathers, and a light from the hand of God passes over a monkey's head in this strange work. Both owls and monkeys are ill omens connected to the black arts. The painting is kept locked away in the church of Mary Magdalene.[16]

West of Aix lies Tarascan.[17] There the legends of Mary and company take a bizarre turn. Martha, whose house Jesus had visited shortly before his death, is given credit for having driven away a dragon that had plagued the people of that city. Every year on the last Sunday of June, a parade commemorating that legend still takes place. From the region of Lyon and Carcassonne west, the trail of the family through France continues to Bordeaux, the city that the Frankish king Dagobert called his Aquitaine capital in the seventh century. In Bordeaux is the Place des Martyrs-de-la-Resistance, a famous cemetary reputedly dedicated by Jesus himself. Bordeaux today is known as a famous wine-growing area, as is nearby Saint-Emilion.[18] Saint-Emilion is the site of Europe's largest underground church, cut into rock. Fertility cults once held their own rites there; later they became Christianized, to a point. In Saint-Emilion there is also a Templar commandery.

At Pomeral is another church to Saint-Emilion cut into rock; this one contains a zodiac, quite an atypical design for a Christian place of worship, since astrology is condemned by the Catholic Church. That did not stop the people of Bazas from naming a cathedral the House of the Astronomer. This church, complete with some very strange carvings supposedly holds the blood of Saint John the Baptist among its collection of relics. Still another odd site is Soulomes. Home to another Templar commandery, Soulomes has depictions of Mary Magdalene and Jesus, of the apostle Thomas, and of Jesus in company with a Templar. These sites describe a "history" very different from the accepted history of both church and state.

The history of Christianity is rife with violence resulting from an organized central authority wishing to force its minions to adhere to a rigid doctrine of belief. The south of France, which may have received the message of Christianity from an early date, is ironically the scene of the worst bloodshed resulting from religious persecution. Even more ironic is the fact that the Church's attacks on fellow believers have been the worst events in the history of religious persecution.

The Visigoths

The south of France, like other areas of the Mediterranean, had a history of invaders and conquerors. The Celts yielded to Roman influence at about the time of the birth of Jesus. Toulouse was a Celtic city that had been settled in ancient times by a group called the Tectosages, which called most of southern France their own before being pushed out by Rome.[19] The Tectosages had raided Greece in 279 B.C. and looted the sacred oracle temple at Delphi. Later on, this tribe went to war with the Ligurians, and Rome came to their defense. Rome raided the Tectosage treasure trove, which was said to hold 110 pounds of silver and one hundred thousand ounces of gold. Before escaping with their reward, they were attacked themselves and their cache lost before reaching Marseilles. Legends of buried treasure abound in the region.

During the reign of Constantine, the Roman Empire began to see the writing on the wall. Hordes of barbarians from the steppes were heading into Europe, pushed ahead by even stronger hordes coming behind them. The Goths made up one group, divided into East Goths and West Goths, or Ostrogoths and Visigoths.[20] They were forced into a collision course with Rome. The Visigoths suffered defeat at the hands of Constantius, the son of Constantine, in A.D. 332. At the same time, they had captured a religious man, Wufila, who converted many of them to Christianity while he was held captive. But the conversion was not complete.

The Visigoths kept their pagan influences, and while they accepted Christianity on the surface, they persecuted those among them who would not worship the older gods.[21] These Visigoths were an unusual blend of heathen Christians who lived by plunder. A religious civil war threatened to divide them, but support from the more powerful Huns saved them from becoming assimilated into more advanced civilizations. By A.D. 390 they were on the warpath again and were soundly defeated by the Romans. By that time the Romans could no longer mount the same caliber army as it once had, and the Visigoths found themselves attacking other barbarians, who were serving as mercenaries for Rome.

Between A.D. 408 and A.D. 410 the Visigoths, under Alaric I, plundered Rome. The first attack was bought off by ransom, but they simply attacked again. During the second attack Rome was completely sacked; part of the spoils was the plunder brought home by Roman centurions who had sacked Jerusalem. The goods looted from Rome actually included the treasures of the Temple of Solomon in Jerusalem. The barbarians headed north in their retreat from Italy.

Alaric, who had survived for years as a land-bound pirate killing and looting, did not survive the rigors of his wedding night. To avoid having his body fall into the hands of his enemies, his lieutenants had slaves divert the banks of the Busento and construct a vault under the riverbed to entomb their leader. The slaves themselves were all killed afterward, to avoid the chance that anyone would find out exactly where the fearless leader rested. The river was then allowed to return to its natural course. While there is no claim to a connection between the Visigoths and the Oak Island treasure, it is interesting to note just what measures they could and would take, seventeen hundred years ago, to protect a burial vault. Similar underwater vaults are located in the Wye River in southeast Wales—one that reportedly had once contained the manuscripts of Shakespeare was discovered to be empty in 1911. Shakespeare himself—or Bacon—wrote of a king buried under the River Soar in England.

Knowing that the Visigoths had looted treasures from Rome, which included treasures taken from Jerusalem, it would not be surprising to find that they had taken even greater measures to protect them than to protect the burial vault of their king. Alaric's brother-in-law, Ataulf, married a captive named Galla Placidia, who was the sister of Honorius of Rome.[22] Honorius was the inheritor of the western Roman Empire, and the marriage raised Ataulf to a greater status. He celebrated his marriage and new status with full Roman rites in Narbonne, in southern France. The name of Ataulf's adopted city, Narbonne, means the "Good Maiden," or "Good Virgin," and it may be there that the Levis, the family of Jesus, met the Visigoths. The historian Origen mysteriously calls Mary Magdelene "the mother of us all" and also writes of her entrance into southern France through the port city of Marseilles.[23] If Mary had been bearing the child of Jesus, that child would have been born in southern France. As late as the twelfth century the Jews of Narbonne claimed that their king (his heir) was living among them.[24] The Arian Visigoths and the Jewish-Christians of the Jesus family both regarded the king in the Davidic line as a man and not a god. Both Jews and Visigoths believed that there was only one supreme God. The Visigoths later became allies of Rome and brought peace to southern France that lasted for centuries.

The next group to be pushed west by stronger barbarians in the east was the Franks. The Huns, under their legendary leader Attila, were much stronger contenders. For this reason, the Franks chose to find greener pastures in France. While the Visigoths were allied with Rome in the south of France, the Salian Franks allied themselves to Rome in the north. This alliance held against the Huns on the Plains of Moiry. The battle was the second serious defeat for the Huns and turned them eastward in retreat (A.D. 451). Peace reigned for a time as the Franks in the north and the Visigoths in the south shared Gaul. Visigothic territory was the richer land, and Euric, the leader of the Visigoths, started to expand his kingdom into Spain in A.D. 470, at the expense of the dying Roman colonies.

The Germanic Franks in the north began to grow jealous of the wealth of their neighbors in the south. Under a system called "Hospitalitas," Visigoths became great landowners in return for having served with the Roman armed forces. The Germanic mercenaries wanted the same. As Rome gave up estates, the Visigoths steadily became wealthier, and conflict with their closest Frankish neighbors, the Merovingians, became inevitable. While the rules of a feudal system were safeguards against conflict, religion became an excuse, a catalyst for conflict.

The Visigoths had accepted the Arian Christian faith that placed the one supreme God above all. This form of the faith had been acceptable to the early Christian Church, as it had to the Jewish followers of Jesus. Later the Roman Church held the First Council of Nicaea (A.D. 325) and adopted the position that Jesus was the Son of God and equal to God. They also adopted the concept of a Holy Trinity, which more closely resembled the Greek mystery religions—but without a female deity. The council declared that any divergent belief was a sin. The Frankish leader Clovis I saw his opportunity to remain with Rome. He declared himself a Christian and was baptized immediately. Immediately after conversion, he sought to conquer his wealthy neighbors in the south.

Besides the wealth of prosperous farms that was held by the Visigoths, Euric also had held the treasures plundered from Rome, specifically those of the Temple of Solomon. Euric adopted Toulouse as his base, and his treasure was hidden there.

After the reign of Euric, his son, Alaric II, took over. Alaric was no heir to his father's and grandfather's fighting ability and constantly yielded to Clovis in the north. The feeble Alaric was resigned to a Merovingian conquest of his region, since the Franks had the support of the Church and Rome. He continued to cede territory rather than fight and surrendered a fugitive Gallo-Roman king to Clovis. The appeasement strategy served only to build Clovis's confidence, and in 507 the newly Christian Clovis himself killed Alaric, to become the king of France. Visigothic Spain and Frankish (Merovingian) Gaul had one last territory to battle over, the border lands between them known as Septimania; the struggle went on for years.[25] The region became home to constant warfare, and religion was ostensibly the reason. Visigothic nobles tenaciously held on to their important centers, like Narbonne, and were backed by the Basques, who still control the mountainous region between the two countries.

The Crusade Against the Cathari

Not far from Aix is the town of Béziers.[26] Just how many people from the east settled there will never be known, but Béziers became a center of what came to be regarded as the Arian heresy and the center of the sect of Christian believers known as the Cathari, who denied the central authority of Rome. They were targeted by the Roman Church as part of the debate over Christ's nature on Earth—was he man or god? Like the Jewish-Christians, the Cathari believed that Jesus on Earth was a man, a prophet. The scions of the Jesus bloodline, too, believed that he was a man. The Church, however, taught that Jesus was God even when he was on Earth—the question was not open to debate.

In 1209 forces of the Church massacred the entire population of the city. Seven thousand Cathari were killed in the church of the Madaleine. The leader of the Christian forces asked the prelate sent by the Pope just how he would know who the Cathari were. The church leader declared, "Kill them all; God will know his own."[27] From there they massacred Cathari and Christians alike in the surrounding towns and villages in a genocidal action that depopulated much of the wealthy Languedoc region of France.

The fortress of the Cathari was their stronghold at Montsegur.[28] Guy de Levis owned the temple at Montsegur, which had been regarded as the "earthly image of their faith."[29] The Cathari held out here against a siege by the Church of Rome, which they regarded as the Antichrist that John had warned about in the Apocalypse. Rome after all, was love (amor) spelled backward and thus the antithesis of everything Jesus had taught. In the Book of Revelation, John had declared that he, too, was of the royal bloodline. "I am the root and the offspring of David."[30] The Church had every intention of stamping out the root and stock of David—such a bloodline had threatened Rome previously. The Church had become the survivor of the state of Rome. In the stamping out of the "sprouts" of the sacred bloodline, the line of David, were the descendants of the family of Jesus among the casualties? There is evidence that they were and possibly this family was, in fact, the target of such a crusade.

During this time the breakup of the Roman Empire left a constantly embattled Europe. There were no banks, Templar or otherwise, and often the wealth of barbaric kings and nobles was portable, in the form of gold and silver. Even the formidable castles and walled cities were no match for the onslaught of barbaric hordes. Wealth earned and stolen plunder shared a need to be buried. Caves, grottoes, and man-made structures served as the predecessors of banks. Very little in the way of records exists to guide treasure hunters to caches that might have been left behind by nobles killed in battle, but there is evidence that such treasures *were* left behind for the lucky to stumble across hundreds of years later.

Chapter 9

THE MYSTERY OF
RENNES-LE-CHATEAU

Sometime between 1885 and 1891, someone was very lucky and unearthed a treasure worth millions. A parish priest by the name of Bérenger Saunière had been posted to a very tiny mountain village at Rennes-le-Chateau. Saunière had been born in a nearby village in 1852 and had been ordained a priest in 1879. This village was his second assignment. It was not a good post for the learned young priest, who is described as having had a taste for the good life. Although larger than his first posting in the village of Clat, where there were twenty-three of the faithful in his congregation, Rennes-le-Chateau was far from Paris and at the time still accessible only by mule path.[1]

There was little "good life" to be had on his income, which was barely enough to support himself and a housekeeper. With a village of barely two hundred souls to look after, young Saunière had time on his hands. Whether it was from boredom or for another reason, Father Saunière decided to use his time to restore the village church, which was in disrepair. The church had been built in 1059 over the ruins of a Visigothic church dedicated to Mary Magdalene that dated back six hundred years, to A.D. 411.

The young priest chose to start his restoration with the altar. He removed the altar stone and the two pillars that supported it. To his amazement, one of the two pillars was hollow and contained three sealed tubes, each holding documents on parchment. The texts were in Latin— two were dated to 1244 and 1644, respectively. Two others were religious texts, but apparently coded. This was not the first time Saunière had come across odd documents that needed translation. Before the discovery of the parchments in the altar, a document that Saunière had found required the help of a local to translate; it supposedly contained property titles. The document was written in Latin, but it was a very old Latin, which the priest himself had not been trained to read. The notary he consulted was known to be well versed in the idioms and subtleties of the language of Virgil's days. It was this document that may have started Saunière on his path to finding a treasure. It might also have been a document that the priest needed to keep secret.

The story is told that shortly after a notary, from nearby Quillan, translated documents for Father Saunière, the two went on an outing, a hike in the rocky mountainside with some village children. Saunière and the notary from Quillan preceded the children through a steep, brush-covered path, where there was an accident. Father Saunière was hurt, and the notary was killed. A police inquest concluded that the death was indeed an accident, as Saunière claimed. Few priests would have been doubted, but it would not be the last strange death in the life of Saunière.[2]

When Saunière found the documents concealed in the hollow columns of the altar, he contacted the bishop of Carcassonne, Monseigneur Felix-Arsene Billard. His bishop sent him to Paris and to the abbé Bieil, the director of Saint Sulpice.[3] In Paris he also made a point of seeking out three paintings that held significance.

One of the paintings, *Les Bergers d'Arcadie* (The Shepherds of Arcadia), was by Nicolas Poussin; it depicted three shepherds looking at a tomb and pointing. The inscription read "Et in Arcadia Ego." The tomb in Poussin's painting and a certain tomb near Rennes-le-Chateau were one and the same. The message itself translates as "And in Arcadia, I am." The significance of this message remains uncertain, but it and others found in the texts of the parchments held great significance to Saunière. Upon his return, the priest visited the local cemetery and removed the inscription. The only reason we know today just what was inscribed on the stone is that the town had kept a record of the gravestone.

Besides the three paintings, it is unknown what exactly Saunière discovered in Paris; there is no question, however, that the paintings led to something of great value. From a parish priest with an income of thirty dollars annually, he became a millionaire. The money changed his lifestyle and Rennes-le-Chateau forever, and according to some the religious-historical significance of his find (genealogies preserving the blood line of Jesus Christ) has the power to change the world. He suddenly went from being an impoverished parish priest to a philanthropist who spent millions on public works for his village. He built roads where before there were only dirt paths. He girded his own village with ramparts, although he was not expecting a siege. Or was he? He modernized the water supply for the ancient village. He founded a zoological garden, restored the church, built himself a library, and put up a tower dedicated to Mary Magdalene. In total it is estimated that he spent the equivalent of five to twenty million in today's dollars. He also began entertaining important guests from all over Europe, from royalty to artists. What attracted such personages as the Hapsburgs and opera singers to Rennes-le-Chateau, we can only guess.

The documents Saunière found were genealogies that traced the lines of certain people backed to Visigothic-Merovingian times, and further still. They may even contain the bloodline of David extending to Jesus and from Jesus through descendants living in France. Whatever was translated by the unfortunate notary led Saunière to the parchments in the altar, which in turn brought him to the cemetery of the tiny village and ultimately to the tomb that was the subject of Poussin's painting—the tomb of one Marie de Negri D'Ables, who died on January seventeenth in the year 1781. This tomb of Marie de Negri D'Ables revealed the message "Et in Arcadia Ego," which had been inscribed by the abbé Bigou, a previous curé of Rennes-le-Chateau, who also composed the coded parchments found in the church.[4] One of these parchments provided the message "To Dagobert II and Sion belong this treasure, and it is death." Sion, of course, was Zion, or Israel. Dagobert II was one of the last heirs to the Merovingian French throne, and Marie had descended from the royal line.

Marie was the widow of Francis of Hautpoul, the lord of Rennes and Blanchefort. She had three surviving daughters; her son had died young. If she was the last of an unbroken line, she found herself in a predicament, being without a surviving male heir to whom she could pass the treasure. Her relationship with her three daughters was described as "acrid," and in them she placed no confidence.[5] And she needed someone in whom to confide. This was one hundred years before Saunière would arrive in the village. His predecessor was the abbé Bigou.

To the abbé Bigou the secret genealogy of Marie and her family tree was passed. On Marie's death her secret was safe. If the family held a treasure, it was not one that she apparently wished to use. Her daughters continued to live in obscurity and lost the family estate to foreclosure. If Marie held a secret or a treasure, Bigou left only clues. The treasure, said the message, belonged to Dagobert. This was the message that fell into the hands of Father Saunière. Many of these documents and messages found by Saunière are confusing. Some were passages from the Bible, but the words ran together, and words not found in the Bible had been added. Certainly much was in code. One message was so complete in its coding that a computer used by the military could not decipher it; this one may have been deciphered by Saunière. Whatever its meaning, it appears that Father Saunière found the key. For us, he, too, left only clues, and some of these are visible in his bizarre restoration of the church.[6]

Over the doorway to the church there is a Latin inscription: "Terribilis est locus iste," which means "This place is terrible." The inscription serves as a warning to the visitor who is next greeted by a statue of the pagan Middle Eastern demon Asmodeus, who reputedly built the Temple of Solomon and is regarded as a keeper of secrets and a guardian of treasure—not a typical feature in a Christian church. Another statue is of the Virgin Mary, with the word MISSION on the pedestal; the letters are separated are to spell MIS SION, possibly referring to the Prieuré de Sion. The altar has two Jesus children facing each other, which could be a reference to the Cathar dualistic belief or, according to one Gnostic author, a reference to the idea that Jesus had a twin. Saunière's church also had a very unusual set of depictions of the Stations of the Cross. One station had Marie looking into a cave. Was he telling us that Marie knew where the Merovingian treasure was secured? Another station featured a child dressed in Scottish plaid. Was Father Saunière leaving his own message that something from Jerusalem was being guarded and that someone in Scotland might be an heir to such secrets?

Saunière also built a home for himself, which he dubbed the Villa Bethania. Its cost in today's terms would be close to five hundred thousand dollars, and it was considered the greatest house in the area. The name itself might be another clue. In Aramaic, *beth* translates to "house" and *ania* to "sky" or "heaven." The close friend of Jesus, Lazarus, who was miraculously rescued from the tomb, lived at his own home in Bethany with Martha. Martha is one of the followers who allegedly went to France with the fleeing companions of Jesus. Saunière left the house, and his secrets, to his housekeeper. Father Saunière's church and home hold only clues—he personally did not reveal much to anyone. His own superiors demanded to know the source of his wealth, and he refused to tell them. When the new bishop of Carcassonne suspended him, the Vatican interceded and reinstated him. He also flaunted his new lifestyle by living openly with his housekeeper. The Church made threats but did nothing. Someone else may have made threats that were taken more seriously.

A priest in the nearby village of Coustaussa, the curé Gellis, was killed in his presbytery in 1893. His murder was brutal (he was finished off with an ax), and he was then laid out "solemnly and respectfully." Even though he kept great sums of money that belonged to the Church, they were left untouched. Only a locked deed box had been broken into. It was not the only mysterious death in the area before or after Saunière's own mysterious death. Abbé Boudet, a close friend of Saunière and an expert in Celtic stone structures helped him decipher some of the local monuments. How much Saunière shared with Boudet is unknown, but

Boudet was healthy when he was visited by "sinister strangers" and died within hours of their departure.[7] In modern times three additional bodies were removed from the ground outside of Sauniere's home.

Sauniere's death was also very suspicious. He had been active and healthy on January 12, when his housekeeper ordered his coffin and paid for it in advance. Then, on the feast day of Saint Sulpice, he suffered a stroke. The date of January 17 is interesting because it is the same date as that on the tombstone of the marquise d'Hautpoul de Blanchefort, which Sauniere had obliterated. Saint Sulpice is also the place where Father Sauniere went to research whatever he found in the altar columns. Before his death he called for a local priest to hear his last confession. Father Riviere is said to have been shocked by what he heard, refused Sauniere the last sacrament, and became ill immediately afterward. He did not go back to work for months. On January 23, Sauniere died.

The housekeeper, Marie Dénarnaud, lived on for years after Sauniere's death. The source of her wealth, of course, was considered to be the treasure found by Sauniere. In 1946 the French government ordered that all old currency be replaced with new currency as part of the rebuilding of its financial system after the occupation by the Germans. Marie was seen burning large denominations of currency. She did not want to explain its source. Without money, she sold the Villa Bethania, the house that she inherited from Sauniere, to a friend. She told her friend and close companion that she would reveal her secret to the buyer when she was near death. To the buyer, Noël Corbu, she said, "My friend you walk on gold, but you do not know it." Marie also told him that what she would reveal would make him a "powerful" man. A mysterious choice of words, points out one writer—she did not say "rich." She later suffered a stroke and was unable to speak. She went to her grave, allegedly, without making any revelation. Corbu himself died in 1968 in a suspicious car accident.[8]

The mystery of Rennes-le-Chateau and the source of Father Sauniere's sudden wealth have been the subject of many theories. The source of the buried treasure alone could point in several directions. Might it be the loot of ancient Celts who raided Europe and then retired to France? Or the treasure of barbarian Visigoths who raided Rome and then settled in the Rennes-le-Chateau area? Or is it Cathar treasure brought to safety at the last minute by a handful of survivors and hidden in caves?

The involvement of the Bishop of Carcassonne, the director of Saint Sulpice in Paris, and later the intercession by the Vatican on behalf of a less than orthodox priest point to a greater secret. What could have been unearthed in a tiny mountain village to bring such great attention to the village of Rennes-le-Chateau?

The Merovingian Dynasty and the Family of Jesus

Dagobert II was the last of the kings of Merovingian France.[9] When Merovingian power was being challenged after his father's death, Dagobert was sent to live in a monastery in Slane in Ireland. He married a Celtic princess, Mathilde, in A.D. 666; she died giving birth to his third daughter. In A.D. 670 he married again. His second wife was Giselle de Razes, the daughter of the count of Razes and granddaughter to the Visigothic king. The wedding was celebrated at Rennes-le-Chateau, her home and the capital of her fiefdom. The Visigoths are the first people after the Gaulish Celts who shared their territory with the exiles of the Holy Lands. The Aramaic-speaking followers of Jesus may have married into Visigothic families—the name "Razes" recalls an Aramaic word *razi* meaning "my secret." Today there remain several villages in the surrounding area with Razes in the name. The Visigoths invaded the south of France during the fall of Rome. They were followed by the Merovingians, whose rule of France was lost to the Carolingians after the death of Dagobert II.

The *Life of Wilfred*, written in the eighth century, is one source that mentions Dagobert II; outside that we see little reference to him. According to *The Merovingian Kingdoms*, "The general silence of the sources . . . suggests that the episode was one over which Merovingians and Carolingians both wished to draw a veil."[10] If Zion and Dagobert shared a treasure, it could be theorized that it was the loot from the Temple of Solomon. The thesis of *Holy Blood, Holy Grail*—whether they shared a secret as well—is that the family of Jesus, exiled to France, had heirs and a dynasty that survived the centuries.

The Carolingians had planned for the Merovingian dynasty to end with Dagobert II. On December 23, 674, he was murdered while hunting in the forest surrounding his northern seat of power at Stenay. A son of Dagobert II could legitimately claim power because he was in a more direct line in the bloodline of kings. The veil drawn by the usurpers was not pierced until the seventeenth century when more evidence of the life of Dagobert II surfaced.

As far-fetched as both the existence and the significance of such genealogies seems today, there is a good body of evidence that shows how much value was placed in such records. The Gospel of Matthew set great store on tracing the genealogy of Jesus back to David.[11] It was the basis of his kingship and his fulfillment of the prophecies. The Old Testament, too, shows genealogies that stretched from Adam to Noah and to Abraham and David. Eusebius records that the family of Jesus expounded his genealogy in the same chapter where he tells of Herod's exile to France.[12] The Romans searched for these genealogies, but we have no record that they found them. They wanted to lay hands on them to destroy any claims to a throne that could be based on their existence.

Another early historian, Hegesippus, writing of the family of Jesus, says that surviving relatives accused the Roman rulers of ferreting out, capturing, and killing the heirs in the Davidic line as well as destroying the genealogies of Jewish nobles.[13] Clearly, the genealogies held great importance. They appear to be missing, and at the same time there is no record of their destruction. We can easily make a case that these historic documents were hidden. Did Saunière find them?

Saunière left the world only clues to a great mystery. One clue to the nature of the treasure of Rennes-le-Chateau was found on the gravestone that Saunière eradicated. "Reddis Regis Cellis Arcis" read the grave marker, which translates loosely to "At Royal Reddis, the cave of the fortress." According to *Holy Blood, Holy Grail*, Reddis (or Rhedae) was the name the Celts had given to what would later become Rennes-le-Chateau. The root *rede* also has the meaning "to guard." This marker may alternatively be translated as meaning "the Caves [at Arques] Guard the Ruler."

The south of France is full of caves and man-made tunnels as well as legends of hidden treasure. It would be possible that the source of Saunière's wealth was something that anyone in the vicinity could have stumbled across. He was only twenty miles from the fortress of Montsegur, from which the Cathar treasure might have been saved at the last moment. The author Jean Blum reports on one cache of gold being found and taken to a jeweler. The jeweler had trouble in determining just what purity the gold was because the objects contained added minerals he had never seen present in gold jewelry. He gave a bracelet to his son, who was an atomic engineer. The son determined that the element added to the gold was cobalt. Since cobalt was added only to African gold, Blum deduces that it was part of the stolen treasures of Solomon.

While any explorer or treasure seeker could have stumbled across such a cache, only Saunière had access to the altar stone and the genealogies and coded tombstone that directed him to the treasure—a treasure possibly owned by Zion and by the Merovingian king Dagobert II. The Frankish Merovingians were part of the huge barbarian wave that was being pushed westward by the Huns from Central Asia. Their history and roots are shrouded in legend. The Merovingian kings have their own telling of the story of their descent from King Clodio. After the king had impregnated his queen, she went swimming in the ocean. There she came upon a sea creature, who impregnated her a second time. The sea creature was a "Quinotaur"; of such a beast we have no description.[14] To the queen a child was born, who carried the blood of kings and the blood of a sea beast. He was named Merovee, which, like the name Mary, has connotations related to the sea.

The legend could be a literary device to explain the intermingling of two great powers. Just as Jesus was the descendant of the priest Aaron and the king David, Merovee, too, had great and powerful ancestors— one a king, who in Europe before the French Revolution would typically claim to rule by divine right, and the other a supernatural creature. As a result of this unusual bloodline, the Merovingians claimed the ability to heal by the "laying on of hands," a power that the Essenes were reputed to command, as did Jesus, whose healing is recorded in the Gospels. Merovingians also believed that their power resided in their hair, which could never be cut. In the case of Samson, too, his hair was the source of his power. When the once long-haired Spartans defeated the Argives in 564 B.C., they forced the Argives to cut their hair in recognition of the fact that the Argives no longer had a claim to the Peloponnesos. Hair also featured significantly for James, the brother of Jesus, who was regarded as holy by Eusebius because "no razor touched his head." We remember also that the words *caesar* and *czar* are derived from the German for "kaiser," meaning crown of hair. The Merovingians, then, were like Jesus, priest-kings with both supernatural ability and a royal bloodline stemming from earthly kings.

The grandson of Merovee, the half-man, half-fish founder of the dynasty, was Clovis, the conqueror of the Visigoths.[15] The comparison with Jesus holds no further coincidence with this brutal ruler. He did not lack in imagination as he plotted to consolidate his role as king of France. He told the son of another king, Sigibert, to murder his father, which the son, Cholderic, did. Cholderic then showed Clovis a chest of gold coins he had taken from his father. While Cholderic bent over the chest, Clovis split his head with an ax. Another minor king was beheaded alongside his son for challenging Clovis.

History tells us that Clovis converted to Catholicism to appease his wife, but a more likely reason was that the diabolical Clovis needed a strong ally and the Roman Church proved such a powerful friend and provided justification for attacking the neighboring Visigoths. Marriage had given him Burgundy. Once an Arian, he stated, "It grieves me that these Arians should hold a part of Gaul."[16] With support, he soon extended France to its historical limits. After the death of Clovis his kingdom was again divided, among his four sons.

The history of the Merovingians is one of murder and treachery. Grandsons of Clovis continued their rule by murder, and Merovingian women were not to be outdone by their men in terms of cruelty. Chilperic murdered his first wife to marry a second. Fredegund, the mistress, even tried to kill her own daughter, Rigunth, who constantly irritated her.[17] The dowager queen Clotild was given a choice, to have her grandsons' hair cut off or to have them killed. She responded that if their hair was cut off, they could not rule, so they might as well be killed.

Later, rule passed down to Dagobert II, the king mentioned on the gravestone at Rennes-le-Chateau. As we recall, he married a Celtic princess, and after her death the Visigothic princess Giselle in Rennes-le-Chateau. The brief record of Dagobert's life tells us that he amassed a large fortune, which aided his efforts to take over the rule of most of France.[18] His inheritance of the Visigothic treasure hoard may have been the basis of this war chest, but his rule did not last forever. On a hunting trip near his northern capital at Stenay, he was stabbed with a lance. The area surrounding Stenay is known as Lorraine, and a later duke of Lorraine became the grandfather of Godfrey of Bouillon, who would be the conqueror and king of Jerusalem.

Later Merovingian kings lost their drive, and as the line lost control, power was seized by the mayors of the palace, regents of the kingdom. Instead of remaining pledged to the cause of the Merovingian line, as the Roman Church had done under Clovis, the Church threw its support behind Charlemagne. The rule of the Merovingians came to an end. There was one heir, Sigisbert IV, who survived the hunting trip to Stenay. He inherited the Merovingian throne (in name) after being rescued from the enemies of his father. It is said that he was brought back to safety at Rennes-le-Chateau. With no chance of taking the crown, Sigisbert was given the title of count of Reddis, duke of Razes. He was not the last of the Merovingian kings, but he was a direct descendant. Sigisbert's progeny took the surname Plantard, which means "ardently flowering shoot."[19] Sigisbert himself became the scion of the Merovingian dynasty, as the Levis were the scions of the Davidic kingship.

One branch of the vine descended through Bera VI. Bera came to be called the "Architect," a name that Freemasons regarded highly. Northern families still went out of their way to marry into the Merovingian line despite the fact that power was no longer theirs. Intermarriage between the house of Lorraine and the Merovingian heirs made sure that Godfrey of Bouillon's veins flowed together with the sacred bloodline of the French kings. It was the Merovingian heirs who conquered Jerusalem. Had they a secret agenda?

One hypothesis of *Holy Blood, Holy Grail* is that the Merovingian dynasty was a continuation of the Davidic line, which flowed through the family of Jesus or even through Jesus himself. The heirs of Jesus living in

France intermarried with the Visigoths. Later ruling families of the Merovingian and Carolingian dynasties would make it a point to marry into the families of the heirs of Jesus. Marie de Negri D'Ables was one of the heirs in the Davidic line. Saunière's secret might have been much more significant to the world than simply the booty of looted Rome and Jerusalem or other ancient caches of Visigothic treasures. The secret may have been that Jesus' heirs were alive and well and ready to assume power when the time was auspicious.

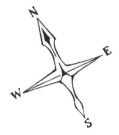

Chapter 10

THE CONNECTING THREAD

Our English word *clue* comes from a much older word, *clewe*, meaning a ball of thread. In the myths of the Greeks, children were carried off each year to Crete, where the evil king Minos had them sacrificed to a monstrous creature, half man and half bull, called the Minotaur. The Minotaur lived underground in a maze of passageways called the Labyrinth. The children, seven boys and seven girls each year, were thrown into the maze, and the Minotaur would kill and devour them. The Greek hero Theseus asked that he be sent to Crete as part of the yearly offering.

In Crete Theseus attracted the eye of the daughter of the king, who fell in love with him. Her love led Ariadne, the princess, to devise a plan to free Theseus from death. She supplied him with a ball of thread, which he could unwind as he traveled through the maze in order to find his way back out.[1] The word took on a new meaning when the "clewe" provided the "clue" to solving the mystery of the Labyrinth. In the mystery of Oak Island it is a long thread unwinding through a labyrinth of history that we must follow to find the source of the treasure hidden in the Money Pit. The trail starts in the Jerusalem of Solomon and David.

David and Solomon

Undeniably one of the holiest places in the world, Jerusalem is claimed as the center and birthplace of three distinctly different religions—Christianity, Judaism, and Islam. Together these religions encompass the majority of the population of the planet—billions of people believe Jerusalem is their cradle. Ironically, this holy city started as a pagan site of worship before these major world religions laid claim to it. The area surrounding Jerusalem had been home to the Canaanites and other peoples who might have settled the area from the sea.[2] The Canaanite religion included many gods—their god of prosperity, Salem, was worshiped in Jerusalem.

David, king of one of Israel's twelve tribes, had understood that by having one fortified city as a base he could unite the twelve tribes into a nation. He chose Jerusalem to be that unifying capital.[3] The young king was experienced in war, having learned the art of war as an ally to enemies of Israel called the Philistines. He understood that the siege of an established, walled fortress like Jerusalem could take years, but through spies he discovered that the water supply of the city came from a spring called Gihon. The designers of the city had planned ahead for a siege that might hinder their ability to obtain water from outside wells. They built a large tunnel underneath the city and connected it to a vertical well. David used their strategy against them and sent his men through the underground water tunnel and up the well shaft. The city surrendered.[4]

David then had himself anointed king of Israel. He was the savior of his people; he was the messiah. The Hebrew people called him the "Shepherd." The title was not descriptive, since David was a warrior and a king, but it had been a custom from as far back as the time of the Sumerians to designate kings as "shepherds."[5] God, too, was a shepherd, and Christians pray to Jesus, the Lamb of God, who takes away the sins of the world.

Monotheistic beliefs were just starting to take precedence over religions with literally hundreds of gods. David was part of the trend; he tried to push his own flock in this direction and to wean them from such customs as idol worship, which was characteristic of premonotheistic religion, and having more than one wife. For himself, he did not wish to change too fast. He kept many wives.[6] His most important wife was Bathsheba, a Jebusite woman, to whom a son was born. The relationship started as an adulterous affair. David promised Bethsheba that her son would rule over the sons whom David had fathered earlier, with his other wives. They named their son "Solomon." Standard translation tells us the name means "peace," but a truer rendering is "Sun God of On."* Worship was not standardized, as it is now and such sanitized versions of the names of religious figures, with little reference to their more pagan forms of worship, would come much later.

With such a great importance placed on bloodline and genealogy, it is odd that the son in whom David placed the kingship of the Israelite people was half Jewish and half Jebusite. The Jebusites were of the groups of peoples that had started settling the area hundreds of years before as invaders. These "sea peoples," as Egyptian texts call them, included tribes like the Shardan and the Peleset. "Peleset" became corrupted as "Philistine"; the Jebusites were a related subset of this larger family of sea kings. The invading sea kings were the downfall of the Hittite Empire, one of the strongest in the region. They might have brought down Egypt, too, if the pharaohs had not wisely hired them as mercenaries.[7]

The bloodline of Solomon, therefore, was a combination of the kingship line of the Hebrews and of another strain extending from a people that came by sea. The bloodline of Jesus was derived from the priestly caste of Aaron and the kingship caste of David. The quality of a priest was often determined by his ability to perform magic. The priest-kings from the east who visited the birthplace of Jesus were called "magi,"

---

*According to Barbara Walker, "On" refers to a city in ancient Egypt, possibly Heliopolis.

Members of the Blair Syndicate circa 1909, including a young lawyer named Franklin Delano Roosevelt (third from right).

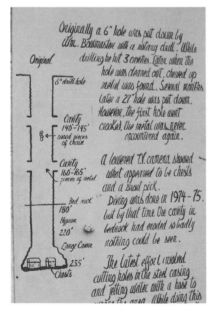

Cross section of hole originally drilled in 1845. During this drilling several platforms of wood and metal were hit before striking what they thought to be a treasure trove.

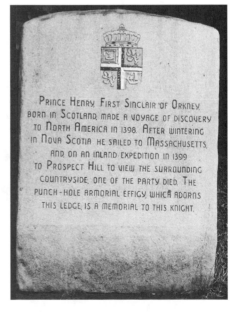

Memorial to Prince Henry, first Sinclair of Orkney.

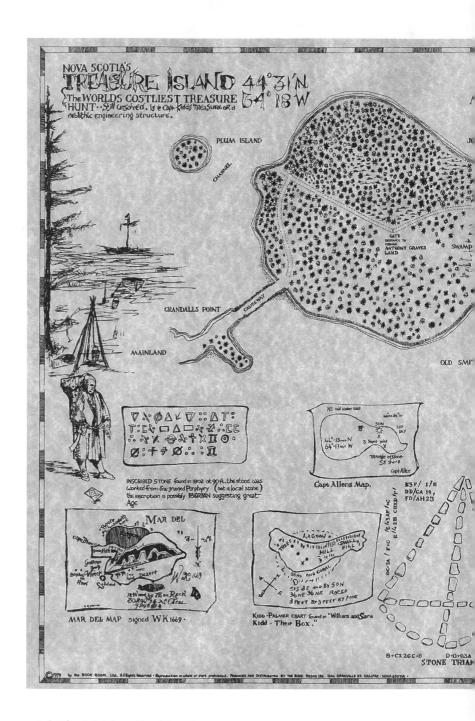

Oak Island, Mahone Bay, Nova Scotia.

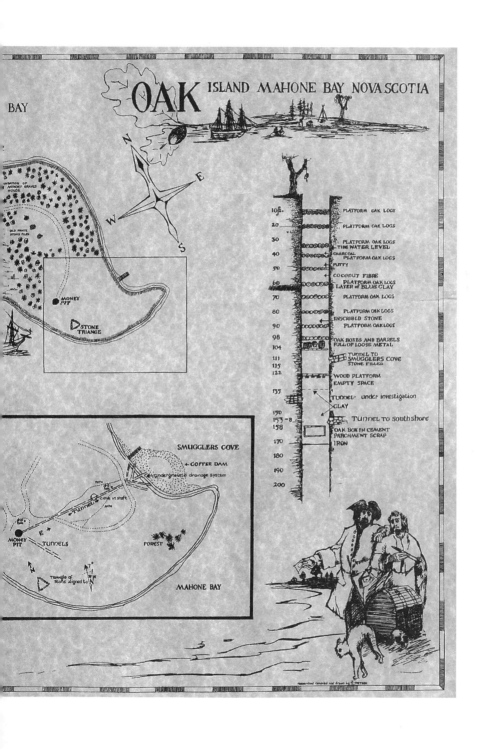

OAK ISLAND MAHONE BAY NOVA SCOTIA

BAY

N · E · W · S

VARIATION OF ANTHONY GRAVES HOUSE

OLD PIRATE STONE PILES

MONEY PIT

STONE TRIANGE

Depth	
10 ft.	PLATFORM OAK LOGS
20	PLATFORM OAK LOGS
30	PLATFORM OAK LOGS / TIDE WATER LEVEL
40	CHARCOAL / PLATFORM OAK LOGS
50	PUTTY
60	COCONUT FIBRE / PLATFORM OAK LOGS / LAYER of BLUE CLAY
70	PLATFORM OAK LOGS
80	PLATFORM OAK LOGS
	INSCRIBED STONE
90	PLATFORM OAK LOGS
98	OAK BOXES AND BARRELS
104	FULL OF LOOSE METAL
111	TUNNEL TO SMUGGLERS COVE
115	STONE FILLED
122	WOOD PLATFORM
	EMPTY SPACE
135	TUNNEL under investigation
	CLAY
150	
153-8	TUNNEL to southshore
158	
170	OAK BOX IN CEMENT / PARCHMENT SCRAP / IRON
180	
190	
200	

SMUGGLERS COVE

COFFER DAM

underground drainage system

PATH

Cave in shaft

MONEY PIT

E

TUNNELS

TUNNEL

FOREST

TRIANGLE of stone aligned to N

MAHONE BAY

Researched compiled and drawn by G. METSON

Inscription found at Oak Island. The chalk-filled grooves reveal Gunn Clan heraldry.

Replica of an inscribed stone found at ninety feet that allegedly tells of a treasure buried forty feet below. The original stone, once a part of John Smith's fireplace, has disappeared.

since magic was indeed the priestly art. Similarly, the heirs of the blood-line of the Merovingian dynasty were born after a queen was first impregnated by the king and then by a mysterious creature from the sea—an "other world" father and an earthly father.

David's energies were spent in planning a great temple as befitting the center of the Hebrew world, but it would be left to Solomon to carry out the plan. A Jebusite farmer owned the land surrounding the sacred site, which was a rock called Moriah. With the god Salem already deposed by the Canaanite god El, a more supreme being, the Hebrew people now accepted El as their own. El had once been a "bull god" that the sea peoples had adopted from contacts across the Mediterranean. At this point El simply became the Father God.[8] The sacred premises of Salem—Moriah—was sold by the farmer to the Jews and it, too, underwent a name change. It became Zion.

Modern Freemasons make the claim that it was Solomon who was instrumental in starting the traditions of their craft.[9] The temple was not the first major work of the ancients, and highly developed technicians were needed to create such large buildings. These technicians were usually found in specialized guilds. The Hebrew herding peoples had no tradition of constructing much more than tents; they had always been a nomadic people. They had to consult with those who had greater ability and experience in architecture. Solomon consulted the Canaanite king Hiram. In Masonic lore, much of which was invented in the seventeenth and eighteenth centuries when Masonry took a decidedly occult turn, Hiram is regarded as the master builder. In reality, Hiram had master technicians at his command.

Hiram instructed Solomon to send thirty thousand workers to learn from Phoenician craftsmen. Hiram took on the role of developer as well and funded the work that soon employed one hundred eighty thousand laborers. In turn, Solomon gave Hiram twenty towns. The temple grew to become a massive structure whose facade opened to face the rising sun in the east. This vestibule received the early light, just as structures from Ireland to Asia were so aligned to receive the first rays of the sun. History and religion conceal the importance of such structures largely because their functions are not understood completely.[10]

From Sumerian times onward, the learned men who were architects believed that the heavens could and should be replicated on Earth in the form of such monumental structures. From Sumeria to Stonehenge, monuments and complete cities were built and organized with such a master plan in mind, representing their highest amalgamation of religion and science. Later "modern" religion came to feel threatened by this science, which was once considered a function of another religion or, worse, "magic." The desire of the master builders, the architects, to replicate heaven on Earth is manifest in the Masonic statement "As above, so below."[11] This undercurrent of science that was forced to remain secret to avoid the wrath of organized religion existed throughout the medieval age.

The Christian cathedral at Chartres is one of the most important monuments to pagan science and to God. It actually measures the date of the summer solstice by strategically placed flagstones that receive the sunlight on that date. One mystery of Chartres is that it was not dedicated to the Virgin Mary but to Mary Magdalene.[12] Both had been given the ambiguous title "Notre Dame," meaning "Our Lady." But they had different meanings to their followers.

When the Christian religion was imposed on the Celtic people, the Church had to overcome the goddess worship that prevailed from India to Ireland. In place of the goddess, they tried to substitute the Blessed Virgin, the Mother of Jesus, but she was not the same as the pagan goddess. The pagan goddess had three aspects, that of maiden (virginity), mother (fertility), and crone (death). She was at once her own trinity, who brought both life and death.[13] This goddess was remembered as Isis, among other names, and her symbol was the dove, as was the symbol of Mary Magdalene, the Cathari, and Saint John the Baptist. The "underground stream," the secret celestial knowledge, was also preserved from ancient religion. Part of this secret knowledge was an understanding of the universe. The Masonic adage "As above, so below" exemplifies the job of the mason to create on Earth a representation of heaven.

This body of knowledge of the celestial world helped create a structure where the sun could penetrate the darkest recesses on a sacred day of the year. Such knowledge was used in structures from prehistoric New Grange and Stonehenge to Jerusalem and Chartres. The original master builder, Hiram in Masonic lore, built the Temple of Solomon according to this celestial outline. On the north, west, and south, auxiliary temples were built around an area called the Ulam. Entering through the facade, one would first reach the nave, sixty feet in length. The main hall was called the Hekal. At the western extreme was the Debir. The Debir was the Holy of the Holies, a perfect thirty-foot cube. Only the privileged could enter, and the way was barred with chains of gold. The Ark of the Covenant holding the Ten Commandments was housed there.[14]

Solomon did not leave anything to chance. In his temple concessions were made to pagan gods and goddesses just in case his own god let him down. He believed in the Supreme God, El (or Jehovah), but at the same time there were other gods and goddesses to appease. The Tyrian sun god Melek (Moloch of the Bible), the goddess of Sidon named Astarte, and the moon goddess Sin (who became male and the source of the word "Sinai") were all included. Solomon built another temple to Chamos, the idol of Moab, and two temples to the great mother goddesses.[15]

The temple itself was formed using the design of Canaanite temples. Two massive columns, thirty-four and a half feet high and eighteen feet in diameter, were built at the entrance. Some have said that these columns represent the sun and the moon. Others say they stand for the Tree of Life and the Tree of Knowledge. Solomon named the columns Boaz and Jachin.[16] In the initiation ceremony of Freemasons, the new inductee is taught that these columns were hollow. The insides were left hollow to protect secret documents from fire and flood. The columns of the altar at Rennes-le-Chateau were also built to hold secret documents, which may have been held there against time and the ravages of invaders until Saunière undertook the renovation of the church.

The palace of Solomon was an engineering feat as well. Underground hydraulic works were employed because David's conquest of the city taught him just what a high price could be paid for making well water accessible. The spring of Gihon was camouflaged, and the cistern was invented to increase the outside water supply and the fertility of the area.

Farming and trade brought great prosperity to Jerusalem. The riches of the city are described in 3 Kings 10: 18–21. It is said there that nothing in the temple is not covered in gold. Solomon was receiving tribute from all over the world. "Two hundred shields of gold, six hundred sixty six talents of gold" were brought to him every year. His throne of ivory was covered in gold, as were other furniture and utensils. The Bible reports that the Queen of Sheba (in Ethiopia) offered both herself and the treasures of her kingdom to him. Solomon's fleets traded as far east as India, where they met with junks from China, and as far west as Spain, where the mines of Tarshish yielded silver.[17] While Jerusalem may have been the wealthiest city in the world during Solomon's time, constant warfare later destroyed the original temple. What we know about the temple today comes from its description as recorded in the Bible. None of the original architecture remains standing.

The massive columns of the temple are described in the Bible but were lost to history. Were they truly hollow? We have no other source to confirm these claims. If they were hollow, did they contain the genealogies of the Hebrew kingship line? While we have more recent evidence in the facts that the columns of the Visigothic altar at Rennes-le-Chateau were used as a hiding place, this finding alone does not verify the lore of the Masons.

Evidence available from sources other than Masonic lore, however, tell of the connecting thread that stretches from Jerusalem to the south of France. It can be verified by the genealogies hidden in the hollow columns of the church at Rennes-le-Chateau, and it is corroborated in legends of the Languedoc region in France. The theme gains support, in part, in the body of Grail literature that became popular during medieval times. The message that seems to flow just under the surface of the Grail literature is that a king was wounded but survived or that a king left us only to return again. Was the king the Messiah the world had waited for, only to see his early death?

Jesus and the Holy Grail

The Holy Grail itself may be a literary device for the vessel that carried the blood, or the bloodline, of Jesus. One Grail romance depicts Joseph of Arimathea as the man who brought the Grail to safety.[18] Was Mary

Magdalene the vessel herself, bearing the child of the executed Messiah? The precise nature of the Holy Grail has been a favorite topic of researchers into Arthurian romances. Most accept the common idea that it was a cup. Some point to much older days, when the cauldron was considered magic. Celtic and Nordic lore is full of such examples. Others believe that the Grail was specifically the cup from which Jesus drank at the Last Supper, when he instructed the apostles in the sacrifice that he was making.[19] The cup contained his blood. Could the Grail be an allegory for the sacred bloodline of Jesus? The central thesis of *Holy Blood, Holy Grail* is that the "Sangreal" is the Blood Royal of the family of Jesus. The Davidic kingship extended through the generations to Jesus and on through his wife, Mary Magdalene, to the descendants exiled in Roman Gaul. The family of Jesus was assimilated into Visigothic culture and in turn into the Merovingian dynasty, whose kings went out of their way to marry Visigothic princesses to continue their own line and merge their family with the family of the Davidic line.

In posting this thesis, the authors go onto say that the Jewishness of the Davidic line was concealed by Visigoths and Merovingians, and later in the dynasty of Charlemagne, because of Christian domination and persecution. This secret group, however, was always aware of its mission and is aware of it even today. To examine the evidence for this possibility, we must return to ancient France, the Gaul conquered by Julius Caesar. Most of the early history of France is centered at Reims. Caesar had made this city his local capital after conquering Celtic Gaul and the Remi tribe in 57 B.C.[20] Reims was still important when Clovis was baptized in A.D. 496, and this bolstered the city's legitimacy as a sacred place where kings would be coronated. Reims also became the overland hub of eight major trading routes.

From their capital at Reims, the Merovingian dynasty in turn conquered Gaul, including the Visigothic south of France, from which the Romans had retreated. When they vanquished the Visigoths, they would have sought to take the treasures of that dynasty, although legends of buried Visigoth treasure attest to the safety of much of it. Both the Visigoths and the Merovingians shared Arian tendencies, since they both had migrated from the east and both the north and south of Gaul were still attracting settlers and refugees from Asia and eastern Europe. This migration may have been well under way for thousands of years. Greek and Phoenician traders left their mark on western Europe. Cannes may have been named for the Canaanites who went to the southern European shores of the Mediterranean from the eastern shores of that same sea. Rock monuments to the Phoenician god Baal were erected in Monaco; this deity was worshiped from the British Isles to Scandinavia to Portugal.[21]

Semitic personal names and surnames were also typical in Merovingian-Visigothic France. Mons Judaicus near Auvergne signified acceptance or at least recognition of the Jewish influence. The Arian-leaning Visigoths and Merovingians lived peaceably with the Jews until alliance with Rome led Clovis to turn on his fellow Arians and Jews alike. Jews were given a choice that intolerance in Europe would offer them several times—convert or leave.[22] Many did convert but remained Jews in spirit, as would many Arians. This may not have been true of the peasant class, which had few choices but to coexist with large intrusive neighbors. Could both the Visigothic and Merovingian kings have been aware of the bloodline of David in their midst? There is evidence to support this theory.

The family of Jewish descendants of David and Jesus would have been highly regarded among their own people. Visigothic rulers who were Arian Christians would have tolerated them because their beliefs would not have been much different from their own. Both peoples believed in a supreme deity, a bible, and a messiah. Furthermore, they might have gone beyond tolerance and acceptance to actual respect for their Jewish neighbors and the highborn bloodline of some of them. When the Visigoths of Spain yielded to the Merovingians in the north, a borderland called Septimania separated France from Spain. In that region was the greatest population of Jews in the south, and intermarriage was commonplace between Jews and Goths. Semitic names like Bera are found frequently among the Visigothic aristocracy. When the Merovingian and Visigoth nobility married, the combined families had even more Semitic names. In some writings the words "Goth" and "Jew" were used interchangeably. The code of laws and proscriptions of the Merovingians, known as the Salic law (complicated rules on where one could live, how not to plough, etc.), had at least one full section that derived directly from the Talmud.

The acceptance of the belief in a royal line of kingship among the Jews and their relations by marriage among the Visigoths and Merovingians became even more common by Carolingian times. After the son of Frankish ruler Charles Martel Pepin III, deposed the Merovingian king in the eighth century, he sought to claim Merovingian descent for himself.[23] He was anointed king in the Hebrew rite and asked the Jewish population of Septimania to recognize his succession. He, in turn, endorsed Theodoric as the rightful king and heir to the line of David in the Jewish stronghold of Septimania in southern France.

There is a good possibility that the son of Dagobert II, Sigisbert IV, had a son who became Theodoric. If Sigisbert IV survived the assassination of his father, his survival may have depended on his remaining anonymous. He was, however, the rightful heir, and when the Carolingian Pepin found out, a deal was struck. Theodoric might have been allowed to live and prosper in a limited role as king in the south of France.[24] Theodoric married Pepin's sister, Alda, giving more legitimacy to the blood ties of both lines.

History records little of Dagobert II and nothing of Sigisbert IV, but Theodoric is mentioned. Research into his biography shows that he came from Baghdad, descended from a group that claimed to be Jews from the Babylonian exile with the most direct line of kingship connection to David. Why would a Merovingian claim to be a descendant from the purest bloodline of David if he were not at least partly Jewish? And why would the Merovingians accept this claim unless, as a people, they had shared a common background with the Asian Semites?

Theodoric, the accepted king of the Jews in Septimania, was married to Charlemagne's aunt (Alda) and ruled in the south. At that time vast estates were given to the Jews in various parts of France. Schools of learning were established at Troyes in the north and Narbonne in the south. Despite the protests from Rome (because even Church land had been given to Jews), tolerance reigned. Theodoric and Alda had a son, Guillem de Gellone, who assumed the title of count of Razes (Rennes-le-Chateau and the surrounding area), among others—titles that would have rightfully belonged to Dagobert's heirs.[25] He was both Jewish and Merovingian and was accepted as being in the royal bloodline of David.

No longer the most powerful family in France, these former Merovingian kings underwent social decline, but kept their reduced wealth and lands. A few generations later, the family received Blanchefort, an estate one mile from Rennes-le-Chateau. They then become known as the de Blancheforts, and this family can be traced into Saunière's day.

Having usurped the power of the Merovingians, the Carolingian dynasty ruled most of France. In northern France the reign of Charlemagne became the most famous of the new dynasty. Charlemagne took steps to legitimize his rule by intermarriage between his family and the older dynasties of France. His recognition of the Jewish blood in his Merovingian and Visigothic predecessors caused him to be known as one of France's most tolerant kings. But his tolerance drew the wrath of Pope Stephen III, who complained about lost Church lands and the fact that Jews owned Christian slaves. He was powerless, however, to move against Charlemagne, who was the protector of Jewish Septimania and even Rome. Charlemagne went beyond mere tolerance and did his best to attract more Jewish immigrants to southern France.[26] On the surface he was decidedly Christian, but at the same time the seal of Charlemagne said, "Rex Solomon."

The son of Charlemagne, Emperor Louis (ruled A.D. 814–840), extended even greater powers and freedom to the Jews and placed them under his guardianship. Their communities were chartered directly by the king and their rights to property protected by him. Their testimony in court was valued equally with the testimony of Christians. Louis's second wife, Judith, did nothing to conceal her Jewish name or her favor for Judaism, atypical in European monarchies. Louis fought against the Roman Church to uphold the equal rights that the Carolingians had granted the Jews, but two separate incidents hurt his efforts. One involved the case of a Christian slave who ran away from a Jewish master, which brought the Church and public opinion down on his policy of tolerance, and the other was the conversion of Louis's own minister to Judaism, which was seen as a sign of weakness. The Church was equally determined to stop such tolerance.

After Louis passed away, his sons divided his kingdom. Charles the Bald continued the protection of the Jews and put many in posts of authority. He fought the Church and refused to have his authority usurped by the clergy. Peace prevailed in France during his reign. It would not be until the Crusades that persecution of Jews began.[27] They were blamed for the poverty of the Christians and for causing the rise of the Muhammadans. In 1095 entire nations lost their collective sanity after Pope Urban II whipped them into a frenzy. Before the crusaders marched to the Holy Land, mobs marched on the Jews in northern France and across Germany. On the fifteenth of July in 1099, when Jerusalem fell, the Frankish crusaders killed every Muslim in the city as well as every Jew. The age of religious tolerance had ended.

In northern France, the area to which the sacred precinct of Reims belonged, was the district of Champagne. There Clovis, king of the Franks, had been baptized. There the first kings of France were crowned. Champagne had been divided under Merovingian rule, and leadership was always shared between the Church and the counts of Champagne. It may have been a balance of power that the count of Champagne wanted to tip in his own favor. The Templars started as almost a private club surrounding the count.[28] While their early history is shrouded in secrecy that nine hundred years protects, we do know that the earliest members of the Knights Templar were all vassals of the count of Champagne. One early grand master was the uncle of Saint Bernard of Clairvaux, a very powerful charismatic leader whose Cistercian order included Pope Honorious.

Behind the Knights Templar was that even more mysterious and elite group called the Prieuré de Sion.[29] The purpose of this small, but very powerful circle is said to have been nothing short of the restoration of the kingship of Jerusalem. The Merovingians in the north, who had purposely intermarried with the Visigoths in the south in turn intermarried with the succeeding Carolingian dynasty. If the family of Jesus, the rightful heirs of the kingship line from David, had become intermingled with the Visigoths, did the Ordre de Sion consciously seek to establish a claim to the throne of Jerusalem as a result? According to *Holy Blood, Holy Grail*, the answer is yes.

Such a goal would not be looked at with favor by the Roman Church, since, at the time, it had no such claim to a legitimate bloodline. The inheritance of the Church was only its claim to be the appointed guardian of the message of Jesus through Jesus' appointment of Peter to that role. The Church, as directed by Constantine sought to stamp out any earthly line of descendants who would threaten its authority. The Church and Rome were one under Constantine, and the followers of Jesus, who could provide an earthly king, were in hiding in France. Understanding just how serious the Church's reaction to such a threat would be, the Prieuré de Sion remained underground. This "underground stream" of knowledge of the royal bloodline was the secret behind the order.

When Jerusalem was captured, Godfrey of Bouillon, we recall, was elected king of the city.[30] He reputedly shared in the bloodline of the legitimate kings, and finally he was king in title. He died in 1100 and was succeeded by his brother, Baldwin, who also took the title king of Jerusalem. It was Baldwin who granted the Templars their official status. The Merovingians at last had reconquered their city and reclaimed the title due them as kings in the royal line of David.

But the Templars and their king made no public claim to anything more than a political title in a troubled area. Their other purpose, looting the Temple of Solomon, may have also served little purpose as a source of wealth. The temple had already been looted and destroyed. Instead, the object of their search might have been more than monetary treasure, including the lost Ark of the Covenant, relics of Jesus or the early apostles, or the Davidic genealogies. The relics may have been the largest booty that the early Templars brought back to France. Such relics were highly valued, and relic collecting was a rage in western Europe at the time. Various bones, skulls, and pieces of hair of important personages; pieces of the True Cross and Noah's ark; and even water from the Jordan were bought, sold, and traded.

If the Merovingian inheritors of David had won a political victory, it was short-lived. The Saracens beat back the crusaders in 1187, and the Knights Templar began to lose their elevated position. According to sources used for *Holy Blood, Holy Grail*, they were also abandoned by their secret organization, the Prieuré de Sion.[31] The core of elite French families behind the Templar organization had separated themselves from the "cover" organization, although some did remain active in both the Knights Templar and the more secretive Prieuré de Sion. St. Clairs had been in both organizations as Hugues de Payens was the husband of Marie St. Clair. Bertrand de Blanchefort, heir to Dagobert II, remained in the Templars and commanded a Templar fortress in Bezu, near Rennes-le-Chateau. The Ordre de Sion was renamed the Prieuré de Sion.

It is this secretive group that claims to be in possession of part of the treasure hoard of the Temple of Solomon and also says it will restore items to Israel when the time is right. They assert that the most important part of their "treasure" is not money, but secrets that, once revealed, will change society. Presumably, the fact that a continuous bloodline exists, complete with authentic genealogies, will be the basis of their claim to a kingship role. It seems more appropriate to the imagination of an aging Hapsburg to believe that such a claim, backed by the appropriate genealogies or not, would induce the modern world to accord even a titular role to such a claimant. It seems to step further into the realm of science fiction to believe that the modern world would turn over power to such a claimant (although not to the authors of *Holy Blood, Holy Grail*). And what of the treasure?

We know that the Templars disappeared from France with wagon loads of the gold and silver entrusted to them. We also know that French Templars turned up in Scotland, where they helped defend that country at Bannockburn. Third, we have seen the Sinclairs of Scotland take over guardianship of the successor organization to the Templars, the Freemasons. In the peaceful interlude between Bannockburn and the Reformation, the Sinclairs consolidated their power in the isles of Scotland, and "Prince" Henry sailed to Nova Scotia. His family was in control of the largest fleet in the north of Europe and vast estates and had an army to carry out their wishes. Did the Sinclair power have at its base the organization that came under its protection? Most likely it did. The guardianship of the Freemasons was further legalized by no less an authority than that of the Scottish king. The role of guardian included the task of protecting whatever treasury still existed. This mission induced the building spree that included underground passageways and tunnels large enough to hide an army. And finally, we have seen the Sinclairs under siege and a family leader disappear along with the treasures that were secreted in the walls of Roslin.

It seems at this point that the Sinclairs' motives were more grounded in earthly objectives, but examining the French side of the family, the St. Clairs, shows that the mysterious side of the equation still has some merit. The second grand master of the newly named Prieuré de Sion was Marie St. Clair.[32] She was descended from another Henry St. Clair, who had fought alongside Godfrey of Bouillion in the Crusades. Her maiden name was Levis, that Merovingian-Visigothic name that hints at a Judaic origin. Knowing the proclivity of the St. Clairs to marry in their class, it is reasonable to connect Marie Levis to the Levis family that owned the Cathar stronghold at Montsegur. The Levis family axis extended from Nîmes, where denim was invented and named (*denim* means from "fabrique de Nîmes") by a modern Levi (as in Levi-Strauss), to Narbonne.

Bertrand de Blanchefort, too, was a Cathar, as was his family. On the surface this would seem to deflate the importance of a Jewish bloodline passing through the Merovingian-Visigothic ancestors of the Blancheforts. Such a bloodline would take on importance only in a historic sense rather than a religious one. If Visigoths were Arians, believing in only one supreme God and a more earthly Jesus, that is, a prophet, then their religion would not be very different from that of the Cathari.[33] Nor would it be so different from that of the Jews, who believed in Jesus as the earthly Messiah. Bertrand's descendants fought alongside the Cathari at Montsegur, but they stopped short of allowing themselves to be immolated for their faith. The St. Clairs and the de Blancheforts featured in events in the Languedoc area hundreds of years later.

Through marriage the family of Marie Levis St. Clair was connected to the de Gisors, the family from which the first and third grand masters of the Prieuré de Sion came. Without question, the Prieuré de Sion was created and run by individuals related to the St. Clairs. The third grand master was in charge in the year that the Templars were ordered arrested and the treasure fleet set sail for Scotland to escape the agents of the French king. Did one St. Clair (from France) correspond with another

Sinclair (from Scotland) for this express purpose? Most likely the answer is yes.

The Sinclair family had become well established in Scotland, and the Roslin branch had for some reason divorced itself from the family of William the Conqueror, but not from their French relations. Throughout the history of Scotland the Sinclairs switched sides often and sometimes appear on both sides of a conflict. This is not to say that they were self-serving or disloyal—it was more a sign of the times in which they lived. Their loyalty was often rooted in their own clan, which was very typical of northern Europe as well as Scotland. As the clan became a larger unit, loyalty was focused on a smaller part within that unit. Despite the code of chivalry, as we know it from literature, the Dark Ages and feudal period of Europe's history features kings and churchmen rarely loyal to their subjects or their flocks. Nationalism did not yet exist. The Sinclairs understood the fluidity of these alliances, and were loyal most often only to themselves. They also understood opportunity.

In 1307, when the fleet of the French Templars left La Rochelle and disappeared from history, St. Clairs had conspired with Sinclairs to gain control of the treasure fleet. The treasure laden ships fled to the protection of the Sinclair domain on the outer islands of Scotland. The Scottish Sinclairs, playing the role of the power behind the throne, added to their own power immensely. They rallied behind Robert the Bruce, who went down in history as a hero, but in many ways they stayed behind the scenes. The Sinclairs did not want the role of martyr. As a reward for their protection of the Templars, the Sinclairs gained from the king the hereditary distinction of protectors of the Masons. Did they inherit the myth as well? Most likely not.

Two hundred years after Bannockburn, the battle in which they threw their resources behind the excommunicated king of Scotland, the Sinclairs of Scotland remained devout at least to their Catholic religion if not to the corrupt popes. At that time it was not a popular position to take. The Reformation was raging through Scotland, and people were losing everything in their defense of their form of Christian worship. If the Sinclairs believed in an Arian Christianity or entertained thoughts of their own descent through the Davidic line, they gave no sign of such heresy. The Sinclairs of Roslin, in fact, lost all for their loyalty to the Roman Catholic Church.

The French St. Clairs might have been more caught up in their own mythology. Medieval times saw such elite families taking elaborate steps to make gods of themselves. Genealogies were rewritten by historians bought and paid for by the family being glorified—a phenomenon that did not disappear from history, although modern genealogies seek less pretentious goals. To claim descent from an ancestor who stepped off the Mayflower is a more realistic goal than to assert a divine right to kingship based on one's ancestor having been a Judaic priest-king.

While there is little doubt that the Sinclairs held to their Catholicism, the Freemasons who were Templars did get caught up in the Reformation and in the mythology that they created for themselves. Before they took on the trappings of being heirs to a sacred body of knowledge—pagan and Christian at the same time—they were simply an organization with military goals and later, by default, more civil goals.

The Knights Templar and their successive organization, the Freemasons, took shape in a Europe that had been almost completely conquered by Normans. Today it is difficult to grasp just how complete the Norman Conquest was, but from Great Britain to the tip of Italy the Normans had thoroughly changed the world in which they lived. No longer were they the Vikings from the north who blazed through Europe looting and pillaging. These forefathers had raided the Irish coast, settled the western isles, and also sailed to Turkey and Russia, where their influence became permanent. Once they established a political base in France, the second wave of "northmen" were no longer called Norse, but Norman, meaning "northmen."

The Normans conquered great stretches of land throughout Europe. They reintroduced surnames, which had faded away, as a means to tax the populace of the lands they came to own. And they brought in their own courts of law, held in their own French-Norman language. In the early fourteenth century the language of the rulers of England and Scotland was Norman French. If a Briton was accused of a crime, he went to a court conducted in this Norman language, not his own. It was not until 1352 that the English language prevailed as the legal language as well as the popular language of the realm.

The fleeing Templars (now Freemasons) preserved their French-Norman language as code words that survive into modern Masonry. John Robinson's *Born in Blood* is a good source for both the development of the code language and irrefutable proof that the Templars hid as a trade guild.[34] While such a real trade guild of masons would not need to post guards at its meetings, an underground organization banned by state and church might. The Freemasons still employ a guard at their meetings, called a "Tyler" in England. But unlike the meaning of the English word—"tailor" (from the French *tailleur*, or "one who cuts"), the Tyler guarding the Freemason meeting was a swordsman. The term "freemason" itself was derived from *frère* (meaning "brother" in French), the name the Templars reserved for each other, and *maçon*, another word for knight.

Another name reviewed in *Born in Blood* is "Lewis." According to the author, this title cannot be translated exactly, but it refers to the son of another mason. General Douglas MacArthur was a Mason who held the "Lewis" title. If the initiate's father was a Mason, the son could be considered a Lewis. Interestingly enough, Lewis is the English version of the French "Levis," also meaning "son of," "scion," and so on. This is more evidence that Masonry is grounded in a secret context and refes to a Davidic vine with "sprouts" secretly growing in southern and, later, northern France.

While it is doubtful that the average fez-wearing modern Shriner believes himself to be an heir to the god kings of Israel, other Masonic-Templar-Judaic trappings are accepted and commonplace among Masons. The initiation tale recited and acted out when a modern member is enrolled in the Masons recalls the name of the master mason murdered while working on Solomon's temple. That name, never recorded historically, is Hiram Abiff, meaning Hiram "who was eliminated." Modern Masons are told that they are inheriting traditions that started with this murdered man.

One word that has defied translation is the Scottish Masonry term *mahabone*. It is considered a secret "Mason's word," and it may have something to do with piracy. After passing through initiation, the newly inducted Mason is told that he is now "a brother to pirates and corsairs." Robinson mentions a pirate port in North Africa used during the Crusades, called "Mahdia." Pointing out that Arab-held Madrid was pronounced Mahadrid, he says Mahadia might have been corrupted into Mahabone. Alternatively, Mahadia the Good, in French, would be Mahadia le Bon. The author also shows a precedent in the corrupted Franco-English language—"Mary the Good" has become "Marylebone," a district of London.

Grail literature might suggest another meaning—in Grail prose "Mahadia" referred to the "desired knight." Galahad was one such desired knight, a reincarnation of his father Lancelot, who ruled the Round Table one year and then died at the altar just after seeing a vision of the Holy Grail. Grail literature is steeped in both Christian and Celtic mysticism, and in some tribes a "king" would serve for just one year, only to be sacrificed afterward. In the sermons of the warmonger saint, Bernard, Mount Galaad in the Holy Land is represented by Christ. This term was employed in a French contribution to Grail literature called *Queste del Saint Graal*, where Galaad is called the "Christ Knight." In *The Grail: From Celtic Myth to Christian Symbol*, Roger Sherman Loomis determined that the name Galahad comes from the source word Galaad, a "reference to the Messiah." He says Galahad was the "long awaited healer" and compares him to Christ. Thus, Galahad, "the desired knight," and Mahadia, might be one and the same.[35]

This author leans toward the pirate explanation. The term *mahonnes* describes a low-lying French corsair favored by pirates. The Masons were brothers to such "pirates and corsairs." And the hiding place at Oak Island that has been credited to pirates lies in Mahone Bay, named for the French pirate ship. Even more fascinating is another Masonic term that has defied explanation—"Heredom," described both as the mother of Freemasonry and a mythical mountain.[36] It is tempting to connect it to Sheerdom Cove, the predecessor of Smith's Cove on Oak Island. Sheerdom Cove is at the edge of the island that contains the booby-trapped water-draining system that has plagued treasure seekers for centuries. It was given the name "Smith's Cove" only after treasure seeker Smith bought the island.

The Sinclairs of Scotland inherited an organization that had served as a front to forward the aims of their French relatives, the St. Clairs. After Bannockburn, Robert the Bruce, their king, recognized the help of the Templars, and their "cover" as a trade guild was given over to the protection of the Sinclairs, who were influential in bringing them to Bruce's (and Scotland's) aid. In 1441, more than a hundred years later, James II appointed the Sinclairs as guardians of the Freemasons and made this title hereditary.[37] At the time, Sir William Sinclair was building his temple at Roslin, which required the work of such masons. James II used this as his reason for the appointment. The Masons had been under Sinclairs' protection for a century, and James, in this way, was merely making his peace with the Sinclairs. He was at war with the Livingston clan at the time and may have needed the Sinclairs' neutrality.

Local history says an influx of "masons" to the Sinclair borough started in 1441, although construction on the chapel did not begin until 1446. Why would workers be needed five years before the start of the project? It is now evident that the chapel of Roslin was a cover for the construction of massive workings underground. Tunnels and secret entrances created to conceal an army were built or extended during that time. The work that started on the chapel continued for forty years and never saw completion. Just what else were masons doing in this forty-five year period?

The chapel perched on a gorge is steeped in Masonic symbolism, complete with carved head of a man with a gash in his skull (Hiram Abiff) and a depiction of the man who killed him. A third head is of the "Widowed Mother," another Masonic symbol that suggests that all Masons are the "sons of a widowed mother."[38] (One masonic hand signal signifies the phrase "Is there no help for the son of the Widow?"—which is a call for help.) This truly bizarre "hallucination in stone" is unlike any Christian church, but it is an example of the ancient art represented in the Temple of Solomon.[39] The message may be that more than one god can be worshiped—a Masonic theme but certainly not a Catholic one. Solomon's edifice allowed space for Semite pagan gods; Sinclairs gave equal time to Green George, the Celtic vegetation god.

Near the chapel at Roslin there is a cave behind a waterfall where a weathered head appears carved into the rock. And in the cliff face is a "dressed window," behind which is a "warren of tunnels sufficient to conceal a substantial number of men." To enter this secret hideout, one has to be lowered down into a well and travel through a tunnel. The same engineering had created the well and tunnel entrance in Jerusalem almost two thousand years before Sinclair's Roslin. And the same shaft and tunnel design was used on a grander scale in Nova Scotia.[40]

The Sinclair family had something of great value that needed to be hidden. There was no Bank of Scotland that could serve as a repository; instead the cliffs and caves and tunnels constructed by the Masons would become their secret vault. Modern treasure seekers using every means available have attempted to discover just what the Sinclairs were hiding. Basements under basements and secret depositories have been uncovered, but nothing has been found.[41]

Where, then, do our clues lead? An elite family with a pretension to a bloodline that starts with David. A sacred vine that extends its sprouts into southern France, where Visigoths, Merovingians, and Carolingians seemingly aspire to a Davidic ancestry. A cover organization, the Templars, concealing a secret and elite inner circle. A succeeding cover organization that combines pagan symbolism with secret handshakes. And an immense treasure that includes the wealth of Europe entrusted to Templar safekeeping in the vaults of a Scottish family who was possibly holding the treasure for itself. All finally leading to an empty vault. Between 1441 and 1482 the treasures guarded by the Sinclairs left their hiding place in the warren of tunnels in the cliffs near and under Roslin. They set sail again, this time for the western lands of the Sinclairs.

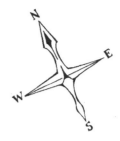

Chapter 11

THE TREASURE
COMES TO OAK ISLAND

$\mathcal{T}$he Sinclair family had grown and prospered in the years
after Robert the Bruce achieved independence for Scotland. They had
signed the Declaration of Arboath in 1320, which decreed Scotland an
independent nation.[1] This is a sign of prominence equal to being a signer
of the American Declaration of Independence, and it highlights the
importance of the Sinclair family. It is an unusual document, in that it
claims an Asian ancestry for the Scottish people and calls Robert the
Bruce a second Maccabeus, referring to a Jewish freedom fighter.

The Sinclairs themselves were fighting for their Templar organization, resisting the efforts of the pope to grant the Hospitalers all of the
Templar lands in Scotland. They claimed that the Templars owned no
lands in Scotland, although they did own more than five hundred individual properties. As Templar lands were being recovered by the enemies
of the organization, the Sinclair family took steps to defend them. The
Sinclairs were in contact with their French counterparts, but repression

against the Templars and a hostile England separating France from Scotland drove a wedge between the two elite families. As this wedge widened, it was the Scottish Sinclair family that held possession of the order's treasures. Thirty years after the last Viking expedition to America, Henry Sinclair and his Venetian first mate Zeno made their first voyage to the New World.

The Guardian Family in Scotland

Between 1398 and 1400 Henry Sinclair made perhaps two trips to the New World and laid plans for a colony. He controlled the largest fleet in the world and, in his role as guardian, the largest treasure in the world. But when he returned to Scotland, hostilities between the ever warring clans were raging out of control. After his return to Scotland he encountered the English, who attacked both Edinburgh and then the chief Sinclair property in the Orkneys, Kirkwall. Kirkwall was a castle with a walled harbor built to protect it against sea raids. Henry lost his life in defense of his stronghold.[2] With Scotland's independence threatened, Henry's son (also Henry) was given the task of guarding the son of the king. Robert III trusted Henry to sail to France and safety, but both Crown Prince James of Scotland and the younger Sinclair were taken prisoner and released later for ransom.[3] The next threat to both the Sinclairs and Scotland would come from within.

Norway had given up domination of the northern islands, many of which had been in Norse control since the tenth century. The clan Donald made a violent bid to rule the north believing themselves to be more powerful than the Sinclairs and other allied clans. Armed with swords, axes, and bows, the Donalds raised the largest army ever to fight in a clan war in the Highlands. After defeating the McKay clan, the wild men of the north marched south toward Aberdeen, plundering everything in their way.[4]

In 1411 the earl of Mar came up against the Donalds in protecting his own lands at Harlaw. The bloodiest battle in the Highlands saw nine thousand of the clan die, and possibly an equal number among the defenders. As a result of this gruesome battle, and irritated by the constant warfare in the north, King James I, the prince who had been imprisoned with Henry, reacted quickly.[5] In 1428 James ordered the heads of forty clans to come before him. He arrested most of them, threw them into his dungeon, and executed three. It was a bold step, and he took an even bolder one in denying the pope's powers. He declared the pope corrupt and, in standing up to Rome, alienated himself from other countries.

In a few short years the king had done much for Scotland and made many enemies. In 1436 he was assassinated in his bedchamber by Robert Graham, a hired assassin.[6] He died with twenty-eight dagger wounds, and his queen sought revenge. Robert Stewart, the son of the earl of Atholl who allowed access to the bedchamber, and Graham were tortured and executed. That same year, Prince Henry's grandson, William Sinclair, was designated admiral. He was already the inheritor of the world's largest fleet and the Templar treasure as well, so it was a designation mostly in name, which seemed to belong to the Sinclairs as a birthright.[7]

After the assassination of James, the country fell into the hands of a child king and a warring regent. The Douglas clan joined with the Livingston family against the Crichton clan, and this time the hostilities were centered around Stirling and the Sinclair base of power at Roslin. The new war and the child king's inability to rule served as an excuse for the English to march north, to Edinburgh and the Sinclair ancestral home. William Sinclair was imprisoned for part of his father's ransom that was never paid. Henry Sinclair (not the prince) had been held in the Tower of London, but was allowed to go free when he agreed to pay a ransom—a ransom he never paid once he was free.

For the Sinclairs this placed the battle on two fronts; they faced both the constant irritation of the English and incessant infighting among the clans, which even had Sinclair fighting Sinclair. It is very likely at this time that Admiral Sinclair made his own trip to North America to see the lands his grandfather had discovered. The secret of lands in the far western Atlantic would have been passed from father to son, along with the role of guardian of the Templar wealth and the surviving Freemasons. A trip to Nova Scotia from Scotland could be made in three weeks' sailing time if the weather was good. Leaving time to confirm and examine firsthand the harbors described by his grandfather, an entire expedition could be made in three months. Between the year he was appointed admiral and 1441, William made his plans.

In Roslin he constructed an edifice that would be worthy of the master masons and craftsmen in his protection.[8] And he built a warren of tunnels and secret depositories to guard his treasure. In Nova Scotia he also built a vault to guard the Templar treasure, in case the civil war and the war with England threatened his ancestral home. It was William who started importing workers for these projects in 1441, five years before he began a job that took forty years to complete.[9]

In a phone conversation, David Tobias, the present owner of the Money Pit, told me that his theory had Sir Francis Drake bringing Cornish miners to Nova Scotia. There they excavated the Money Pit and created the treasure vault. Where would Sinclair find miners? He certainly would not find them in the English-owned Cornwall area. Researching Roslin further, I discovered that it had once been a mining village. Importing workers for his chapel and tunnel system five years before the actual work took place concealed Sinclair's ulterior motive. The new workers were, in fact, replacing more trusted workers, who had been sent to Nova Scotia.

Only an Englishman as powerful as Sir Francis Drake, and in command of a private navy, would be able to conceal such a project. William Sinclair might have been at least Drake's peer. He was powerful, in command of both a private navy and the national navy, and capable of enlisting the needed talent. Sinclair had the means, the wealth, possibly a much more trusted workforce, and certainly a stronger motive. At some time between 1436 and 1441, Sinclair ships took on boatloads of miners from the home borough of Roslin and began a settlement near Oak Island, perhaps on one of the larger islands in Mahone Bay.

In addition to laying the groundwork for the secret vaults at Roslin and in Nova Scotia, Sinclair also started an elite group of fighting men called the Scots Guard.[10] Like the Templars before them, the Scots Guard was made up of young men from wealthy and noble families. It pledged itself not to Scotland but to the king of France—and nominally at that. Their loyalty was given directly to the Valois rulers and a subset of Valois, the House of Guise. Finally, William Sinclair was reappointed as grand master of the crafts and guilds and orders of Scotland by James II. This office remained hereditary until the Lodge was formed three hundred years later. Strangely enough, Sinclair also appointed himself protector of the gypsies. Each year, from May to June the gypsies of Great Britain would migrate to the Sinclair home at Roslin. There they were given land to camp on and were allowed to perform their summer pageant, a play about Robin Hood and the May Queen. The Protestant Calvinists believed this to be nothing but pagan rites in disguise and protested fiercely.[11]

William Sinclair would have everything but peace. When James II was crowned king at age six, he was under the tutelage of Sir William Crichton and Sir Alexander Livingston. Stewarts and Douglas vied for rule of Scotland and, fearing a power play, the two tutors had the young earl of Douglas killed.[12] A decade later, when James came of age, he said he wanted to reconcile with the Douglas clan. He had learned that William Douglas had gone abroad to meet with both the pope and the English, and he feared that a rebellion with English support was imminent. He invited Douglas to dinner at Stirling, the royal castle, and asked the head of the clan if he could discuss affairs without the presence of Douglas's bodyguards. Douglas rebuffed him, and James stabbed him in the neck. Other court attendants rushed to plunge their daggers into Douglas as well. Another Douglas rose to take William's place and marched on Stirling with six hundred men. The king defeated the Douglas clan, but in one of many continual skirmishes with the English, a cannon exploded, killing James II. His son, James III, took over the rule of Scotland in 1460.[13]

It is very likely that while the Douglas clan rebellion and the continuing attacks by the English were going on, the Sinclair inheritance was being moved to the New World. The Sinclairs stood by their kings but at the same time saw that the opposition was mounting. Young James III was kidnapped after inheriting the throne. Upon his escape he married Margaret, the daughter of King Christian of Norway and Denmark.[14] The following year he made a deal with another William Sinclair, Henry's great-grandson, buying the earldom of Orkney. The castle of the Sinclair sea kings at Kirkwall was traded for Ravenscraig in Edinburgh, although several Orkney estates stayed in Sinclair hands. While lucrative properties remained in the Sinclair domain, this William came to inherit the nickname the "Waster" for trading away the family property.[15]

In 1475 the stonemasons of Edinburgh received a charter from the king, which was ratified at Mary's Chapel in that city. This would later be known as Lodge One, but the Sinclairs were still recognized as the patrons and guardians of the Masons, despite this early recognition of autonomy.[16] In 1488 the Douglas rebellion was rekindled. James III went to battle himself, was wounded, and fell off his horse. He was carrying the sword of Robert the Bruce, but this time it failed him. Fearing he was near death, he rushed from the battlefield, where he met a priest. When he asked the priest for final absolution, he was instead stabbed to death.

The thirteen-year-old James IV became king. He would be remembered as a Renaissance man who tried to keep peace with England. In 1503 he married the twelve-year-old Margaret Tudor, daughter of Henry VII and sister of the man who became Henry VIII (in 1509). At this point, the Reformation was making Christian Protestants turn against Christian Catholics. Protestant Henry VIII and Catholic France went to war. Scotland, loyal to France, invaded England in 1513. At the Battle of Flodden the Scots were beaten badly, and for the Sinclairs it was a major personal blow.[17] Forty Sinclairs had marched to Flodden with their earl and king; only one would survive. Since that disastrous day, no Sinclair has ever worn the color green—the color worn that day—to battle again.[18] James IV allegedly died at Flodden as well, although the body purported to be the king's was missing his ever present iron chain of expiation (worn around the waist as a symbol of piety), leading many to speculate that James had survived.

War and the massive building and rebuilding projects of the Sinclairs were beginning to take a toll on the family's seemingly inexhaustible resources. The Sinclairs had once been the puppeteers running their country's affairs from behind the scenes; now the weak kings were pushing them to the front. It cost them dearly in terms of their own lives and their property. Oliver Sinclair was a favorite of James V. His protection of Sinclair and his marriage to Mary of Guise ensured his loyalty to the side of the Catholics, but the religious revolution that was under way in the form of the Reformation was causing trouble between England and Scotland. Henry VIII tried to convert his relative to the Protestant side, but James would not repudiate his faith. In 1542 the Battle of Solway saw Scotland defeated and Oliver Sinclair captured. James V was horrified and declared that all was lost with the loss of Oliver. At the same time that he heard of the defeat at Solway, he also heard of the birth of his daughter, Mary. He predicted the dynasty was over and himself died shortly afterward.[19] His daughter Mary would become known to history as Mary, Queen of Scots.

While the new queen was under the protection of the Sinclairs, Oliver was furloughed from prison in England. He was allowed a short visit home, but instead he disappeared from Scotland and history—forever.[20] The year was 1545. The regent, Mary of Guise, worked closely with (still another) William Sinclair. She would go far to show the Sinclairs that their alliance was with the House of Guise-Lorraine. In the same year that Oliver was supposed to report back to prison in England, the Sinclair family was ordered by Reformation bishops to turn over the treasures of the Scottish Catholic Church. Since the family had commissioned and paid for many of these religious objects, they had taken them under their protection. The property of the Catholic Church also included relics that the Sinclairs had brought back from the Crusades, including a piece of the True Cross. The Reformation mobs everywhere were looting Catholic churches and stealing and destroying such relics. The Sinclairs refused to allow this to happen at Roslin.[21] The same year that Oliver disappeared, so did the sacred objects under the care of the Sinclair family.

William Sinclair allowed only the Guise family to be privy to his greatest secret. Mary of Guise proclaimed a "bond of obligation" to William, stating, "We shall be loyal and true masters to him. . . . His counsel and secret shown to us, we shall keep secret." What secret? Andrew Sinclair, biographer of his ancestors, asserts that the secret was that there was a room beneath the chapel at Roslin that contained a repository with the sacred relics.[22] After devastating vandalism by Protestant mobs and twentieth-century excavation that uncovered many secret vaults, no such relics have turned up. It is more than likely that every castle and every cathedral in medieval times had a hidden tunnel or chamber. The absence of one would be uncommon. William Sinclair and Sir Oliver Sinclair harbored a much greater secret. That secret was Oak Island. Oliver, commander of both the army and the navy, had set sail for the concealed vault and secluded country of the Sinclairs in 1545, never to return.

The fortunes of the Sinclairs in Scotland and the Guise family in France would be hurt badly in the religious wars that followed. William Sinclair was made Lord Justice General by Queen Mary of Scotland and traveled back and forth to France. Mary of Guise died in 1560. François, duke of Guise, was assassinated in 1563.[23] Mary, Queen of Scots, was executed by Queen Elizabeth I in 1587 while her own son stood idly by. His lack of concern earned him both the throne of Scotland and, later, the throne of England when Elizabeth died. The year after Mary's execution, François of Guise's son, the new duke, and his brother, the cardinal Guise, were both assassinated on the orders of Henri III of France. In 1589 the Guise family, in turn, had Henri III assassinated.[24] The religious wars caught up to the Sinclair family in Roslin as well. In 1615 the head of the family, William Sinclair, was ordered condemned to death for allowing a Jesuit priest to conduct the Catholic Mass at Roslin. The priest was hung and William pardoned to an exile in Ireland; mobs destroyed the Sinclair home and chapel.[25]

This act by the Sinclairs seems to indicate that despite the paganistic-Masonic trappings of Roslin, they were devout to the Catholic religion and loyal to their faith. They were also loyal to their role as guardian of secrets and treasures whose care they had inherited. The massive Templar treasure that included objects once looted from Jerusalem was not dissipated, nor was all the Sinclair wealth spent. It disappeared. The relics, as well as the treasures of the Scottish Church, were never uncovered. Everything had vanished; so had Oliver Sinclair. The Sinclairs had been transferring the objects in their care for more than a half a century to their vault in Nova Scotia. In 1545 that transfer was completed. The only document we have mentioning the "secret" is that order from Mary of Guise. How much did Sinclair allow the Guise family to know? At some point a parting of the ways took place between the French families that made up the Ordre de Sion, later known as the Prieuré de Sion, and the Scottish Sinclair family. The schism was not complete, but the Scottish contingent appears to have taken control of the Templar treasure hoard.

The Guardian Families in France

The Guise family and the Sinclair family remained united by a greater bond, the secret Prieuré de Sion. This group was truly an elite network of a very small number of French families.[26] The first grand master of that group, after the split with the Templars, was Jean de Gisors. He took control after the "cutting of the elm" in 1188, which symbolically divorced the Templars from the Prieuré de Sion, and for the first time the Templars and the Prieuré de Sion were not controlled, at least in name, by the same person.

The second grand master was Marie de St. Clair, who had descended from the Scottish branch at Roslin. Her maiden name was Levis, indicating that St. Clair, too, had married into the kingship line of David.

The third grand master was Guillaume de Gisors, who had started another secret society, the Order of the Ship and the Double Crescent. He was related to the St. Clairs and connected to the temple at Paris from which the vast Templar fortune had disappeared into history. His sister married into the des Plantard family, who gave their name to the Plantagenet dynasty. The Plantards, too, claimed descent from the Davidic bloodline, the word *plantard* being French for "flowering shoot." In the Apocalypse, John had said that he was the root and stock of David; so, too, were Levis and Plantards. Two members of the de Bar family held the grand master title next. One of them, Jean de Bar, had owned the land around Stenay where the last Merovingian king had been murdered. The de Bars were related to the family of René d'Anjou and to the Coucy family of Picardy. The lords of Picardy were described alternately as kingmakers or challengers to the throne as the subjects of Barbara Tuchman's study of the medieval world, *A Distant Mirror.*[27]

The sixth grand master was again a St. Clair, this time from the French side of the family. He was a minor figure, but it shows the relatively tight circle that was in control of the Prieuré de Sion. The ninth grand master was a major figure in medieval history, René d'Anjou, whose multitude of titles included the count of Guise. He was the most important force behind the Renaissance of Europe and was called the "Good King René" by his subjects. He was married at the age of twelve, to Isabella of Lorraine in a political alliance. While most court-arranged marriages do not last, René was dedicated to Isabella for thirty-three years, until her death. René composed music, learned languages, studied mathematics and geology, learned the law, and reformed his own lands. As the true Renaissance man, he brought to his domain new and modern trends in learning and science. He took part in one mania of the day, which was the collecting of relics. His prize possession was a cup that had been used at the marriage at Cana (which may have united Jesus with Mary Magdalene). He claimed to have obtained the cup in Marseilles.

René d'Anjou was a member of several secret orders, including a revival of the de Gisors' Order of the Ship. One member of that order was the father of Leonardo da Vinci's patron. Da Vinci, too, became a grand master in the Prieuré de Sion. In an age of chivalry, d'Anjou was a promoter of the pageantry and the chivalric display of his times. He participated in the Tarascon festivals, in which the town celebrated Martha's driving away the dragon that had plagued the town. He also staged what were called *pas d'armes*, medieval combinations of plays and tournaments. Often the theme would evolve around the central idea of the earthly Garden of Eden, Arcadia, and an underground stream. Well before Jacopo Sannazaro's poem was published, the Arcadia theme was important to d'Anjou. Each year his mistress played the role of shepherdess.

It was the work of Nicolas Poussin that captured the ideals of the Arcadia theme, replete with trappings of a mystical and idyllic life. And it was his painting *Les Bergers d'Arcadie*, (The Shepherds of Arcadia) that took Father Saunière to the Louvre in Paris to find clues to his treasure hunt in Rennes-le-Chateau. That clue brought him to a tomb that he deemed so important he obliterated the engraving on it. The message that took Saunière to Paris to seek the work of Poussin was "Poussin holds the key." That key was a code employing pentagonal geometry, which was used to conceal the directions to the treasure in the village of Rennes-le-Chateau. The lines forming the pentagon had at their central point the forehead of the shepherdess. What made the shepherdess so important to Poussin and to René d'Anjou?

The painting itself depicts three shepherds and a shepherdess looking at an ancient tomb. Two of the shepherds have their fingers extended, pointing to part of the tomb with the message "Et in Arcadia ego." The shepherdess could be Mary Magdalene (as she was the wife of the shepherd Jesus). Mary showed the apostles the tomb after discovering Jesus was not there. Now in Poussin, she is saying, he is here, and he is dead (il est mort). That specific tomb is six miles from Rennes-le-Chateau, and it held further secret codes and clues to the mystery of Father Saunière.[28] In 1448, when d'Anjou established his Order of the Crescent, the revival of Order of the Ship and the Double Crescent, William Sinclair was in the early stages of building Roslin and starting the construction at Oak Island. Related by marriage, brought together by the secret societies in which they both participated, united by a religion under siege, it is tempting to speculate that there might have been correspondence from William Sinclair to d'Anjou, telling him of the land the natives call "Acadie." It is also tempting to speculate that the reports of Sinclair's western explorations found their way to another man in the service of d'Anjou, young Christopher Columbus. And it is tempting to read more significance into another coincidence.

René d'Anjou's daughter, Iolande de Bar, had taken over as grand master of the Prieuré de Sion after her father. She hired Georges Antoine Vespucci as tutor to her son. Another Vespucci, Amerigo, gave his name to the map of the "discovery" of America, brought back by Columbus. Iolande's son was also named René, and he inherited several titles, including duke of Lorraine. The younger duke, as well as the Vespucci family, were patrons to both Leonardo da Vinci and the artist Sandro Botticelli. The patrons of Botticelli included the Medicis, Gonzagas, and Estes, who were all contemporaries and peers of the Zeno family in Venice. Botticelli incorporated the Arcadia theme into his own work and played an active role in the Prieuré de Sion.

Like Botticelli, Leonardo da Vinci counted the Estes and Medicis among his patrons and grew in stature and prominence with their help.[29] When he was a struggling painter he became acquainted with the wealthy Florentine family of Vespucci—he had followed Amerigo Vespucci's grandfather around the streets to sketch his face. As a reward for his talent, Vespucci helped Leonardo gain admittance into the inner circles of the rich families in northern Italy. One such family was that of Ludovico Sforza, whose father was in René d'Anjou's order. Leonardo also served as grand master to the Prieuré de Sion from 1510 to 1519. In 1515 da Vinci took employ with this viceroy of Milan and Languedoc. While he started his career as an artist—and art is central to his greatness—he was also an inventor, physicist, geologist, and engineer. It was in the latter capacities that he was employed. As a military engineer, he designed an underwater suit and was able in the art of hydraulics. Water always played a role in his scientific pursuits—from its use as a power supply to its harnessing for agriculture to its potential application to weaponry. Da Vinci was a student of botany as well.[30]

Did da Vinci play a role in designing or building the complex system of flooding tunnels, artificial beaches, and clog-proof drains protected by eelgrass that became the Money Pit? One invention of this grand master was what he called the "cogged bracket," a movable sluice. Grouping these sluices together, he said, could act as a barrier to the current. He could cause water to rise and fall. A series of sluices and dams could control the widest bodies of water, depending on just how many were used. He also invented a portable dredger that floated on two rafts.[31]

In 1510 he wrote that he had decided to cut short his work on anatomy into order to put more time into his mechanical inventions. His writings may have served as a blueprint for his design of such a complicated vault and protective trap. Could a bay like Mahone in Nova Scotia be held back by a sluice of his design? Upon his death, thousands of pages of his notebooks were spread around Europe as collectors' items. Many were illegible, and many were coded. Da Vinci had a shorthand that divided or combined words for reasons known only to himself. Some notes were written backward with his left hand so that a mirror was needed to read them. It is said that despite all the work that

Leonardo da Vinci completed in his capacity as engineer and inventor, there is no monument, no completed work of his architecture that bears his name.

A recent book on one of the most controversial icons in Catholic history, the Shroud of Turin, declares that Leonardo da Vinci was the artist behind that sacred relic. The shroud, which is not claimed as a true relic by the Catholic Church, has been dated to medieval times or earlier. The provenance of the shroud is questionable; it arrived in France some-time after the Crusades but was denounced by the bishop of Troyes as a fake. It was then given to the House of Savoy and suddenly appeared again on exposition in France in 1492. The authors of the *Turin Shroud,* Lynn Picknett and Clive Prince, believe that da Vinci had invented a sort of proto-camera and captured his own image.[32] Improved carbon dating now dates the shroud to an earlier period than was previously thought. But the authors of the *Turin Shroud* tell a very interesting biography of their own candidate for creator of the alleged fake.

An alchemist and a necromancer, da Vinci was troubled by his lack of sexual identity. The son of an unmarried Cathar woman, he may have been homosexual; he was accused of heresy along with a group of young men. At that time, such a charge was often taken to mean that the crime was sodomy, according to Picknett and Prince, who mention other indi-cations of his orientation. His connection to the Medici family saved him.[33] *Turin Shroud* also asserts that, like many other alchemists, da Vinci was a devotee of the goddess Isis, the Black Madonna worshiped in secret in Christian Europe and venerated in hundreds of churches, grot-toes, and caves. Whatever da Vinci's shortcomings, there is no question of his being a master of many trades and, as a scientist, someone who could be considered a borderline heretic and magician. At the same time, he was a grand master in the same order that tied together the wealthy elite of France and Scotland.

If the moving of the treasure guarded by the Sinclairs took place at the time of the construction of Roslin, then it is possible that later in that century, when further discoveries of the western lands took place, the Sinclairs and their Guise counterparts in France felt there was a threat to its discovery. It was on the Feast of John the Baptist in 1497 that John Cabot, sailing from Bristol, England, landed in Nova Scotia. If fishermen from Europe had not been sailing to the Grand Banks of Canada earlier, they were now. Such fishermen were not potential colonists, although their tiny shacks dotted the Saint Lawrence Seaway, but Cartier and others threatened the secret lands with invaders. A simple mining tunnel and shaft might have been regarded as no longer safe for the treasures of the Templars. If the entire complex, complete with false beaches and flooding tunnels, had not been put in place earlier, there was suddenly a reason for it. In the dual role of Prieuré de Sion grand master and military engineer, could da Vinci have designed and planned for the protection of the treasures that the elite families controlled?

It is said that history is written by the victors. Those in power in Europe were a handful of elite families married to each other, if not always allied. They were the patrons of the arts and often had artists use their faces as those of religious personages. They commissioned the sciences, and they supported the writers, who in turn acted with due caution in not biting the proverbial feeding hand. Most likely, we will never know the full extent of the effect they had on history as it has been preserved for the twentieth-century reader.

The Prieuré de Sion and the New World

If these select families had a secret society that mysteriously placed great value on Saint John the Baptist, it is more than coincidence that John Cabot, Jacques Cartier, and Samuel de Champlain all reached the New World on his feast day. Is it then design that the capital of Newfoundland (Saint John's), the original name of Prince Edward Island (Île-St-Jean, or Isle Saint John) and the capital and harbor of New Brunswick (Saint John) all commemorated that saint? Even the naming of the new continent leaves us with questions. John Cabot's principal backer was Sheriffe Richard Amerike. The same year that Columbus reached America, relatives of his ex-employer sent Amerigo Vespucci to Seville to protect their interest. Vespucci, in the employ of the Medicis drew extensive maps for the newly explored lands. The duke of Lorraine's salon in Sion-Vaudemont, that sacred pilgrimage site, bound the maps into books with two famous mapmakers on the cover—Ptolemy of Greece and Amerigo Vespucci. The editor of this atlas commented that the continent should be named for Vespucci, a man of great ability. We are told in history books that the name "America" was an accident. Because it was placed on the map as someone's name, people misinterpreted it to be the actual name of a place.

In *The Mysterious History of Columbus*, John Noble Wilford points out just who might be responsible for such an accident.[34] "In those days, a small group of scholarly clerics lived in obscurity at the ancient village of St. Die on the slopes of the Vosges Mountains in Lorraine." These "obscure" clerics were not too obscure, since they had a printing press in the very early days of the availability of that invention, and they had a patron, René, duke of Lorraine. It is possible that the naming of America was more by design of the duke of Lorraine and his relatives, the heirs of "Good King René." The duke of Lorraine married the sister of Connetable Bourbon, who was then grand master of the Prieuré de Sion. His brother-in-law was the employer of da Vinci. It could have been that Columbus, having left the employ of René d'Anjou and his group, discovered the continent for a rival Spanish dynasty. And it may have been pride that led the "salon" of the duke of Lorraine to deny Columbus the credit and instead give it to a current employee of their tight circle.

Later historians claimed that Vespucci actually sailed to the New World, and deserves a certain amount of credit for his own explorations, but the basis of this statement is flimsy. A letter in the possession of René, dubbed the Soderini letter, describing the voyage of Vespucci to America has proved to be a fabrication. Vespucci never left Europe, but he had powerful and well-connected friends.[35] It is possible that it was the wish of this tight-knit group that the continent was best left secret. D'Anjou, and the St. Clairs had no interest in their secret lands being uncovered. Neither did their Italian contingent—the Medicis, the Sforzas, and the Estes. These Italian families shared control of northern Italy with the Zeno family, who had been equally secretive about the discovery. The voyage of Columbus changed all that. Suddenly, the Prieuré de Sion needed to assert their prior claim. They wanted the New World to be named by them and possibly even controlled by them.

In 1524 an Italian banker in the circle of the Medicis, Bonacorso Rucellai, backed another expedition to the New World. Rucellai was based in Lyons, where the Carolingian dynasty was no longer able to protect the Jews against the avarice of others who sought their property. Many Jews had converted, often more in name than in spirit. Rucellai hired a captain from another noble family to take charge of his exploratory journey. The Captain was Giovanni da Verrazano. The family crest of the Verrazanos was, remarkably, the six-pointed Star of David, a symbol of the bloodline of that Jewish king and those who claimed descent.

Verrazano took the Prieuré de Sions' passion for the Arcadia theme to the New World. Sailing by a coast with tall trees, he said that it reminded him of Jacopo Sannazaro's idyllic Greek land, and called the place Arcadia. The harbor now called Newport he dubbed Rhodes after the harbor in Greece. Rhode Island's modern harbor city still debates the origin of the "Viking Tower" that Verrazano labeled as a "Norman villa" on his map. The secret lands of the Sinclairs were becoming less secret.

When Oliver Sinclair set sail in 1545, the grand master was Ferrante de Gonzaga, son of the Duke of Mantua and Isabella d'Este, da Vinci's patron. Both Ferrante and Leonardo da Vinci assisted Charles de Montpensier in military operations in France.[36] France and England were at war, and Scotland was dragged into the fray. After Oliver Sinclair left, the duke of Somerset attacked Scotland on the River Esk. Ten thousand Scots nobles and commoners were slaughtered in the action.

Mary Stuart, through her emissary, William Sinclair, asked France to send help, but France, even while declaring that Scotland was now part of France, failed to support her ally.[37] England and Queen Elizabeth did not want a French queen on the Scottish throne, and Scotland, almost leaderless, was unable to protect itself. Scotland and the Sinclair family were backed into a corner.

King James IV of Scotland, who allowed his mother to be executed by Elizabeth without protest, was persuaded as the inheritor of the Scottish crown to grant land in the New World to those in his court. But he was no friend to the Catholic Sinclairs; instead, he distributed land and baronies to those Protestant members who later came to the support of

Elizabeth in England. Sir William Alexander was given a charter for Nova Scotia—New Scotland—and even Sir Francis Bacon was numbered among the friends with a land grant in the New World.

Officially, Sir Francis Bacon was the Lord Chancellor and Keeper of the Great Seal. Unofficially, he was connected to the "Invisible College" we have spoken about—the collection of scientists and alchemists, physicians and writers, that served as the conduit for an underground stream of knowledge. In those days, such knowledge could get one excommunicated or worse.[38] This group resembled the Prieuré de Sion but held no Catholic leanings like the Guise-Lorraine families. Bacon was not able to reveal his secret side until he left government, and, as discussed, he very likely was a critic of the divine right of kings and the government in general in his disguised authorship of the Shakespearean texts. Under his own name he published an interesting work, *The New Atlantis*.

The so-called new Atlantis was very much like the Arcadia of the Catholic d'Anjous and St. Clairs—a utopia where the true Renaissance man could be free to publish and study science without fears of a censoring government or a church inquisition. The name of this utopia was Bensalem. Jerusalem means "Foundation of Salem," and Bensalem means the "Son of Salem," in the context of a second holy place. Here in "New Salem," said Bacon, a secret society resided, to which few were admitted and even fewer were privy to the secrets. Was this Masonic-like society similar to the Prieuré de Sion? This secret society had as its founder a wise king, and the order this wise king started was called Solomon's House. Bacon made a point of declaring that Jews were allowed to reside on the secret island and practice their arts and sciences.

In Bacon may lie the connection to a Merovingian-Davidic dynasty, forced underground first by Rome and later by the Roman Church. Even after England turned to the Protestant Reformation, this secret Jewish group still feared the repression of Europe. The secret society could also just have been a refuge for those who practiced astronomy, anatomy, geology, or just about any science and who would have been branded as heretics or witches—for whom Europe reserved its cruelest punishments. Or perhaps they were simply members of the Invisible College who wanted academic freedom. While this argument seems more credible, it was Bacon's own declaration that the secret society and their utopia were both very Jewish in background and tolerance.

In his writings Bacon discussed flasks of mercury as part of a system for hiding documents. On Oak Island such empty mercury flasks have been found.[39] And, of course, so has a most complex feat of engineering, which may have been designed by another true Renaissance man, Leonardo da Vinci. Sir Francis Drake had the means and the money to put together an expedition to the Money Pit with the members of the Invisible College and even to bring along the designs of da Vinci to use in such a place. On the surface, it does not seem likely that devout Protestants and devout Catholics would act in collusion. The writings of Bacon and the Masonic concept of accepting common ground, however, suggest that a joint undertaking might have taken place, especially as a means to stop the monopoly over science, learning, and free thought that religion had seemingly claimed for itself.

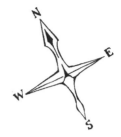

Chapter 12

OAK KINGS,
SEVERED HEADS,
AND THE SECRETS OF THE ANCIENTS

$\mathcal{D}$arkness has fallen, and the light of the bonfire blazes. The entire village surrounds the fire, and the young men take their turns jumping through it. One stumbles and falls, obviously due to the weight of his transgressions throughout the year. Chosen to wear the hide of a cow or goat, he walks at the head of the New Year's Eve procession through the village. Anything but orderly, the procession goes to each house as the other young men beat on the sinner and on each house while circling it. Three times they march around each house, clockwise, always keeping the house to the right of the "leader." At each house a strip of meat, still hot from the bonfire, is given to the occupants. The Winter King, the human sacrifice chosen by his failure to leap across the fire, is kept alive until the new year. Then he is given to the fire, and every villager takes part of that fire home to restart their own hearth. Welcome to Hogmanay, the New Year's Eve of the northern Celts. This festival is still celebrated in Scotland and the offshore isles, but with a twist—the Winter King is not really beaten or killed.[1]

Remnants of such barbaric customs survive in many of our own. This rite was conducted to ensure that the sun would return and to celebrate the new sun. When the Julian calendar was still in use, the New Year, as well as the corresponding death and rebirth of the sun, was celebrated on December 25. According to the *Golden Bough*, the celebrants would cry, "The Virgin has brought forth." The goddess had given birth to a new sun.[2]

The major religions of the world—Christianity, Judaism, and Islam—have all sought to impose their own dogma, myth, and tradition on older beliefs. In this interest, they are not often free to create everything anew. Instead, cathedrals are built over pagan sites, male god trinities replace threefold goddesses, and river gods become saints. In the fourth century the Catholic Church decided they had to celebrate the birth of Christ. While they did not known what day of the year it had occurred, assigning it to the pagan birth celebration of the sun seemed fitting. The guardians of the Church chose Christmas, the birth of the Son of God, to be that same day the non-Christians celebrated the birth of the sun. The Roman Church also replaced a Roman state religion called Mithraism. As a result, the holy day of the week came to be "sun" day, instead of the Jewish Sabbath, which was traditionally on Saturday. Those who are in power get to write history.

The Guardians and the Holy Grail

The elite families of France and Scotland, the Prieuré de Sion on the Continent, and the survivors of the Knights Templar in Scotland, changed the world. They also attempted to bring about a major upheaval in religion and government. They attempted to alter the Roman version of Christianity with a style more dominated by the purity and dedication of the earliest Christians. A corrupt state and a corrupt church had allowed religion to be marked by abusive power, harsh taxation, and harsher penalties for those who searched for freedom of thought and expression. With the aim of finding such freedom, the Sinclair family and their European counterparts influenced not only the exploration of the New World, but also the single greatest body of literature to emerge from the medieval world. What has come down to us as the myth history known as the Grail romances of Arthur and his court is an inspired body of fiction placed on top of true historic events.

Arthur was a minor "king" who fought back the Saxons when all sense of order left England with her Roman overlords. Arthur's family had been of Roman nobility and Celtic stock. When Rome abandoned England, barbarians sought to conquer the Celtic inhabitants. Ensuing warfare threw England into the Dark Ages.[3] The historian Gildas was the first to write (c. A.D. 540) of the son of a Romano-Celtic family who stood up to the invaders, but he did not cite Arthur by name. A second text, the Welsh *Gododdin*, mentions the same event and calls the hero a king; again, he is not named. Finally, in A.D. 800, Nennius identified the king as Arthur. Welsh tales that were passed through generations by storytelling were finally put to parchment in the same century and developed the story of Arthur in the *Annales Cambriae*.[4]

At this point the Arthurian legend was mostly a realistic tale of a leader battling invading Saxons. Then Geoffrey of Monmouth added magic and mysticism to a story that once took place in northern England and Wales and transported his mythical version to the south of England. While some believe that Geoffrey was true to some sources that were available in his day, and have since been lost, he more likely added a liberal mixture of Welsh and Celtic lore into his "history." Geoffrey wrote in Oxford, which may be why the story migrated to the south with his retelling.[5]

In France, in the province of the count of Champagne and the duke of Lorraine—the center of influence of the elite families of the Prieuré de Sion—the highly fictional narratives introduced the knights Lancelot, Gawain, Perceval (or Parsifal), Galahad, Kay, and Malegant.[6] The French version of the Arthurian literature played down the role of Arthur himself and added pieces of Celtic myth to the Grail romances commissioned and written there. Marie de France may have been the first to demote Arthur. The king himself was less important; the men and women surrounding Arthur were all important. Her work is entirely fiction, and her critics believe her goal was to praise the ideals of her time. The main theme of her romances we call "courtly love." In an age when many marriages were arranged political mergers, women of the court could be as adulterous as the men. While this loose morality was condemned by the Church, it was a natural reaction to the loveless marriages that were commonplace.

The Grail romances also attempted to validate, or invent, a religion born in Jerusalem and carried to the south of France by a contingent of Jesus' followers.[7] One French Grail writer even says that the knight Perceval descended from Joseph of Arimathea. Writing in the twelfth century, Robert de Boron declared that Perceval, a knight of the Round Table, was Jewish.[8] If an armed band of Jewish knights were not enough of a surprise, the genealogy of de Boron had another shock. This new bloodline included a certain Laziliez (Lazarus), who was related to Mary Magdalene.

Robert de Boron wrote of the "three Worthies" of the west: Arthur, Charlemagne, and Godfrey of Bouillon. Arthur was named because he was the inspiration for all of the Grail stories and Charlemagne because, through marriage to a Merovingian princess, he was an heir in the royal bloodline. The third "Worthy" was Godfrey, who not only was a direct descendant in the Merovingian line, but also became the king of Jerusalem as a result of the Crusades. While the genealogies of Charlemagne and Godfrey could be traced to the Merovingians, Arthur fit in as a link to the survival of Celtic knowledge and legend that had been superimposed on the Roman Church. If the secret Prieuré de Sion manufactured a body of literature from its base in Champagne and Lorraine to represent the survival of a Jewish-Christian religion, it was not meant to be consistent with the mainstream Jewish religion.

The Jewish-Christian blend of thought preserved the ancient knowledge and myths that the modern Roman institution, the Church, had tried desperately to erase. While the Church had built its edifices over Celtic sacred sites, so had many stories of God, the family of Jesus, and the numerous saints likewise been conceived to disguise the ancient pan-European Celtic myths. The myths themselves are meant to convey knowlege on various levels. On one level a religious story can embody a moral lesson, while to an initiate it may be a device to pass on esoteric knowledge. In one form or another almost all civilizations have an annual ritual of death and rebirth. This most important mystery pervaded all of life. Why did crops grow in the spring and die in the fall? Why are babies born, and why do the old die? Each day the rising and setting of the sun signals a birth and a death and then a cycle of rebirth. Each night the moon follows the course the sun takes during the day.[9]

From very early on, humans recognized that the moon had a cycle of twenty-eight days—a life that lasted for a month. First there was the white new moon, then the red full moon, and finally a dark, dying moon. Humans also understood the connection between the cycle of the moon and female fertility. The sun provided heat, while the moon controlled the tides of the sea, the female menstrual cycle. The theme that was played out daily and regularly in the heavens was also was played out on Earth, and humans recognized this mystical similarity. The seasons of the year marked birth, fertility, and death.

The Church of Rome had never been sure of the dates of the events in the life of Jesus. They were, however, waging a campaign to fit the old religions into the new. The Resurrection of Jesus, possibly the most important date in the Church year, was fixed by the spring solstice— and then named for a Celtic pagan feast day that the Church wished to eradicate.[10] Easter was named for Eostre, goddess of the east, the spring, and of course, fertility. She was depicted with a rabbit.

Christmas, also imposed over a pagan celebration, kept the trappings of the old way. Holly, sacred to the goddess worshipers; mistletoe, flowering from the oak and particularly favored by the Druids; and the Yule log, as well as Christmas tree, all were retained—although their functions changed to reflect the new beliefs."[11] The Christian Church then attempted to accomplish what the Jewish religion had tried a thousand years earlier, the assimilation of the old into the new. The Jewish religion came to fruition at a time when goddess cults were prevalent everywhere. The moon goddess was called Sin. Her name exists today in the Sinai Peninsula, which separates Israel from Egypt. The Hebrew faith first made Sin a male lunar god and then dropped all such multiple gods. "Sin" came to signify something evil.

To ensure the rebirth of the sun, primitive humans, and possibly even primitive peoples in modern times, conducted the ritual of choosing a king annually. He ruled with his queen for a year, as did the sun in its cycle. The rite was symbolic of the Earth as female married to the male sun. Each year both king and queen were picked anew. The king would have every benefit that came with being king, for twelve months only.[12] The annual ritual in Greece started with a celebration that is preserved in part by the myths. A race was run by fifty contestants; the fastest of the fifty was chosen to be the high priestess, representative of the Earth Goddess. She became the queen and mate of the king for the year.

The new king would be chosen by the priestess for his virility. The mating of the high priestess and her chosen king was a joyous one if received well by the goddess, and the reward was a fertile Earth. The summer king, who had reigned during the previous year, would not be so joyful—his rule was over, and his fate was death. This would become the chief celebration of the Celtic year, and it occurred on June 24, Midsummer Day.[13] We find this date celebrated from Asia to Ireland. The Celts began to migrate in 2000 B.C., and they ranged from India to Ireland, but the practice of the annual choosing of a king might have been even older.

With the Bronze Age, more modern man discovered that he was at least as important as the female in the continuity of life and fertility. The sun (male) cults took ascendance over the moon (female) cults, but the change was not abrupt. The Achaean peoples of early Greece had had a female-dominated culture that survived in the Olympic Games. The old king, often called Hercules (from his devotion to Hera, the Mother Goddess), was put to death. The new king, "Green Zeus," mated with the winner of the footrace. The death of the old king (not necessarily an old man) was a sacrifice to the goddess and was meant to preserve the fertility cycle.[14]

As the celebration was further modernized, the king sacrificed his first-born son instead of himself. The biblical representation of Abraham and Isaac suggests a break with the lunar cults of ancient Judaism, which demanded that a son of the king be murdered. God (now decidedly a male) stopped Abraham at the last moment and said he no longer required such a ritual. In the more "civilized" world, an animal sacrifice was made in place of the ritual murder of a living person. The animal would placate the god or goddess, dying in expiation for the people's sins. The scapegoat was put to death for the faults of every person.[15]

In Celtic Europe and early cultures of the Levant, the oak tree represented knowledge. This throwback to nature religion never truly died away. The first letters of the alphabet in Celtic Europe were established for corresponding objects in nature. "D" in the Ogam alphabet was the seventh letter, *duir*. From "D," we get our word for the product of the sturdy oak, the "door." The early male gods were all oak kings. Hercules, Jupiter, Thor, and even Jehovah held sacred this mighty tree. In Rome the oak king was Janus. This two-faced god represented the door between two years, the old and the new. One face peered into the past, one faced looked to the future. His name is immortalized in the name of our first month, January, the dividing line between the years.[16]

Halfway through the year, the month of Jupiter began on June 10, and extended to July 7. And halfway through this midyear month, the oak king would be sacrificed. He could be burned to death, pierced, or beheaded. His wake would start on June 24 and end on July 1. As bizarre as this custom appears, in one form or another it has survived into modern times. In medieval days the week of the wake would be a time of hiring fairs all over Europe, where men would apply for employment for the harvest or in their crafts as masons and tradesmen. For the Celts it was the beginning of the year. In Masonic belief, Saint John the Baptist is the old king, the oak king.[17] He is sacrificed (beheaded) shortly after anointing the new king (Jesus), who began not only a new year but a new era.

The Druids also took their name from *duir* the name of the sturdy tree.[18] Druids were literally "Oak Knowers," practitioners of an ancient art of worship. Their rites were conducted in circles, as in Greece. The *cyrkles* were sanctuaries of their magical practice, which was often directed to the goddess Circe (Kirk). The word for a circle used in magical practice later became *kirk* and then "church." Churches today (circular only in Templar structures) are the sanctuaries where we can worship our god in ritual form. The original structure of the cathedral at Chartres was the round (female) church, which was later built over. The round church itself had been built on a pagan site of goddess worship.[19]

The more important deity of the pre-Celtic Druids was that of the goddess.[20] Representative of the female, the goddess shared the characteristics of the female in her different aspects. She was sometimes the maiden—young, beautiful, ready for mating. Later she would be the mother, giving birth to and instructing her children. And then she would be the crone, the grandmother—no longer able to attract men or give birth, but jealous, dangerous, and horrible in appearance. When the male gods were imposed on the female, so were the words for god altered. Dia-Meter (god mother) became just Deu (god). Crone (aging goddess) was changed to Cronus (father time).[21] Those devotees of the underground stream understand that the sciences were invented when the goddess reigned supreme. The word for mother and the root of the measurement "meter" are evidence of this correspondence.

Mathematics is derived from the science of numbers named after the mother. The learned would "matriculate," a word still used today. For such mysterious peoples as the Druids, the measurement of time, space, and distance was a sacred science. Words associated with these sciences entered our language and remain. *Chronology* derives from the name of the goddess who determined time. From India to Ireland, this dark goddess was "Kali," who measured both time and the lives of humans. We take our modern word *calendar* from her books of time, the Kalends.[22] From the mother goddess herself came the word *calibrate,* meaning "to measure," and *caliber* which is the diameter (of a projectile). The *circle,* named for the goddess Circe, was divided by the diameter (Dia-Meter).[23] In its center was the *core,* named for the goddess Kore. *Radius* takes its name from the course of the sun (Ra) crossing the circle to its center, or core.

In Ireland, Kali's priestesses responsible for watching the skies wore green (kelly green). Our word *month* is from *moon,* which in the time of the goddess measured divisions of time. The word *hour* derives from the temple prostitutes of Babylon, each assigned one period of time to stand watch and make herself available to passersby and strangers. The "ladies of the night," those assigned temple duty in the evening, became the "whores." Our word *horoscope* comes from *horos*, meaning "time," and *scope* meaning "watch." The horoscope is the product of the "time watchers." Night itself was named for the goddess Neith, who was known by that name from the Atlantic to Egypt. In Mexico and Europe the fertility goddess shares the moon and knitting as symbols of her work.

The goddess had other duties besides protecting the sciences. She blessed men with good fortune in the hunt and in war. Artemis in her early forms was the huntress.[24] Women may not have taken part in the hunt, but the goddess was responsible for the fruitful hunt. To Artemis, especially in Arcadia in Greece, the bear was sacred. It was called Arktos (Arctic) because it came from the north. To kill a bear, one required great skill and luck and the blessing of the goddess. Before embarking on a bear hunt, and after the completion of the hunt, men were expected to conduct a ritual honoring the bear. From the Ardennes, named for Arduina (the Germanic name for the huntress), to the south of France, bear hunters left sanctuaries to their patroness. In France, figurines and skulls of bears were found in caves, leaving us only to guess just what ritual was conducted. Drinking from bear (and human) skulls was one custom.

In war, the fearful goddess Hera protected her own. Those faithful whom she blessed with courage and strength would become "heroes" in her name. The goddess blessed the farmers as well. The blessing of Kore was the "cornucopia," which was "plenty."[25] Corn may have been named for the goddess, and cereal was a grain product from the goddess Ceres. Between the time of David and the time of Jesus, crop and hunting magic began to be replaced by state religion, institutionalized magic. Unofficially, noninstitutionalized magic still survives in various forms and customs: blessings before meals, scarecrows, hex signs, and horseshoes on barns are just a few examples.

The ritual beheading of the king and the actual beheading of Saint John may have had nothing to do with each other, but the symbolism is appealing to those initiated into a world of magic. Going back to the Ogam alphabet, where each letter corresponds to a tree, the letter after "D" is "T." Whereas "D" symbolizes June, the month of the oak king's execution, the month for "T" is July, when the new king takes the throne.

With "D" representing John and "T" representing Jesus, the fact that the "T" is symbolized by the Cross is significant.

Jesus starts as the "Green King," the young king, whose tree is the holly.[26] Such tree magic survives in that holly and Christmas are inseparable. Jesus' ministry started a short time after the beheading of John. June twenty-fourth is the death of John and June 24 to June 30 "the wake"; Christ's ministry then started on July 1 in the symbolic Masonic mystery. The event appears to take on even greater cosmic importance. In the writings of the early Christian historian Nennius, the world will have seven ages. The fourth epoch began with David and the building of the Temple of Solomon. The fifth started with John the Baptist and the sixth with Jesus.

The Hebrew religion outgrew its pagan roots and was monotheistic by the time Jesus was born. The Hebrew people were not looking for another god, but the earthly Messiah, a king who would deliver them from the Roman yoke as they had been delivered by Moses from Egypt and as they had been libertated from Babylon. The concept of Jesus as God was not understood or accepted by the Jewish people in general, and for the most part it was not understood or followed even by his own family or village. After the death of Jesus, Paul became the follower turned leader who opened the door of the new religion to the same pagans that the brother of Jesus, James, wanted to exclude. While the Pauline Church grew and prospered under European rule, the Asian religion stuck to the belief in one god and the Asian-Islamic concept that Jesus was important only as a prophet.[27] His own words were used as proof that he was not a god: "For the Father is greater than I" (John 14:28).

Britain had not yet outgrown its own pagan roots, but it shared one thing with Israel—foreign oppression. Britain and Israel both had the need for a king. The Jews wanted an earthly king to emancipate their people from Rome, as Britain needed one who would free the Britons from Roman and then Saxon oppression. The earthly Jesus failed to liberate Israel from Rome and died in his mission. His empty tomb offered the hope of his return. The Camelot of Arthur, too, failed to last. In legend Arthur was wounded and carried away, presumably to return again.

The similarities of Jesus and Arthur do not end there. As the mysterious magician Merlin had prepared the way for Arthur, Saint John had prepared the way for Jesus. Arthur's wife, Guinevere, was named for a great white goddess and was considered unfaithful by the Grail writers. The companion of Jesus, Mary Magdalene, whose symbol, the dove, is reminiscent of the goddess Isis, was also regarded as a sinner and a prostitute by later Christian writers. As women attended to Jesus in his tomb and were the first to reveal that he had departed, so also would women deliver the wounded Arthur from the last battle and take him to Avalon by boat.

Hundreds of books have been written that show the comparisons among the Celtic myth cycle, the life of Arthur, and the life of Jesus. It is not coincidence that the Prieuré de Sion families and their commissioned writers strove to identify the connection. The Grail romances served to bring back the higher purpose in life. The Arthurian quest for the Grail can be compared to the Greek search for personal excellence, *arete*. It was the quest for the Grail that was important, rather than the attainment of the Grail. Greek devotion, too, was never fulfilled, yet always strived for. Jesus taught in a similar vein. The law was made for man and woman not man and woman for the law. One's highest goal was the love of God and neighbor for its own sake.

These values were not part of church or state in the medieval age; the Grail literature was an attempt to revive them. Bringing all religions together was one step—the Freemason credo of worshiping any supreme deity was an example. And bringing the true message of Christ to the world through the Grail literature was another. But there was still a third step—incorporating the older beliefs into the modern. Celtic Christianity still had one foot in the world of Druids, vegetation gods, and mysterious magicians.

The strange character of Merlin formed a bridge between the misty Celtic past and the medieval age. Once the "wild man," the "Green George" of the Britains, Merlin became almost Christianized. Merlin's birth story is even stranger than that of John the Baptist, who was born to a "barren" mother. As revenge for Christ's victory over hell, a demon is sent to torment a religious family.[28] The family, already bankrupt, has nothing left save three daughters. The demon compromises the chastity of the youngest two but is resisted by the third. This oldest daughter, still a virgin, is raped by the demon on a night that she has forgotten her evening prayers. The child Merlin is born—a human, but completely covered with black hair. Such tales are symbolic devices, although their full meaning has been lost in time. The Frankish Merovingians had their own odd tale about their ancestor, Merovee, who was miraculously conceived by both a king and a sea creature.

The Welsh patron saint is David (Dewi in Welsh), which means "waterman."[29] The calling of the waterman in Christian Wales was to baptize the Welsh people. Saint John's mission was also to baptize. The name John stems from the Greek "Ionnes," which in turn derives from the Babylonian "Oannes." Oannes was a half-man, half–sea creature who brought civilization to the ancestors. The name Merlin also has water connotations in that *mer* means "sea" and *lin* often has a water meaning as well (pool). What ancient tradition unites these three watermen? Modern humans may never know. Almost every culture has a legend of a man bringing civilization who arrives from the sea. From the Incas and Mayans to Native Americans to Egyptians and Babylonians, a stranger arriving from over the water gives human beings the arts of building, writing, agriculture, and healing. The waterman is always the civilizer. Were Merlin, Merovee, and John outgrowths from shared myths?

The Masonic explanation of their tradition is that Solomon himself, the king who built the temple, founded a secret society of Masons that survived through three millennia. A more likely aim of Freemasons, Rosicrucians, the "Invisible College," and other such orders was to create a more free society. Europe was a melting pot of peoples—Christian and pagan, Asian, Islamic, and Celtic. State governments and religions tried to deal with such differences by imposing a regime of vicious repression. The Roman Church and the Norman state together made dissension very dangerous.

Europe was just entering into the Dark Ages. Barbarian invaders from the west finally turned back at the Battle of Troyes in A.D. 451, and the Huns were stopped. But it was too late for the Roman Empire, which had given way to successive hordes of Visigoths, Vandals, and the Frankish Merovingians who ruled western Europe. The Norse Vikings and the Norman invaders ruled the British Isles and parts of Europe. The conquerors practiced domination by death and mutilation and ushered in one of the cruelest ages in modern times. Statecraft and churchcraft meant torture and execution for those who refused taxation and uncompromising obedience. The taxing state offered no protection of law to its oppressed citizens, only war. The Church, too, offered no earthly reward and comfort and instead forced upon the people taxation and conscription to its religious wars.

Even the oppressors themselves were oppressed, since kings and the elite handful of families that governed Europe could easily be ostracized by mean-spirited popes whose decrees of excommunication would lead to an invitation to be attacked by neighboring enemies. For kings who decided to question the doctrines of religion, which included intolerance, the risks were great. But there were certain places where the candle of learning would not be dimmed. The monastaries of Ireland saw the books of the world preserved and copied. In Islamic Spain there were great advancements in medicine, mathematics, and other sciences. And in the north of France, the city of Troyes somehow emerged as a learning center, where new ideas were welcomed. The bishop Lupus created a library that guarded two hundred thousand volumes and three thousand original manuscripts. And this learning center also condoned freedom from religious persecution.

The counts of Champagne invited Jews fleeing from Spain to emigrate to France. The rabbi Solomon Isaac, who is given credit for having preserved the Talmud, was born there in 1025.[30] Rashi, as he was called, started a yeshiva that attracted scholars from all over the world. His school was not limited to Jews, and it is said that he had the French priests singing in Hebrew. Hebrew teachings at the time included an esoteric set of mystical teachings, the Cabala, which had come to France and Spain through the Diaspora, the migration of Jews fleeing the revolts in A.D. 70 that saw the destruction of the temple. The quickest way to exit Israel was via the Mediterranean Sea, and the Cabala traveled first west and then spread north. It was not meant to be taught to everyone but only to a learned few. To this elite were given the secrets behind the written language, the cipher for interpreting the meanings were hiding in the letters. The Cabala had very strong ties to the teachings of the Essenes. Among the Essenes, too, only a select few were able to receive the sacred teachings. The Essenes hold central the idea of a "teacher of righteousness," who was a "nezer"—a "sprout" in the sacred bloodline.

Max Dimont, a modern scholar, writer, and student of the Jewish people past and present, calls cabalism the "subterranean stream underneath the Torah." It mixes faith with reason, logic, and science, to bring human beings close to their deity.[31] But not everyone.

Science and writing were pursuits of an elite few. In medieval times writing was a craft dominated by the Church and the state. Those who could write were in the employ of one or the other. Writers outside the mainstream risked being branded as heretics, traitors, or witches. But even those in power soon grew weary of the corruption. It was a noble class, not above corruption itself, that commissioned the Arthurian romances. The same families that banded together in the Prieuré de Sion, which brought about the creation of the Templars, were the ones to commission the works of Arthur and the history of an idealistic, if also mysterious world.

Even Geoffrey of Monmouth, writing from England, was not outside their realm. Geoffrey was the first to truly elaborate on King Arthur. He dedicated his *History of the Kings of Britain*, written in about 1135, to the English king Stephen, a grandson of William the Conqueror. Stephen of Blois had sworn fealty to Matilda, daughter of Henry I, but then took the English throne himself. Matilda married Geoffrey IV of Anjou and had a son (Henry II) who was later named as Stephen's heir. It is this Geoffrey IV who gave the family of the counts of Anjou their surname, Plantagenet—the flowering shoot of the royal bloodline.

Geoffrey of Monmouth had placed the Arthur story in the south of England; later French writers, and rivals, would relocate the Arthurian romances to France. Geoffrey died in 1155.[32] Shortly afterward the entire body of Grail literature came into being. Most of the Grail works were completed in a fifty-year period, from 1180 to 1230.[33] *Lancelot*, written by Chrétien de Troyes, was commissioned by Marie de Champagne. Marie's mother was Eleanor of Aquitaine, whose second husband was Henry Plantagenet, duke of Normandy and count of Anjou. When Chrétien followed the dictates of Marie, says the prolific Grail historian, Norma Lorre Goodrich, he was not being true to his sources, and the result did not "work."[34] To set a historical Welsh-British king in a medieval background subverts both history and art, as the story is contorted to fit the dictates of the master.

The real Guinevere was a warrior queen, but she becomes reduced in status to a level that suited the life of the countess of Champagne. Guinevere was a Pict, and in her culture she could pick and choose husbands at will and dismiss them as easily. In courtly Troyes, countesses and queens alike were often married without their consent, resigned to their loveless marriages, and unable to do anything about their plights. Guinevere, who could, is considered unfaithful when she has a love affair with the knight Lancelot. Her "desertion" of Arthur is considered adultery in the Troyes version.[35]

The reader of Chrétien is also left without an understanding of why the knight Lancelot brings a severed head to his princess. Just as their ancestors preserved the heads of bears whom they had hunted, the Celts kept alive the custom in preserving the heads of important enemy chiefs. The Norman reader of the twelfth century, seven hundred years after the historic Arthur, may not have understood the custom. Chrétien may have understood it since he was more well-read than his readers, and he may have included such old customs to be true to the source. But the dilution of the Celtic mystical history that was required to please his wealthy patron could be the reason *Lancelot* was left incomplete. Goodrich believes that Chrétien simply lost heart.

Did Chrétien de Troyes finally decide to leave behind his Arthurian works and the employ of Marie of Champagne? In 1188 he died, from unknown causes, and a mysterious fire destroyed most of his work and his sources. We can only wonder if either of the two events was the result of a falling out. One year before his death, in 1187, Jerusalem fell to the Saracens. Many blamed the Templar order. The stress of the loss and the tide of popular opinion hurt the order. The secret organization of the French families behind the Knights Templar split with the knights.

The Lorraine families most likely still exercised some control, but disassociated themselves publicly with the group.

There is little way of shedding light on a death that is eight hundred years old, but we know that if Chrétien's patrons were unhappy with his refusal to finish the work in the style demanded, there were others who would proceed without the baggage of conscience. He could easily be replaced. Just before his death he had been told to place certain genealogies in his works. This act became a trend in later Grail romances. It was two years after his death that Robert de Boron introduced the genealogy of Perceval, which extended from Joseph of Arimathea.[36]

Robert de Boron, the successor of Chrétien, is suspected of having been the new tool of the elite Prieuré de Sion in their attempt to create their own legitimacy as kings and inheritors of the sacred bloodline. It is Robert who cites the Holy Grail as a sacred item removed from a hostile foreign land to the protection of new guardians. It is from this writer as well that we learn of a new Grail castle being built to protect the sacred cup. Was the Prieuré de Sion documenting its ownership of a sacred object that had been removed from the temple in Jerusalem?

If we interpret the Holy Grail as the sacred bloodline, the Grail itself may comprise the documents, the written genealogies of the David-Jesus family. De Boron says the Grail was taken to an isolated land 454 years after the death of Christ. Since it is said in certain legends that the family of Jesus had escaped immediately after the Crucifixion, what happened four centuries later? That brings us to the time of the Visigoths' entry into southern France. The Visigoths brought to France items stolen from Rome, which had been looted from Jerusalem. These items were secured at or near their capital at Rennes-le-Chateau.

In the same way the Cabala is written for certain readers to understand on a surface level and for initiated readers to take greater meaning, so were the works of the Prieuré de Sion. The knight Perceval is called the "son of a widow," a term that has very important meaning for the secretive Masonic society.[37] As mentioned, it carries the connotation of a fellow Mason and is used when one Mason requires assistance from another. In the Conte del Graal, another Chrétien tale that was finished by unknown writers, Perceval is likened to the Saracen "Mahdi," the "Desired Knight" who can cure others. Both Jesus and Perceval were considered the Desired Knights, and both had the power to heal. Mahdi as "mahadia" survives as another secret Masonic word.[38]

A few years after Chrétien and Robert de Boron, Wolfram von Eschenbach, a knight from Germany, wrote about the most mysterious Perceval of all, in *Parzival*. He places his story in Poitou. Wolfram had very carefully planned his work, down to the mathematics of the number of chapters, leaving us to wonder about the hidden messages. Poitou was part of the domain of Eleanor of Aquitaine and Henry of Anjou, and Wolfram was writing with his patrons in mind. He claims the most complicated genealogy of the Grail romances, with Perceval's father descending from Arthur and his mother descending from two Grail kings, Frimutel and Titurel. And he openly uses the terms "Templar" and "Knights Templar" enough to make one wonder if he was perhaps making a late attempt at public relations for this out-of-favor order.

Wolfram also tells of Perceval's sister, Sigune, who is amazed at how little the Desired Knight knows. He had seen the bloody spear that was used to ensure that Jesus was dead, the silver platter that held the body of Christ, the Host and the Grail that represented the chalice with the blood of Christ. He had met the Fisher King, the wounded God/King who could no longer rule. Sigune wonders how it was that her brother failed to understand the implications of all he had seen. His uncle, described as a hermit, had told Perceval that Christ himself had prophesied that Perceval would inherit the job of keeper of the Grail. Wolfram's was the boldest Grail story in the way that he informed us of the Templars, those other desired knights, and that the temple in his time may have been in the south of France.[39]

The customs of the Grail fellowship dictated that they were to be part of a secret society. Since the Templars themselves were not yet outlawed, and not a "secret" society, it could have been the Prieuré de Sion, the order within an order, that was the "secret society." In this society, the few who were admitted were never allowed to declare their genealogies. In twelfth century Europe one very logical impediment to declaring a genealogy would be if it was rooted in a Jewish ancestry. While being able to claim a link to David or Joseph of Arimathea might have seemed an honor, it also could lay some of the wealthiest families in France open to suspicion and persecution.

Marie de France also reiterated that the Grail keepers had to conceal their genealogies. Was the lack of understanding on Perceval's part his failure to see or accept his Jewishness? Wolfram seems to confirm that point. He said that the original Grail castle was in the Pyrenees, the land of Septimania—the land that was owned by William de Gellone. William, we remember, was a contemporary of Charlemagne, of the usurper dynasty of Carolingians that replaced the Merovingians. This new line of regents did all they could to legitimize their kingship. Charlemagne's son married William's daughter. Through such strategic marriages, William's family became the connection between the Visigoth and Merovingian royalty in the south and the Plantard family, the root of the Plantagenet kings. Further marriages drew the Alsace-Lorraine families into the bloodline.[40] The family of William owned the land surrounding Rennes-le-Chateau and the castle of Blanchefort.

Wolfram went out of his way to correct assertions made by Chrétien, who had fallen out of favor with his patrons. He gives credit to his own sources, who were from the south of France and from Spain. One important source is Kyot of Provence (a well-known master in Book IX of *Parzival*), who had "found" the true history of the Grail in Toledo, Spain.[41] The story had been recorded by a Hebrew scholar who had become Christianized but whose family seemed neither Jewish nor Christian. The father of the Hebrew scholar, Flegetanis, worshiped a calf, and Flegetanis himself studied the Cabala. He understood how the stars rose and set and how they determined the lives of human beings. The Grail, he said, was read in the constellations.

Wolfram also said that there were a few Christianized noblemen in the service of the Grail charged with the obligation of being the Grail keepers. If we substitute the idea of the Grail as a Celtic cauldron or a chalice with the concept of the Grail as a body of knowledge, it makes more sense. This knowledge then is preserved and passed down through history by an elite handful known as the guardians. Among the Jews, that body of knowledge deals with astronomical secrets, possibly so complex that they are understood by only a few rabbis, who study and memorize this sacred knowledge over the course of years so that they can function in the role of guardian. These same secrets may lie behind the more "orthodox" form of Judaism and combine with the astronomy from the land of the Magi, Buddhist doctrine (which may have been inherited by the Essenes), and Celtic religion from a time when the Celts ranged from India to Ireland. In Britain and Gaul such secrets had been kept and preserved by the Druids, secrets, so complex that it took a lifetime to commit them to memory. To the uninitiated, part of the mystery could be told in the same form most religion and history was passed along—in myths, parables, and folktales.

Matthew wrote his Gospel to make sure that the life of Jesus conformed to the prophecy of the Old Testament. The elite families of Sion paved the way for the Messiah to emerge from their circle. Did they have in mind a more earthly kingdom as their goal?

There are several possible raisons d'être for the Prieuré de Sion. One would be the advancement of the bloodline of Jesus and Mary Magdalene. If such a bloodline did extend back two thousand years, the number of "heirs" would be in the millions. Would it be practical for one of these heirs to claim any kind of unique distinction that would give millions a reason to believe in him or her as a god or king? Another, more secretive agenda would be to promote the worship of a more ancient god. Perhaps the goal was to foster the advancement of a religion wherein the goddess would be represented by Mary Magdalene, mated to a god-king represented by a Saint John, a Templar/Masonic–style higher authority that would unite the world in one Holy Empire. The rule of such an empire might be claimed by the "heirs."

The establishment of a secret society is also an end in itself. Societies such as the Prieuré de Sion, the Masons, and hundreds of others often have numerous levels of "achievement" and rank. The higher one is elevated, the more secrets he is privy to. Membership in the P-2 in the twentieth century may have paved the way for an individual's success within the group. The P-2 was a masonic group in Italy so powerful that it was said that whoever controlled the P-2 controlled Italy. However, after the exposure of the organization and its alleged crimes, members soon found out that the elite pinnacle group was both corrupt and a terrible embarrassment to the membership.

Similarly, individual Masons, as they become more deeply involved, are almost blackmailed into staying and concealing the secrets of bizarre religious ideas and practices. Did the Prieuré de Sion and their Scottish relatives conspire to create a Masonic kingdom on Earth?

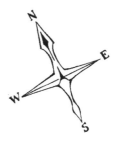

Chapter 13

THE GRAIL GUARDIANS
AND THE MODERN WORLD

Secret societies have always existed and have always been feared by kings and presidents and the general populace alike. They thrive on myth to create an illusion of strength and power and to ensure the loyalty of the members. The main aspect of Masonry that is different from other secret societies is the complexity of its myth history and its ladder of initiation that members must climb to further immerse themselves in the myth. Seen from the outside it appears as innocent as the local rotary. From the inside it is meant to resemble a religion.[1]

This secret society of Masons has a membership of more than one million men (and no women) in the British Isles alone. In the United States there are currently sixteen thousand lodges and several million members. England and Wales has six hundred thousand members, and there are perhaps another hundred thousand in Scotland. Stephen Knight, writing in *The Brotherhood*, a study on the effects of Masonry in England, detailed the corruption that Masonry has wreaked on the police department and the court system there. For most low-level members, Masonry is a social club, a self-help society, and a mutual assistance organization to help in getting a job and attracting customers and clients. Members are initiated into the lower levels and told that there are three in number. After reaching what they think is the highest level, they find that there are thirty more levels to achieve. One student and critic of the organization said that there are most likely three even higher levels that are never mentioned and that are protected by a strict discipline of secrecy. Some believe Stephen Knight's work led to his mysterious death shortly after it was published.[2]

Initiates are schooled in the "sacred geometry" of the ancients from the time of the master Hiram. The earliest Masons would have had to have been knowledgeable in remedial geometry to have done their job. A master mason would have had to have been skilled in higher mathematics to have planned and overseen the construction of cathedrals and churches. In that same fashion initiates would have shared in a small degree of secrets and more advanced levels would have been initiated into higher forms of such sacred knowledge. Members can ostensibly reach the thirty-third degree, but this makes little sense in a mystic scheme where thirty-six is half of the sacred seventy-two degrees.[3] Ex-presidents Gerald Ford, William Howard Taft, Franklin Delano Roosevelt, and Harry Truman as well as such notables as J. Edgar Hoover, Melvin Laird, Nixon's defense secretary, and Steven Bechtel (the construction magnate) all reached the thirty-third degree.[4] What did these people know that was so secret?

In *Genesis*, David Wood explains that Freemasons regard the number thirty-three as the sum of eighteen (an Isis number) and fifteen (for Osiris).[5] Such sacred connections are significant in this pseudo-religion. The number five is a sign of feminine power associated with the pentagram. The number eight is also sacred to Isis, possibly the oldest universal goddess. Eight is recognized as being symbolic of both birth and infinity. And the number fifty-eight (five and eight) is held holy by the Templars and the modern-day Prieuré de Sion. Five plus eight adds up to thirteen, a number deemed bad luck for Christians in light of its goddess association. While eight can be a positive or "lucky" number for Christians, thirteen can only represent the goddess. The goddess letter "M" is the thirteenth letter of the alphabet and it is used as a symbol for the female constellation Virgo. Friday the thirteenth in the year 1307 was not lucky for those Templars who were arrested on that day. Is this magic significance of numbers just silliness?

There are two explanations for such myths and magical numbers. Most likely in the craft of architecture, little was written down. The significant numbers all had stories behind them used as memory devices simply to make recalling a lesson easier. We get our own measurement systems from the oldest civilization we know, the Sumerians. They divided the circle into 360 degrees and the hour and minute into units of sixty. They established the twelve-inch foot and the count of a dozen for eggs. They measured time and space in this number system based on sixty. They measured time by space as well.[6] The time it took for the shadow of the sun to cross a given area, for example, would allow a mathematician (and architect) to determine its distance.

Such measurements took on cosmic significance.[7] The equinoctial sun occupies each house of the zodiac for 2,160 years. A complete cycle of the zodiac would take 25,920 years. On the 360-degree circle it takes seventy-two years to shift one degree. The complete cycle of the zodiac (25,920 years) divided by 432 (a number Berossus uses much as Euclidian geometry uses π), gives the answer 60, the number on which the whole mathematical system is based. Certain key numbers would be remembered with the help of legends.

The Norse Valhalla had 540 doors, through which eight hundred warriors would enter; multiplying these two numbers gives 432,000. Chinese tradition claims that the history of the cataclysm that created the Earth was written in 4,320 volumes. And the Babylonian mystic and historian Berossus says there were 432,000 years between the first king and the Flood. In the Rig Veda of India there are 10,800 stanzas with forty syllables in each (or 432,000 syllables). In the New World certain numbers featured prominently as well. The Mayan time measurement one *katun* was 7,200 days, and five *baktuns* were equal to 720,000 days. The legends behind numbers may simply have ensured that this sort of knowledge could be concealed within myths and not forgotten. Sacred geometry was in fact simply geometry that would be required knowledge for anyone in the building trade.

On the other hand, the occult nature of Masonry was later exploited to control members more fully. Swearing allegiance to strange pagan gods and playing roles in secret ceremonies were enough to get one burned at the stake in relatively recent times. Membership in a Masonic organization has broken political careers in Italy even today. It is evident that use of manipulative methods and blackmail can be a very effective means of controlling members. In certain organizations and movements secrecy and control are very important.[8]

Manly P. Hall, an expert on Masonic law and history, may have been the first to point out just how many founders of the United States were high-ranking members of the Masons.[9] In fact, it appears that the notion of the United States as a country was that of the Masons' in Europe. Independence was the culmination of a long-term effort by the society, which secretly backed and financed the establishment of the United States and outwardly joined the military effort to ensure its survival. The architects of the American Declaration of Independence and the writers of the Constitution were almost all Masons, as were the governors of each of the thirteen colonies. The leading military, both organized and underground, were Masons. And the first president was a prominent Mason. Even the military supporters of the Revolution, who hailed from diverse countries in Europe and came to America to join the war, were Masons.[10] Coincidence? It is doubtful.

The seeds of what flowered into the American Revolution were planted when European colonies were formed in the New World. While the mass of immigrants harbored no ulterior motives, the movement toward revolution and the establishment of a utopian society were orchestrated by a select elite in Europe. The idea of such a freethinking world was supported in the philosophy of contemporary writers, and the words were soon followed by deeds.

The list of Masons who participated in the revolution reads like a *Who's Who* of American history.[11] Patrick Henry and Richard Henry Lee were said to be Masons. John Hancock, Dr. Joseph Warren, and Paul Revere were members of the Scottish Lodge, which in America had a degree of rank called the "Knight Templar." Paul Revere was also part of the Sons of Liberty, connected to Saint Andrew's Lodge, which was behind the Boston Tea Party. Benedict Arnold and his father-in-law, the high sheriff of New Haven, were Masons in that small city's lodge. Benjamin Franklin was the grand master of the Pennsylvania lodge and a member of a lodge in Europe whose name suggests a secret society within a secret society—the Royal Lodge of the Commanders of the Temple West of Carcassonne. Carcassonne, we remember, was central to the Church's war against the Arian Cathari. In an effort to prepare for war, Benjamin Franklin went to France. His mission was to keep open trade with France that would provide the colonies with the needed munitions. He was received by Dr. Jacques Barbeu-Dubourg and Sieur Mountaudoin. Franklin's meeting with the Montaudoin family of Nantes, a Mason stronghold, led to a deal that lasted for three generations, shipping illicit arms and other goods to America. Mountaudoin was a member of the Royal Academy of Sciences and a fellow Mason. Before war broke out, the colonies were already being armed for the coming conflict.

In January of 1775 the French ship *Jean Baptiste*—a fitting name for a Masonic enterprise—carried weapons to Portugal, which were then put on a Dutch ship heading for America. The cargo included a thousand muskets, five hundred pairs of pistols, and barrels of powder. When open warfare finally broke out after the years of rebellious skirmishes, many foreign Freemasons rushed to the aid of the new country. Baron von Steuben, Kazimierz Pulaski, and the marquis de Lafayette were several such notables who joined the war effort. There were Masons on the British side as well, and a student of the Revolution might suspect that they sabotaged the British effort. The British constantly had Washington and the American forces in general on the run—outgunned and outmanned—yet they lost several key battles and thus the entire war.

General Arthur St. Clair, who was descended from William Sinclair of Roslin, had served with the British military leader Sir Jeffrey Amherst in Nova Scotia.[12] When the cause was France against Britain during the American Revolution he chose the British side. When asked to fight against the American colonies, he resigned his commission and was made a major general of the American army. He later fought against the Indians for his new country. He married the daughter of a wealthy French family but died in poverty. His tombstone inscription reads, "This stone is erected over the bones of their departed brother by the members of the Masonic society."[13]

General Horatio Gates, who had fought under Amherst and was George Washington's friend, married the daughter of the grand master of Nova Scotia. Ironically, he was chosen over Washington for the position of commander-in-chief by a cabal that included Charles Lee of Virginia and John Adams of Massachusetts.[14] George Washington had been sworn in as a Mason in 1752, when he was only twenty, and rose quickly through the Masonic ranks as well as the military ranks. He eventually became grand master of the grand lodge of Virginia. Lafayette himself observed how committed Washington was to his fellow Masons and noted that he rarely awarded independent commands to those who were not Masons. His generals Horatio Gates, Henry Knox, and Israel Putnam were fellow Masons. Washington used Masonic tradition and brotherhood as a way to keep the army together and conducted lodge ceremonies even at Valley Forge.

George Washington prevailed against the British and American conspirators and was soon elected president of the new republic. He was sworn in by the grand master of New York, Robert Livingston, with the Bible of the Saint John's Lodge of New York.[15] The dollar had and still has Masonic symbols, including the unfinished pyramid, the "all-seeing eye," and a scroll proclaiming a "new secular order." The first U.S. attorney general, Edmund Randolph, was a Mason as was one of the first chief justices of the Supreme Court, John Marshall. Masonry triumphed in the United States. There the utopia of Bacon came to fruition.

Bacon and the New World Order

Several writers were instrumental in developing the idea of freedom and democracy, but Bacon was one of the few elite who could further the exploration and settlement of the New World. He was a true Renaissance man in terms of both political thinking and science. In his book

The New Atlantis, he called for openness in the arts and sciences, freedom from persecution for Jews, and higher ideals for all. Written at the same time, another work, a play that defied the divine right of kings, cost a friend of Bacon's his life. For this reason, it is speculated, not all of his work could be published under his name. That was the motive for allegedly giving an illiterate actor the credit for such works as *Richard II.*[16]

As we have seen, Dr. Orville Ward Owen of the United States traveled to England to search for the original Shakespeare-Bacon manuscripts. With clues from the writings of Bacon and Shakespeare, Owen scoured the countryside for fifteen years. Bacon's *Sylva Sylvarum* had described preserving documents through the use of mercury, placing parchments in quicksilver for long-term preservation. Owen looked for ruined castles, hidden stairways, and secret chambers where boxes sealed in mercury might be hidden. His search led him to a tunnel under the Wye River and a nearby castle. In the silt of the river Owen found a vault of cement and stone as large as a room, but empty.

Owen's conclusion was that Bacon had used this vault but that he, or someone else, had moved the manuscripts to a safer location. In *Sylva Sylvarum,* Bacon also wrote of constructing artificial springs by using stone, sand, and ferns. Was the refuge of Bacon in Nova Scotia? Bacon and two of his closest friends had received land in eastern Canada. One was William Rawley, who protected Bacon's manuscripts until his death in 1660. The other was Thomas Bushell, a mining engineer whose expertise was in extracting ore from flooded mines.[17] Both may have had a role in keeping the Shakespearean plays of Bacon from seeing the light of day.

In the tight-knit circle of Bacon and his friends, we find the group that constitutes the Invisible College. They were the thinkers and the doers of the Elizabethan court. But they operated in a world that regarded science as magic and heresy—crimes that were punished by torture and death. The idea of a utopia that did not ban experimentation and theorizing appealed deeply to them. The line between science and magic, apparent to modern readers, was very thin in the Elizabethan age. One might be rewarded handsomely for a new discovery or thrown to the Inquisition for heresy. A good example was in the early study of medicine.

Bacon himself studied the human body. He incorrectly stated that there was no norm for body temperature. Another Renaissance pioneer who agreed with him was the explorer Sir Walter Raleigh. Their circle included Dr. Robert Fludd, who asserted that the Bible recorded the use of a thermometer in measuring human temperature.[18] While such theories would be laughed at today, science was coming out of a sort of dark age, and wild theories precede finding truth. Another in their circle was William Harvey, who was soundly criticized in his time for pioneering the use of cadavers for medical and scientific research, but who is remembered with distinction today.[19]

Dr. Fludd was a Rosicrucian.[20] This secret society, which first appeared in Germany in the early seventeenth century, claimed as its founder Christian Rosenkreuz, who wrote *The Chemical Wedding*. Works on alchemy, such as this one, could earn their author execution. The true author, Johan Valentin Andrea, feared the Church and wrote using a pseudonym. The text of *The Chemical Wedding* discusses the Templars, Grail literature, and the lost royal lineage. Being associated with a secret science of the "Rosy Cross" did not endear Dr. Fludd to modern science. Fludd's father was treasurer to Elizabeth I and served in her court along with Bacon. At that time the court was sending aid to France, whose finance minister was Louis de Nevers. Fludd himself tutored Henry of Lorraine's children in Marseilles, including Charles, the duke of Guise. Charles of Guise, whose family had commissioned the Grail romances, married Henriette-Catherine de Joyeuse, who owned the village of Couiza, near Rennes-le-Chateau. And Fludd, de Nevers, and Andrea were all linked in another way—they each served as grand masters of the Prieuré de Sion.[21]

In England, Bacon and his circle seemed to be pressing Elizabeth for their own "New Atlantis" agenda. Dr. John Dee, another in the circle of the Invisible College, had the ear of Queen Elizabeth.[22] While he is not noted for his science of navigation, his work, *The Perfect Art of Navigation*, led Sir Francis Drake to believe it was possible to sail around the world. Dr. Dee, however, was more noted for his work as a magician. Among other tasks, he was astrologer to Queen Elizabeth. She chose her coronation day only after Dr. Dee pronounced a fortuitous date. She and her ladies-in-waiting traveled to the estate of Dee in Mortlake, where he kept his magic mirror that could see the future.[23] Witnesses to its magic were never able to describe what they had seen.

In his laboratory Dr. Dee experimented with alchemy and wrote on this secret science and on the Cabala. His library reputedly contained more books than any other in Europe—many on forbidden arts that today might be regarded as science. When discussion of the Drake voyage first emerged, backers of the scheme enlisted Dee to help. Through the use of some convoluted logic Dee convinced Elizabeth that she was a linear descendant of Arthur and was entitled to be the queen of America (and Scandinavia and Russia for good measure). Elizabeth and other backers put up the funds for Drake's secret mission. The voyage of the *Golden Hind* yielded a 4,700% return for the investors.[24] Dr. Dee's collection also included the charts and maps of the Zeno-Sinclair expedition; the explorer Sir Martin Frobisher had obtained these from Dee. In the end, Dr. Dee's magic did not always work on his behalf—a mob attacked his house, destroying his library, when they heard he was using familiars to perform his magic.

Still another member of the Invisible College, the scientist Robert Boyle, took over as grand master of the Prieuré de Sion after Johan Andrea. Both had studied alchemy. Boyle was connected to the Medici family and to Isaac Newton and philosopher John Locke. Locke was connected to the Guise family and became a student of the mysterious history of Rennes-le-Chateau (long before Saunière's nineteenth-century discovery). Boyle's work on alchemy passed to the hands of Newton.

Among Newton's writings was a study of Judaism, which was said to include divine knowledge that had been lost. Newton was aware that astronomers from Egypt, Babylonia, and Greece had built temples to serve as models of the universe, preserving cosmic knowledge in microcosm. Solomon was the first. Newton wrote of the significance of the dimensions of Solomon's temple, which itself revealed certain secrets. The Apocalypse of Saint John and Ezekiel further taught Newton the value of following the exact plan of the temple. He believed that a select few had possessed the philosophers' stone throughout history, and this group included Solomon, Moses, Plato, Hermes, and Jesus. He himself believed in God but followed the Arian doctrine that stated that Jesus was not equal to God the Creator.[25]

Newton's own belief mirrors the Masonic mythology that Solomon had been aware that he was creating a structure that would resemble the universe. Solomon was preserving within the structure the arcane knowledge of secrets meant to be understood only by a few. Those few included Persian magicians, Babylonian priests, and Greek philosophers, who passed on this knowledge through history. When Newton died, most of his writings were scattered and lost. The English economist John Maynard Keynes came across Newton's papers in 1936 at an auction and studied them in detail. He concluded that Newton was the "last of the magicians."

After one hundred years, the leadership of the Prieuré de Sion, once in the hands of scientists, returned to men of more political orientations. In England the Catholic Stuarts were returned to the throne in 1660. Because they had the support of Freemasonry, that secret society was allowed to conduct itself more openly. Charles Radclyffe, active in Scottish Freemasonry, became the grand master. He was cousin to the Bonnie Prince Charles, who was active in the Royal Society. The Royal Society, the Invisible College, and Rosicrucianism were all reactions to the oppression of church and state and the general fears of the populace, who put their faith in the Church. The patronage of such groups by members of royalty allowed them to further their ideas about science with less fear of being branded as witches or heretics. And these fears were not exaggerated—Galileo was imprisoned, threatened with torture, tried, and confined to his home for life for stating that the Earth moved around the sun.

Freemasonry came out into the open during this era. On June 24, 1717 (Saint John's Day), four London lodges went public. In 1725 a lodge in Ireland followed suit. Finally, in 1737, under Andrew Ramsay, who was in the French order of Lazarus, the Scottish Lodge officially entered the world. Ramsay linked the Templars and the Freemasons by calling the new organization "returning Crusaders." He educated Bonnie Prince Charlie in the ancient mysteries of Freemasonry, which he believed were connected with the goddesses Ceres, Isis, Minerva, and Diana. His agenda was more political and similar to that of the Sinclairs—he wanted to unite France and Scotland again.[26]

At that time, however, the Scottish Masons were no longer devout to the Catholic Church. The Church in Rome condemned the Freemasons and excommunicated all Catholic members. Pope Clement XII declared in 1738 that the true purpose of the Freemasons was to subvert the Catholic Church. This pope may have understood Masonry as an Arian heresy. Today we know that once a Mason rises in rank above the first three degrees, he is initiated into an indoctrination of a religious nature. He is told, as all initiates are, that the organization accepts members of any religion that believes in a supreme god. Later he is told that there is only one god and that Jesus is not part of the godhead. Nor is the god of the Freemasons the same god as in the Catholic religion. God is Jabulon, a mystic combination of Jah (or Yahweh, Jehovah of the Jews), Ba'al (god of the Phoenicians and Celts), and On (a god of Egypt, Osiris).[27]

Stephen Knight has discussed the god of the Freemasons in a chapter entitled "The Devil in Disguise." The god of the Masons was the Great Architect who built the universe. The further one progressed up the Masonic ladder of initiation, the more of the nature of this god would be revealed. Few would talk to Knight about this, since outside their organization Masons belong to more accepted religions. It is difficult to resolve one's "visible" religion with one's membership in an order that believes in Hebrew and pagan gods at the same time.

Bacon had failed to create his utopia, Dr. Dee had failed to gain the rulership of the entire New World for Elizabeth, and Drake had failed to do more than build up his own coffers and those of his queen with the booty of the Spanish galleons. The new utopia, which visibly sought to end religious prejudice and the religious grip on all matters of learning, crumbled in a world where Christians now fought Christians and religious persecution took even more novel forms, as in the prosecution of witchcraft. The intellectual side of Freemasonry had failed. The military side of the order took precedence again. America in the eighteenth century was moving toward the Baconian ideal, but Europe was moving further away.

The Success of the Guardians in America

It was a Scottish Freemason who was instrumental in bringing what is often called the "craft" to the New World and preserving Nova Scotia.

Sir Jeffrey Amherst led a regiment called the Royal Scots and drove the French out of Nova Scotia in 1758.[28] It was Amherst, wishing to increase the population, who divided the territory and created the document known as the Shoreham Grant, one year later.[29] Oak Island for the first time officially had an owner.

Threat of revolution in America brought many New England families north to Nova Scotia. Many Highland families from Scotland migrated to "New Scotland" as well. Where Amherst went, Freemasonry followed. His unit chartered the first British lodge in America and trained such fellow Masons as Ethan Allen, Benedict Arnold, and George Putnam. Serving under Amherst was a Lieutenant Colonel John Young. Young had been appointed deputy grand master of the Scottish Lodge by none other than William St. Clair of Roslin. In 1761 Young turned over the lodge to another Lieutenant Colonel, Augustine Provost. Provost became the grand master for all the Scottish lodges in America.

The Freemasons would take a leadership role in diplomacy behind the scenes and the military resistance that became the American Revolution. The utopian dream of a free country, where religion and the state were separate, was realized. The success of the American Revolution brought such revolutionary ideas to France. The revolution that started with the philosophy of the elite degenerated in France into a mob-run slaughterhouse. By this time the secret treasures of the Sinclairs, the Templar treasury, the loot of the Temple of Solomon, and the relics of the Scottish Catholic Church were all guarded by the secret society, which operated within the frame of militant Freemasonry. The Oak Island repository was a part of Nova Scotia that was threatened by the hostilities of the French and English.

The Failure of the Guardians in Europe

In Europe the elite families that made up Prieuré de Sion were not the self-sacrificing heroes who risked their own wealth and their lives to bring about their ideals. The European elite were seen as self-absorbed, power-hungry, and greedy. The aristocracy became the first target of the mob, and soon all wealthy individuals were considered antirevolutionary. Members of the family of Lorraine who survived the revolution came to hold the title of grand master, but surviving was accomplished only by maintaining a very low profile. Meanwhile, the title of grand master was invested in artists and writers, most likely figureheads being paid by their patrons to avoid the risk that such patrons might attract.

Charles Nodier, a major literary figure in nineteenth-century France tried to revive interest in the Merovingian dynasty and in secret societies in general.[30] He indicated that his group was based both in biblical and Pythagorean philosophy. But such secret societies began to suffer a backlash that a Masonry-related scandal in America and the bloodshed of revolutionary France had caused. After Nodier's term, the writer Victor Hugo and the composer Claude Debussy were at least the titular heads of the underground Prieuré de Sion. Victor Hugo certainly fits the profile of a known artist with less than orthodox religious learning. His family was from Lorraine, and he was attracted to both secret societies and the occult. Regarded as deeply religious, he did not believe in the Trinity or the divinity of Jesus. He married in the Saint Sulpice church in Paris (where Saunière was sent after his discovery) and vacationed in the Pyrennees. He was anti-pope and pro-Freemason when the Italian patriot Giuseppe Garibaldi and the Masons were opposing the pope in Italy. His best-known work, Les *Misérables*, earned him his wealth during his lifetime, but his greatest literary effort was the very unusual *La Légende des Siècles*. This work, rewritten twice, is a treasure story that starts with Adam and Eve and moves to the south of France, specifically the Rennes-le-Chateau area, according to several researchers.[31] Claude Debussy, too, was immersed in the occult, and it was he who introduced Emma Calvé to Father Saunière.

Both of these grand masters, Hugo and Debussy, kept interesting company. One of their circle was Jules Doinel, the bishop of a neo-Cathar church in Languedoc, France, and the librarian of Carcassonne. His heretical church was consecrated in 1890 at the home of Lady Caithness, wife of the earl of Caithness, Lord James Sinclair. The social circles of Doinel, Debussy, and Hugo included Emma Calvé, a famous diva of her day, also immersed in the black arts and occult sciences; she became a frequent visitor to Father Saunière after their introduction through Debussy.[32]

During Debussy's term as grand master (1885–1918), the Catholic modernist movement embarrassed the Church in Europe, and the reaction of the pope was to brand the modernists as Masons. The center of this modernist movement may have again been Saint Sulpice. Those who believe the Prieuré de Sion did not last through the ages, as asserted by the authors of *Holy Blood, Holy Grail*, say that the organization became the Compagnie du Saint-Sacrament.[33] This group and its acivities are well documented, and its members included the founder of the seminary of Saint Sulpice. In the outer world this organization claimed good works as its purpose, but gathering intelligence and manipulating the business of church and state were its real goals. It was a true secret society and often took an anti-Church stance. Whatever the true aims of the Compagnie, it is interesting that Saunière was sent to Saint Sulpice with his discovery.

After Debussy, the French writer Jean Cocteau became the next grand master. His overt connections with the other grand masters are few, but he had a fascination with monarchy, specifically the Hapsburgs. The Hapsburgs and Masonry are connected in that the family played the same role in Germany that the Sinclairs took in Scotland. They were guardians to the Teutonic Knights, the survivors of the Knights Templar that ruled in Germany.

One of Father Saunière's most important visitors was Archduke Johann von Hapsburg, cousin to the emperor of Austria. This contact came in a very crucial era for monarchs. Not too long before, America had overthrown the English monarchy, and France had followed by chopping off the heads of her rulers. The Hapsburgs were, at the least, threatened by the civil wars that raged throughout most of Europe during the nineteenth century. By the twentieth century the threat had escalated.

The dynasty that had begun in the tenth century lost everything in the twentieth. The Hapsburgs had risen to prominence in the Alsace region, neighboring the Lorraine province of the Prieuré de Sion. At their peak they owned Austria, Germany, Spain, parts of Italy and the

Middle East, and even lands in the New World. Hapsburg and Lorraine united in 1735, when François, duke of Lorraine, married Maria Theresa of Austria. Masonic groups had been on both sides of the antimonarchist actions in Europe, and the group known as the Illuminati had plotted against the Hapsburg dynasty during the French Revolution. But the Hapsburgs prevailed until the twentieth century when an assassin's bullet brought down the archduke Franz Ferdinand and triggered World War I. Emperor Franz Joseph's death in 1916 left his cousin Karl and Karl's wife, Empress Zita, as the Hapsburg heirs, but the war found them in exile first in Switzerland and then in Portugal after two attempts to restore their monarchy failed.

When Zita died in 1989, thousands attended her funeral in Vienna, and millions watched the ceremony, four and a half hours long, on television. Her titles were read aloud; among the fifty-two that she had kept was "Queen of Jerusalem." Her life's work—reclaiming the throne for her son Otto—remained unaccomplished. Otto is now a member of the European Parliament and holds the dynastic titles of his family, which is still called the house of Hapsburg-Lorraine.[34]

The death of Cocteau in 1963 left the post of grand master apparently vacant. The organization has complied with the rules of the French government requiring that all such societies file statements of purpose and provide lists of their officials. *Holy Blood, Holy Grail* says that the next grand master was a Pierre Plantard de St. Clair. Unlike his apparent predecessors, he was not unusually wealthy or on the way to becoming famous as a writer, playwright, or alchemist. In his favor, he owned land in the Rennes-le-Chateau area as well as near Stenay in the north, where Dagobert II was killed. He had been in the French Resistance in World War II and fought behind the scenes as a supporter of Charles de Gaulle. When he finally made himself available to be interviewed, he claimed that his organization did, in fact, "hold the lost treasure of the Temple of Jerusalem." But his reign as grand master was not destined to last for life. The publicity of *Holy Blood, Holy Grail* and concurrent media attention on Rennes-le-Chateau played a part in St. Clair's resignation from the post. Today the post is held by a lawyer in Barcelona, and the organization has once again become publicity shy.[35]

The Power of the Secret Society

For better or worse, secret societies have always existed. Often they work on behalf of good causes, but some also have an insidious side that breeds corruption and favoritism, attributes not necessarily monopolized by organizations. Revolving around the Catholic Church are several cultlike groups—not surprising in an era of great change—whose nature and size are certainly eye-opening. The Opus Dei (the "Work of God") is a very right-wing group that counts seventy-three thousand members in eighty seven countries.[36] While their size is not considered huge, their commitment extends way beyond anything required of a Mason. Members swear to unquestioning obedience and celibacy and conform to a daily ritual that includes self-flagellation. There is at least one documented case of a parent hiring a deprogrammer to extricate a child from the group. Opus Dei boasts that it influences 487 universities and high schools, fifty-two radio and television stations, and almost seven hundred publications. While they are most influential in Spain, Mexico, Columbia, and Peru, they are also represented in major cities in the United States.

Comunión y Liberación (Communion and Liberation) is another, less secretive group that boasts six thousand members; its aim is to change Italian society.[37] About one tenth of its members are priests. Chapters have sprung up in New York, Washington, and Boston. They are more traditional Catholics who refuse to work with less traditional groups, such as Catholic Action. Described in the *New York Times* as "armed, active and tough," Catholic Action is not tough in its anti-abortion stance, which is one reason they are alienated from Communion and Liberation.

The most influential group in the Catholic world is the Knights of Malta. Penny Lernoux describes the group as the "old boys club for European aristocracy and the political right in the United States and Latin America."[38] The Knights of Malta was founded on the wealth of the order that it destroyed, the Templars, and it is now headquartered in Rome. There are fifteen hundred American members. Past and present members include William Casey (CIA director), William and James Buckley, Clare Boothe Luce (publisher of *Life* magazine), William Simon (former Secretary of the Treasury), Frank Shakespeare (Radio Free Europe and CBS), Lee Iacocca (CEO of Chrysler), Republican senator Pete Dominici, Alaskan governor Walter Hickel, and J. Peter Grace (conglomerate magnate). The Sovereign Military Order of Malta and its knights have played roles in protecting Nazis during the war crime trials after World War II, in the coup against Salvador Allende in Chile, in right-wing coups in Italy, and in handling logistics for the Contras in Nicaragua.

The Catholic Church, however, has no monopoly on secret societies. From the American Order of Rosicrucians to black magic occult groups like A. W. Waite's Golden Dawn and Aleister Crowley's Order of New Templars, there are also a wide range of goals. All boast secrets that are meant never to be revealed to the uninitiated and have goals that can affect politics. Many have ritualistic initiations. Such groups have always been both active and present in spiritual and governmental affairs. The Prieuré de Sion is just one more such "elite" group, with its own goals and its own history, real or contrived.

The Prieuré de Sion has played a very important role in the mystery of Oak Island. They were the secret core of the Templars, instrumental in bringing wealth and organization to this military order. But the religious wars that tore apart families and governments in Europe may also have served to divide the organization into two. The Sinclairs, once an all important family in the Prieuré, became the guardian family for the Templars. It is under the guardianship of the Scottish contingent that the treasure was brought to the new Scotland. And it would be a Sinclair who held the key to the treasure.

The Grail Treasure and Oak Island

The Sinclair family had the motive and the means to bring the treasure to North America. And they had the treasure itself. The acceptance of the runaway Templars and their treasure fleet by Robert the Bruce in the early fourteenth century meant that the wealth of the Paris temple found its way to Scotland. The temple, like its counterpart in Jerusalem, was the repository of all that the world's first bank guarded, and more—the sacred relics of Christendom brought home by crusaders, the artifacts of first-century Jerusalem looted by Rome, and the sacred treasures held by the Cathari at Montsegur, including the sacred Grail, considered to be either the cup of the Last Supper or the genealogy of the sacred bloodline of Jesus.

All were put in the care of the Sinclairs, as was the role of hereditary protector of the Templars' successor organization, the Freemasons. Acting in accord with their role, the family built an elaborate warren of caves and tunnels under and around their once proud fortress at Roslin.

A century later, religious reformation turned the tide against the Sinclairs. The treasure, along with religious articles of Scotland newly in the care of the family, was moved to Nova Scotia. That treasure has never been found.

Today the Oak Island effort continues. Its construction was intricately planned to defy intruders and was carefully executed in an effort that took years. Modern intruders, armed with present-day science and millions of dollars, have so far found themselves to be outgunned by an older, if not ancient, science and the labors of fifteenth-century masons and miners.

A recent article in *Macleans* magazine described the latest partnership as raising money for the "final" assault, but such optimism has not proved warranted for two hundred years.[1] The latest assault has taken the form of a large and deep shaft called Borehole 10X. The drillers believe it to be next to the original shaft. Until very recently, tourists could visit the island and hear the clanking of the machinery bringing up rock and dirt from almost two hundred feet underground. The current treasure hunters have become more scientific and are not using the dig and drill methods of the past, but the task is infinitely complicated by the numerous shafts that were dug, drilled, and flooded over the centuries. Worst of all, generations of treasure hunters reworking the ground have managed to obscure the location of the original Money Pit.

One company, called Underground Research, brought forth a plan to dig an enormous shaft, eighty feet in diameter, down two hundred feet into the ground. The plan would involve moving one million cubic feet of dirt and rock. A pump, working at eight thousand gallons per minute, would be required to remove the inevitable water flooding into the shaft. The best possible result of digging such a shaft would be the opportunity to look for side tunnels. The discovery and translation of a simple code found on the inscribed slab at ninety feet indicated that a treasure was located forty feet below. It may have been an invitation to dig just a little further, where the diggers would hit the booby trap that led to the disastrous flooding. It is very likely that the route to the vault lies in a side tunnel branching out from the ninety-foot area.

And what if the new supershaft fails? One writer wryly commented that the island itself might be the real treasure in terms of its value as coastal real estate. In recent years Nova Scotia's land values have escalated; the entire island is now worth about four million dollars. While engineers and excavators are working to get to the bottom of the Money Pit, history may provide clues to get to the bottom of the mystery itself.

Jerusalem

Jerusalem provides the first stop. We know that the Holy City was built over a pagan site and that it eventually held great treasure. The pagan owners of the real estate that became the world's most significant religious site had built a system of tunnels that provided water to the city without visibly exposing the source. This fact is recorded in the Bible and other sources. Later, an even more elaborate structure, the Temple of Solomon, was built there, only to be torn down and erected again. We know, too, that the temple was broken into and looted several times, significantly by the Romans, who in turn lost the treasure to the Visigoths, and also by the Templars.

The treasure trove of Solomon held enormous wealth, the result of the tribute from the surrounding countries and the rewards of a trading empire that for a brief time belonged to Israel. There was gold from Africa, silver from Spain, and religious articles deemed sacred by the Jewish nation, possibly including the Ark of the Covenant. These articles were concealed in a massive warren of vertical and horizontal shafts, camouflaged by whatever nature provided. Such passages protected both the city and the treasure, and we know that the knowledge of building such systems predated the builders of the temple. The Knights Templar, and their inner core, the Prieuré de Sion, knew that there was something to be found and spent years digging under Solomon's stables. Just what was brought back remains uncertain.

Jerusalem, of course, fell to Islam. The once sacred temple is now equally sacred, but it does not rest in Christian or Jewish hands. It is sacred to Islam. The area is now called the Kaaba. The Kaaba is forty feet wide, thirty-five feet long, and fifty feet high. Although it is claimed that Abraham built the Kaaba, this is unlikely in light of the fact that the temple has been destroyed and rebuilt. At that site, of course, there will be no excavation or invading treasure hunters—it would not be permitted. In place of Hebrew or Christian icons, the "Black Stone" is protected in this most holy Muslim precinct. Like the Holy Grail, which Wolfram's *Parzival* described as a stone that fell from heaven, the Black Stone, eight inches in diameter, is the most important relic in Islam, believed to have been brought to Abraham by Hagar, Sarah's handmaiden. Ironically, the Black Stone once figured in goddess worship, and priests in that pre-Islamic faith were known by a name reminiscent of the Templars—as Sons of the Old Woman. Any treasure hunting here would be bound to cause an international incident.

The Vale of God

The south of France is the second stop. The Rennes-le-Chateau area was the capital of the Visigoths, who had taken the treasure of Solomon from Rome. Coincidentally or otherwise, this area is the scene of pre-Christian architecture on (at least) an equally massive scale. Here, a second huge underground and above-ground complex exists. This complex is both massive and invisible.[2] Above the ground there are five mountaintop structures that form a gigantic pentagram. Rennes-le-Chateau is one such peak. The Templar site of Bezu is another. The ancestral Blanchefort home is a third, and two other points of reference, Serre de Lanzet and La Soulane, complete the pentagram. The measurements are exact, and they correspond to the movements of the planet Venus over an eight-year period The goddess Venus, known by many names, is also Isis. Her planet makes a five-pointed pattern every eight years (remember that the numbers five and eight signify fifty-eight in Templar numerology).

It is possible that the Celtic Tectosages, or a pre-Celtic people who built the five points of the Rennes-le-Chateau pentagram and the tunnels underground, were part of the same wave of peoples who came via the Mediterranean Sea from 1800 B.C. to 1200 B.C. The Philistines, as the Bible calls them, were the Peleset according to Egyptian records. Such "Sea Peoples" might have been responsible for monument building all along the European coastline. The important point is not so much who built the sites but whether there is a connection relating to secret knowledge being passed down through time—knowledge that might provide a clue to these structures.

Henry Lincoln, one of the three authors of *Holy Blood, Holy Grail*, went his separate way to delve deeper into the mystery, and it is his belief that the pentagram points to the little village of Arques in Normandy. This may have great significance relative to the message "And in Arcadia I am." At Arques there is a chateau that was constructed over the ruins of a seventh-century fortress. Author David Wood believes position of Arques on the map holds the clue to understanding the geometry of the pentagram.[3]

In the center of the five-pointed star is the "womb" of the pentagram, a circle surrounded by another circle. The geographic location marked on the map of France is Le Cercle, should the significance be missed. Flowing through the womb is the Sals River. *Sal* in Sumerian means "womb." Directly in the center of the star and its womb is an ancient mine, certainly a place where a treasure could once have been concealed. The authors of *Holy Blood, Holy Grail* say that at one time German miners had been brought to the area and were not allowed to have any commerce with the locals. Were they searching for a treasure? The gold once mined in the area was recorded as having been mined out. Another possible location for a former treasure site exists. The site is a man-made pool that is the entrance to an underground tunnel system. The pool is located at a place called Lavaldieu, the "Vale of God," which remains on the map today, an area within the pentagram and in which the buried treasure is reputed to be hidden.

Were the builders of the ancient tunnel system of Rennes-le-Chateau and the Temple of Solomon aware of each other? It is very possible that they were either contemporaries or that this special knowledge of architecture—"sacred" special geometry—was inherited and passed on to modern builders. The concept of combining what nature has provided with the architectural talents of humankind is evident in both the sacred city of Jerusalem and the region surrounding Rennes-le-Chateau. This second treasure site, Rennes-le-Chateau, fell to the armies of a new Rome, the Roman Catholic Church. The "Good Christians," as the Cathari called themselves, were nearly exterminated. Toulouse and Carcassonne were re-built after the genocidal onslaught, but Montsegur is a deserted shell save for the New Age tourists and the odd neo-Cathar who occasionally makes a solitary pilgrimage. Rennes-le-Chateau itself is a mecca for tourists, among them, modern occultists, sun worshipers, neo-Nazis, aging hippies, and self-styled Druids. The cottage industry catering to the New Age that is burgeoning here includes a bookstore (the Arcadia Center) run by a de-scendant of the eighth president of the United States—Elizabeth van Buren.[4] Treasure seekers have dug in secret, destroyed tombs, and created a nuisance for those who are not profiting from the new popularity of the region as a tourist site.

Roslin

Our third stop is the third place where the same architecture exists, com-plete with underground tunnels. While the chapel at Roslin was not built in ancient times, it is truly a "holy place" if one is a Mason. It, too, combines the benefits of what nature created and humankind built upon. Roslin, like Jerusalem, was not concealed but existed in plain sight. Both were very important places in their realms. And both would be subject to significant attention. All three places used tunnels, water systems, and man-made edifices to provide a repository for protected secrets and wealth. All three would suffer the effects of assault by changing times and political powers. Roslin was the last to fall.

The treasure hidden in the underground warrens of Roslin was cer-tainly that entrusted to the Templars, along with the relics of the Catho-lic Church in Scotland. Did it include the Visigothic hoard from Jerusa-lem? We are less certain. The Templars were, oddly, more loyal to the Cathar cause than to the Roman Church. This was the only documented instance that the order opposed the pope, perhaps the result of the Blanchefort family's being Cathar or at least having Cathar sympathies. It could also be that the Templar religious beliefs tended to be of an Arian nature and thus similar to Cathar beliefs.

That same family had a Visigothic heritage. Two treasures might have been protected by the Blancheforts—the one that the Cathari took from

Montsegur and the other left behind by the Visigoths. At least part of this treasure might have been under the protection of the Templars. Saunière may have found gold and silver, but no record exists of any sudden appearance of historic religious articles during or shortly after Saunière's life. At least the sacred part of the treasure may have been taken aboard the Templar fleet that left from La Rochelle hundreds of years earlier.

Roslin, too, fell to invaders. Today the masters are gone, the Sinclairs having lost their direct descending male line and their castle. Modern-day treasure hunters comb the ruins of the castle and the chapel in the hope of finding the Templar treasure, the icons of Catholic Scotland, the relics of ancient saints, and the Holy Grail. A house was built over five stories of collapsed ruins in the seventeenth century, making excavation a tough job. Recently, however, a subsidence in the ground revealed a secret buried circular stairway.[5] The discoverers hoped that the Templar treasure would be at the bottom, but Roslin gave away no such secret.

The castle also hints at secret places waiting to be found, but so far these treasure troves have proved elusive. An ancient dining hall with a now exposed chimney lies over fifteen chambers and dungeons that were used to store food for the inevitable siege. Andrew Sinclair, biographer of his distant ancestors, says that the food was hauled up by a rope, in a contraption that might be the world's first dumbwaiter. The chapel itself contains the burial vaults of twenty Sinclair knights in full regalia, which is what makes this such a sacred site in Scotland to the inheritors of the Templar mantle, the Freemasons. In August of 1991 the Knights Templar, a Masonic organization from Nova Scotia, made the pilgrimage across the Atlantic to consecrate the tombs of their fellow knights, who were martyred in their cause. Carved into the stone of the tomb is the Holy Grail and a sword. Another tomb was identified as that of the William Sinclair who had fought at Bannockburn and died in the Crusades. Most of the chapel's odd fifteenth-century depictions are gone, but the legends of Roslin remain alive.

One legend is of a white lady who will someday be summoned by a trumpet note and reveal the way to the secret treasure. But the most valuable secret in the chapel may be the confirmation of the Sinclair's voyage to America. Among the other effigies in stone is the very distinct depiction of Native American corn carved into the archways. Other American vegetation is depicted as well. The treasure, if any remains, is more likely in the hidden passageways that were formerly reached from the chapel. Like Solomon's temple or the underground passageways through rock found in Languedoc, Roslin's underground complex was massive. But there has been little in the way of rewards for treasure seekers there. The treasure that Roslin once held had been moved again.

Oak Island

Our fourth stop then is Nova Scotia. There is no record of sacred articles being taken from Roslin when it was attacked and destroyed by anti-Catholic mobs. If the relics from Solomon's temple, a "Holy Grail" of the Cathari, or even the more mundane, more modern artifacts of the Scottish Catholic Church had been found by a mob, it would not have remained a secret. Nor is there any record of a mob recovering wealth in coin, currency, or gold bullion. The treasures from Jerusalem, from Montsegur, and from the Templar treasury in Paris and the religious relics of the Sinclairs are all unrecovered.

The guardian family, the Sinclairs of Scotland, discovered and explored Nova Scotia long before anyone took an interest. They had the motive to create a hiding place and the means and opportunity to bring the needed workers and supplies. The family never revealed the location of its new land to anyone and, more significantly, kept the secret knowledge limited to only a handful of the family. This may have ensured that Oak Island would remain a secret. It may also have been the reason the Sinclairs could never claim the island or their treasure. The guardian died before passing on the secret. At some point the last Sinclair may have envisioned a new Roslin, a new ancestral home complete with a new chapel in their residence in a new Scotland. But it was not to be. Death on a battlefield, in a prison cell, on an unrecorded sea voyage probably took the last guardian before such a secret could be handed down to the next Sinclair.

Nova Scotia (New Scotland) provided refuge for the Sinclairs and their allied families, the fourth holy place, Arcadia. Oak Island became the needed repository for the sacred treasure. Nova Scotia itself could not be kept secret, but Oak Island was—until three young people stumbled upon the site. Who holds the key to the secret of Oak Island? A late grand master of the Prieuré de Sion, Victor Hugo, spent most of his life writing and rewriting his *Légende des Siècles*. In this work he tells the reader that only one man knows where the treasure is hidden. Was the secret passed down through the Sinclair family? Or was the secret lost to an untimely death?

It is very possible that the ultimate secret was not passed on but died an untimely death, which was tragically typical of the guardian family. William, the second earl of Caithness, fell in battle at Flodden along with forty other Sinclairs. John Sinclair, the third earl, died in battle in the Orkneys. John Sinclair, "master" of Caithness, died imprisoned in Girnigo Castle. George Sinclair, nephew of the earl, was killed in a landslide started by the enemy in a battle in Norway. Could the secret have died in such a way?

After the ancestral home of the Sinclairs was destroyed in the mid-seventeenth century, surviving Sinclairs and their trusted Scottish relations—the Ramseys, Douglases, Setons, and Sutherlands—migrated en masse to the New World. The Sinclairs made a name for themselves there, but they were not known for their wealth. General Arthur St. Clair, whose name graces several geographic sites near Detroit, suffered the worst American military defeat against indigenous Indian tribes before George Armstrong Custer's rout at Little Bighorn. Only fellow Mason George Washington saved him from a board of inquiry. He died in apparent poverty in western Pennsylvania.

Major Samuel Sinclair, a master Mason who fought at Ticonderoga, whose name is immortalized in Sinclairville, New York, also died in poverty. His tomb, complete with such Masonic trappings as the square and compass, was visited even by Lafayette, who went to show respect to a fellow Mason.[6] One of the more interesting lines of Sinclair descendants was that of a certain James St. Clair, who was related to the general. He had twelve children, including a son named Levi and a daughter named Polly. Polly married Hezekiah Whitney and had a son who was named Levi St. Clair Whitney.[7]

Levi's children included Henrietta May Whitney, who was gifted from birth. May, as she was known, could read at age three and published her writings starting at age nine. Her pseudonym was "Egypt" because of her love for things Egyptian. She started the Society de Sancto Claro and promoted the idea that the Norse discovered America, which was accomplished "by the kinsfolk and ancestors of the family." One of her books was entitled *The Origin and History of the Norse Arvel Cup, or Holy Grail*.[8] But neither she nor the hundreds of Sinclairs from Maine to Barbados would ever exhibit any massive wealth that might derive from ownership of the treasure of the Money Pit.

The most likely scenario is that the secret of the Money Pit was lost. The Sinclairs who built it and who were the overseers of its expansion were also the Grail keepers. And the Grail knowledge, the secret of just what lies in the pit and how to gain access to the treasure, was lost because of the death of the secret bearer. If not a Sinclair, who else could be privy to the key to Oak Island?

The date of the construction that the Sinclairs had supposedly started in the fifteenth century was confirmed by radiocarbon testing. The treasure was brought to Oak Island in intervals afterward. It is also very possible that the pit was then expanded upon and protected by the designs of Leonardo da Vinci. In 1510 da Vinci wrote his *Codex Atlanticus*, where he put on paper his military engineering and hydraulic designs. Seven years later he became completely devoted to his engineering work. While he never traveled to North America, Prieuré representatives, miners, and engineers in Nova Scotia followed his designs. The two most likely candidates to have brought the needed workers to Nova Scotia are Sir Francis Drake and Sir Oliver Sinclair.

Drake is a candidate because he was intricately tied to the Elizabethan court and the surrounding intrigues of alchemists, secret societies, schemers, and plotters. If Drake played a role in transporting workers and treasure to America, it is still possible that a Sinclair was guardian, or gatekeeper. Oliver Sinclair disappeared from England and from history in 1545. While he could have hidden in the Orkneys or the Shetlands, even those refuges were under attack. It is more likely that this commander of the country's army and his own navy sailed to North America.

A small colony, or temporary camp, near Oak Island but not on it may have housed the workers.

The existence of such a camp is not easily uncovered. Some claim that there are actually two Oak Islands, where oak trees were planted on purpose to distinguish them from the numerous other islands in Mahone Bay.[9] The northern "Oak Island" is no longer an island because a man-made dike changed it into a peninsula in the 1930s. Midway between the two Oak Islands lies the ruin of an ancient structure that was likely the base for these pre-Columbian explorers. The ruined castle is intriguing, as are claims of two islands. (It should be noted that a local author claims that oak trees dotted the coast of Mahone Bay and the offshore islands until the late nineteenth century, when a plague of black ants started killing them.)

The fact that the camp of the workers has not been found does not constitute proof that it was not there. Viking settlements existed in eastern Canada, but only one has been found, and that was a complete farming village. The camps of the first Sinclair-Zeno voyage and subsequent Sinclair voyages might still turn up. Someone did construct the Money Pit. And someone excavated a shaft connected to flood tunnels. Likewise, someone inscribed stones, placed flood drains, laid oaken platforms, and then hid all from view. The most important question may be "Did the guardians of the Money Pit ever remove their treasure?"

The vault that is the Money Pit may have remained accessible from 1441, at the beginning of its construction, until the 1630s, when Huguenot families started to settle nearby Lunenberg. After that, the steadily increasing population and heightening tensions between England and France made trips to the Oak Island vault risky. Sometime after 1630 the single guardian of the vault passed away.

The two secret societies, linked together (but not closely because of constant war), knew they possessed a treasure. The two groups, one cabal based among the Freemasons of Scotland and England and the other among the French Prieuré de Sion, collectively believed one of their number was the guardian, but because such a secret had to be kept secret, no one would even be aware that the gatekeeper was dead and the secret buried.

As our clues led us from Jerusalem to Rennes-le-Chateau to Roslin and finally to Oak Island, all along the way treasure and sacred artifacts have disappeared. With the notable exception of Father Saunière's wealth, none have surfaced. While it is difficult to keep secret the sudden appearance of wealth, hiding the discovery of other relics would be nearly impossible. The treasures of the Templars have not yet been recovered, and they must still lie deep underground somewhere on Oak Island.

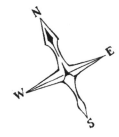

Notes

Chapter 1

1. D'Arcy O'Connor, *The Money Pit: The Story of Oak Island and the World's Greatest Treasure Hunt* (New York: Coward, McCann and Geoghegan, Inc., 1978), and his 1988 updated edition, *The Big Dig* (see note 3), serve as the authoritative texts on Oak Island's numerous excavations.
2. Robert I. Nesmith, *Dig for Pirate Treasure* (New York: Devin-Adair Co., 1959); p. 117.
3. D'Arcy O'Connor, *The Big Dig: The $10 Million Search for Oak Island's Legendary Treasure* (New York: Ballantine Books, 1988), p. 12.
4. William S. Crooker, *The Oak Island Quest* (Hantsport, Nova Scotia: Lancelot Press, 1978), p. 31.
5. Douglas Preston, "Death Trap Defies Treasure Seekers for Two Centuries," *Smithsonian* vol. 19, no. 3 (June 1988): pp. 52–62.

6. Nesmith, *op. cit.*, p. 117.

7. Cameron Platt and John Wright, *Treasure Islands* (Golden, Co.: Fulcrum Publishing, 1995), pp. 1–39; Steve Proctor, "Island of Controversy," *Macleans*, vol. 108, no. 34 (August 21, 1995): p. 54.

8. Crooker, p. 57.

9. Preston *op. cit.*, pp. 52–62.

Chapter 2

1. Ruth Holmes Whitehead, *Stories from the Six Worlds* (Halifax, Nova Scotia: Nimbus Publishing Ltd., 1988), pp. 1–6.

2. Barry Fell, *America B.C.* (New York: Simon and Schuster 1976), p. 257.

3. Harold Harwood, *Newfoundland* (Toronto: Macmillan, 1969), pp. 130–32.

4. Francis Parkman, *The Jesuits in America* (New York: The Library of America, 1983), pp. 146–47. Parkman's work was written in 1867.

5. Patrick Huyghe, *Columbus Was Last* (New York: Hyperion, 1992), p. 201.

6. Harwood, *op.cit.*, pp. 130–32.

7. Parkman, *op. cit.*, pp. 155–57.

8. John Noble Wilford, *The Mysterious History of Columbus* (New York: Alfred A. Knopf, 1991), pp. 62–63.

9. Parkman, *op.cit.*, p. 150.

10. Samuel Eliot Morison, *The Great Explorers: The European Discovery of America* (New York: Oxford University Press, 1978), pp. 147–51.

11. Barry Fell, *Atlantic Crossings Before Columbus* (New York: W. W. Norton, 1961), p. 190.

12. Parkman *op. cit.* pp. 145–47.

13. Ibid., pp. 175–86.

14. Magnus Magnusson and Hermann Palsson, *The Vinland Sagas: The Norse Discovery of America* (New York: Penguin Books, 1965) p. 9.

15. Ibid., pp. 11–43.

16. Hans Holzer, *Long Before Columbus* (Sante Fe, N.M.: Bear and Co., 1992), pp. xi–xiv.

17. Dean Snow, *The Archeology of North America* (New York: Viking Press, 1967), p. 196.
18. O'Connor, *The Money Pit*, p. 227.
19. O'Connor, *The Big Dig*, p. 220.
20. James A. Williamson, *Sir Francis Drake* (London: Crief, Lives-Collins, 1951) pp. 49–59.
21. Derek Wilson, *The World Encompassed* (New York: Harper and Row, 1977), p. 199.
22. James Bailey, *The God-Kings and the Titans* (New York: St. Martin's Press, 1973) p. 29.
23. Colin Wilson, *The Encyclopedia of Unsolved Mysteries* (Chicago: Contemporary Books, 1988), pp. 237–48.
24. Ibid.
25. Sir Edwin Durning-Lawrence, *Bacon Is Shakespeare* (New York: John McBride Co., 1910) p. 178.
26. Wilson, *op.cit.*, pp. 237–48.
27. Durning-Lawrence, *op.cit.*, p. 137.
28. O'Conner, *The Money Pit*, pp. 131–32.
29. Ibid.
30. Catherine Drinker Bowen, *Francis Bacon: Temper of a Man* (Boston: Little, Brown & Co., 1963), pp. 61–62.
31. O'Connor, *The Big Dig*, pp. 81–82.
32. Robert C. Ritchie, *Captain Kidd and the War Against the Pirates* (Cambridge: Harvard University Press), pp. 173–82.
33. O'Connor, *The Big Dig*, pp. 98–102.
34. Wilson, *op.cit.*, p. 161.
35. William S. Crooker, *The Oak Island Quest* (Hantsport, Nova Scotia: Lancelot Press, 1990), pp. 169–87.

Chapter 3

1. Frederick Pohl, *Prince Henry Sinclair* (New York: Clarkson Potter, 1974), p. 130.
2. Peter Firstbrook, *The Voyage of the Matthew* (San Francisco: KQED Books and Tapes, 1997), pp. 87–105.

3. Magnus Magnusson and Hermann Palsson, *The Vinland Sagas,* (New York: Penguin, 1965), p. 8.

4. Ibid., p. 22.

5. Frederick Pohl, *Atlantic Crossings Before Columbus* (New York: W. W. Norton, 1961), pp. 38–39.

6. Tim Severin, *The Brendan Voyage* (New York: Avon, 1978), pp. 11–35.

7. Patrick Huyghe, *Columbus Was Last* (New York: Hyperion, 1992), p. 142.

8. Magnusson and Palsson, *op. cit.,* p. 19; Hjalmar Holand, *Explorations in America Before Columbus,* (New York: Twayne Publishers, 1958), p. 104.

9. Pohl, *Atlantic Crossings Before Columbus,* p. 137.

10. Hjalmar R. Holand, *Explorations in America before Columbus* (New York: Twayne Publishers, 1958), pp. 79–88.

11. Arlington Mallery and Mary Roberts Harrison, *The Rediscovery of Lost America* (New York: E. P. Dutton, 1951), pp. 138–140, 163–66.

12. Holand, *op. cit.,* pp. 154–60.

13. Huyghe, *op. cit.,* p. 154.

14. Peter Schledermann, "Eskimo and Viking Finds in the High Arctic," *National Geographic,* vol. 159, no. 5 (May 1981): pp. 575–601.

15. Mallery and Harrison, *op. cit.,* pp. xiii–xv.

16. Huyghe, *op. cit.,* p. 142.

17. Barry Fell, *America B.C.* (New York: Simon and Schuster, 1976), pp. 283–84.

18. Severin, *op. cit.,* p. 13.

19. Charles H. Hapgood, *Maps of the Ancient Sea Kings* (New York: E. P. Dutton, 1966), pp. 124–32.

20. Harwood, *op. cit.,* pp. 130–32.

Chapter 4

1. Anna Ritchie, *Viking Scotland* (London: B. T. Batsford Ltd., 1993), pp. 44–76.

2. Lawrence Millman, *Last Places: A Journey in the North* (New York: Vintage Books, 1990), pp. 54–60.

3. Deanna Swaney, *Iceland, Greenland and the Faroe Islands* (Hawthorn, Victoria: Lonely Planet, 1994), pp. 528–29.

4. John Julius Norwich, *A History of Venice* (New York: Alfred A. Knopf, 1982), pp. 254–55.

5. Frederick Pohl, *Prince Henry Sinclair*, pp. 81–83. The late Frederick Pohl had been on the trail of the Sinclair expedition since 1943. In several works he wrote of the Sinclair-Zeno voyage, and they are the most extensive modern source on the voyage.

6. William Herbert Hobbs, "The Fourteenth-Century Discovery of America by Antonio Zeno," *Scientific Monthly*, vol. 72 (January 1951): pp. 24–31.

7. Severin, *op. cit.*, pp. 107–9.

8. Swaney, *op. cit.*, p. 518.

9. Pohl, *Prince Henry Sinclair*, pp. 110–11.

10. Hobbs, *op. cit.*

11. Ibid.

12. Pohl, *Prince Henry Sinclair*, pp. 130–31.

13. Andrew Sinclair, *The Sword and the Grail* (New York: Crown, 1992), p. 147.

14. Pohl, *Atlantic Crossings Before Columbus* p. 196.

15. Lawrence F. Willard, "Westford's Mysterious Knight," *Yankee* 42 (April 1958): 61–62.

16. Frank Glynn and T. C. Lethbridge, personal correspondence.

17. Herbert B. Livesay, *The Gunn Salute*, vol. 17, no. 3 (March 1987).

18. North Ludlow Beamish, *The Norse Discovery of America.* Edited by Rasmus Anderson. (London: Norroena Society, 1906) p. 239.

19. Hjalmar R. Holand, *op. cit.*, pp. 218–25.

20. Sinclair, *op. cit.*, pp. 144–47.

21. Holand, *op. cit.*, pp. 216–18.

22. Pohl, *Atlantic Crossings Before Columbus*, pp. 171–72.

23. Samuel Eliot Morison, *The European Discovery of America: The Northern Voyages* (New York: Oxford University Press, 1971), p. 504.

24. Arlington Mallery and Mary Roberts Harrison, *The Rediscovery of Lost America*, (New York: E. P. Dutton, 1979), pp. 154–59 of the 1979 edition.

25. Arthur M. Reeves, in Anderson, ed., *The Norse Discovery of America*, p. 31.

26. Mallery and Harrison, pp. 154–55.

27. Charles H. Hapgood, *op. cit.*, pp. 124–32 of the revised 1979 edition.

28. Ibid.

29. Mallery and Harrison, *op. cit.*, p. 154.

30. Morison, *The European Discovery of America: The Northern Voyages*, p. 504.

31. Ibid., p. 608.

32. Mallery and Harrison, *op. cit.*, p. 158.

33. Pohl, *Prince Henry Sinclair*, pp. 132–54.

34. Mallery and Harrison, *op. cit.*, Appendix C, pp. 239–42.

35. Pohl, *Prince Henry Sinclair*, pp. 132–54.

36. Barry Fell, *America B.C.*, pp. 247–51.

37. Mallery and Harrison, *op. cit.*, Appendix C, pp. 239–42.

Chapter 5

1. Leonard A. Morrison, *A History of the Sinclair Family* (Boston: Damrell and Upham, 1896), p. 37.

2. Frederick Pohl, *Prince Henry Sinclair*, p. 172.

3. Andrew Sinclair, *op. cit*, pp. 127–50.

4. Morison, *The European Discovery of America: The Northern Voyages*, pp. 5–6.

5. Pohl, *Prince Henry Sinclair*, p. 178.

6. Charles H. Hapgood, *op. cit.*, pp. 128–29.

7. Samuel Eliot Morison, *The European Discovery of America: The Southern Voyages* (New York: Oxford University Press, 1974), p. 97.

8. John Noble Wilford, *The Mapmakers* (New York: Alfred A. Knopf, 1981), pp. 73–77.

9. Ibid.

10. Morison, *The European Discovery of America: The Northern Voyages*, pp. 157–80.

11. Christopher Hibbert, *Venice: The Biography of a City* (New York: W. W. Norton, 1989), p. 39. Also see John Julius Norwich, *A History of Venice* (New York: Alfred A. Knopf, 1982), pp. 249, 252, 254–55.

12. Pohl, *Prince Henry Sinclair*, p. 82.

13. Jean Markale, *Celtic Civilization* (London: Gordon & Cremonesi, 1978), p. 69.
14. Inge Ingus, *Baedekers Great Britain* (London: Jarrold and Sons) p. 282.
15. Pohl, *Prince Henry Sinclair*, p. 86.
16. Morrison, *op. cit.*, p. 55.
17. Pohl, *Prince Henry Sinclair*, pp. 179, 181.
18. Morrison, *op. cit.*, pp. 17–30.
19. Ibid., p. 17.
20. David C. Douglas, *The Norman Achievement* (Berkeley: University of California Press, 1969), pp. 173–74.
21. Sinclair, *op. cit.*, pp. 27–35.
22. Ronald McNair Scott, *Robert the Bruce: King of Scots* (New York: Peter Bedrick Books, 1989), pp. 15–16.
23. Ibid., p. 73.
24. Ibid., pp. 145–65.
25. Sinclair, *op. cit.*, pp. 45–50.
26. Morrison, *op. cit.*, p. 37.
27. Douglas, *op. cit.*, pp. 35–36.
28. Morrison, *op. cit.*, p. 37.
29. Sinclair, *op. cit.*, pp. 77–86.

Chapter 6

1. Michael Baigent and Richard Leigh, *The Temple and the Lodge* (New York: Arcade Publishing, 1989), pp. 195–96.
2. Ibid., pp. 34–37.
3. John J. Robinson, *Born in Blood: The Lost Secrets of Freemasonry* (New York: M. Evans and Co., 1989), pp. 153–55.
4. Ibid., pp. 141–43.
5. Ibid., pp. 63-78.
6. Peter Partner, *The Murdered Magicians* (New York: Barnes and Noble Books, 1987), pp. 3, 4, 8–10.
7. Michael Baigent, Richard Leigh, and Henry Lincoln, *Holy Blood, Holy Grail* (New York: Dell Publishing, 1982), p. 418.

8. Robinson, *Born in Blood*, p. 66.

9. Ibid., pp. 67–68.

10. Ibid., pp. 62–65.

11. Ibid.

12. Robert Payne, *The Dream and the Tomb* (New York: Stein and Day, 1984), pp. 125–26.

13. Malcolm Barber, *The New Knighthood* (Cambridge: Cambridge University Press, 1994), pp. 64–114. Barber describes incidents of almost suicidal bravery, including the Battle of Hattim, where only five knights survived, and the Battle of Ascalon, where forty knights attacked a city.

14. Norman Cohn, *Europe's Inner Demons* (New York: Basic Books, 1975), p. 22, 55–58.

15. Zoe Oldenbourg, *Massacre at Montsegur* (London: Weidenfeld and Nicholson, 1961), p. 361.

16. James Henderson, "In the Steps of Unrepentant Heretics," *Financial Times*, March 18/19, 1995.

17. Robinson, *Born in Blood*, pp. 123–26.

18. Ibid.

19. Ibid., pp. 150–51.

20. Baigent and Leigh, *op. cit.*, pp. 1–13.

21. Richenda Miers, *Scotland* (Chester, Conn., Globe Pequot Press, 1989), p. 473.

22. Partner, *op. cit.*, p. 138.

23. Baigent, Leigh, and Lincoln, *Holy Blood, Holy Grail*, pp. 82–83.

24. Lionel and Patricia Fanthorpe, *Secrets of Rennes-Le-Chateau* (York Beach, Maine: Samuel Weiser, 1992), p. 91.

25. Geoffrey of Monmouth, *The History of the Kings of Britain* (New York: Penguin, 1969), p. 222.

26. Robert Bain, *Clans and Tartans of Scotland* (London and Glasgow: Collins, 1938), pp. 112, 280.

27. Ian Grimble, *Scottish Clans and Tartans* (New York: Tudor, 1973), pp. 101–2.

28. Lloyd and Jenny Laing, *The Picts and the Scots* (Dover, N.H.: Alan Sutton, 1993), p. 5.

29. Norma Lorre Goodrich, *Guinevere* (New York: HarperCollins, 1991) pp. 5, 50–58.
30. Scott, *op. cit.*, pp. 81–85.
31. Ibid., pp. 85–89.
32. Baigent, and Leigh, *op. cit.*, pp. 63–76.
33. Ibid., p. 117.
34. Ibid., pp. 101–2.
35. Miers, *op. cit.*, pp. 148–49.

Chapter 7

1. Frances Gies, *The Knight in History* (New York: Harper and Row, 1984), pp. 108–19.
2. Claude Marks, *Pilgrims, Heretics and Lovers* (New York: Macmillan, 1975), p. 286.
3. Baigent, Leigh, and Lincoln, *Holy Blood, Holy Grail*, p. 386.
4. Ibid., p. 344.
5. Morrison, *op. cit.*, pp. 20–21.
6. Sinclair, *op. cit.*, p. 167.
7. Ibid., pp. 179–80.
8. Fitzroy Maclean, *Scotland* (London: Thames and Hudson, 1970), p. 78.
9. Baigent, Leigh, and Lincoln, *Holy Blood, Holy Grail*, pp. 111–30.
10. John J. Robinson, *Dungeon, Fire and Sword* (New York: M. Evans Co., 1991), pp. 36–39.
11. Michael Grant, *Jesus: The History of Ancient Israel* (New York: Charles Scribner's Sons, 1984), p. 19.
12. Jerry M. Landay, *The House of David* (New York: E. P. Dutton, 1973), pp. 219–35.
13. Samuel Sandmel, *Herod: Profile of a Tyrant* (Philadelphia: J. B. Lippincott, 1967), pp. 210–11.
14. Michael Grant, *An Historian's Review of the Bible* (New York: Charles Scribner's Sons, 1977), pp. 153–68.

15. Graham Hancock, *The Sign and the Seal* (New York: Crown, 1992), pp. 360–64.
16. Ibid., pp. 409–11.
17. Ibid., pp. 64–66.
18. Baigent, Leigh, and Lincoln, *Holy Blood, Holy Grail*, pp. 306–9.
19. Malachi Martin, *The Keys of This Blood* (New York: Simon and Schuster, 1990), p. 519.
20. Baigent, Leigh, and Lincoln, *Holy Blood, Holy Grail*, pp. 316–22.
21. Grant, *Jesus: An Historian's Review of the Bible*, pp. 68–77.
22. John J. Robinson, *Born in Blood*, pp. 214–15.
23. Hugh J. Schonfield, *The Passover Plot* (Netherlands: Bernard Geis, 1965), pp. 37-38.
24. Grant, *Jesus: An Historian's Review of the Bible*, pp. 45–61.
25. Gospel of Mark 3:34–35 (also Mark 6).
26. Grant, *Jesus: An Historian's Review of the Bible*, pp. 68–77.
27. Ibid., pp. 7–29.
28. Hugh J. Schonfield, *The Original New Testament* (Rockport, Mass.: Element, 1985), p. 11.
29. Eusebius, *The History of the Church* (New York: Penguin Books, 1989) p. 59.
30. Ibid., p. 38.
31. Schonfield, *The Passover Plot*, p. 52.
32. Eusebius, *op. cit.*, pp. 79–82.
33. Baigent, Leigh, and Lincoln, *Holy Blood, Holy Grail*, pp. 333–38.
34. Ibid., p. 338.
35. Ibid., pp. 366–67.
36. Barbara W. Tuchman, *Bible and Sword* (New York: New York University Press, 1956), pp. 13–21.
37. Ibid., p. 14.
38. Eusebius, *op. cit.*, pp. 65–104.
39. Baigent, Leigh, and Lincoln, *Holy Blood, Holy Grail*, pp. 398–413.
40. Lynn Pickett and Clive Prince, *Turin Shroud* (New York: HarperCollins, 1994), p. 71.

Chapter 8

1. Baigent, Leigh, and Lincoln, *Holy Blood, Holy Grail*, pp. 99–103.
2. Hugh J. Schonfield, *The Passover Plot*, p. 100.
3. Ibid., pp. 129–42.
4. Tuchman, *Bible and Sword*, pp. 13–21.
5. Paul MacKendrick, *Roman France* (New York: St. Martin's Press, 1972), pp. 18–21.
6. Ibid., p. 73.
7. Tuchman, *Bible and Sword* pp. 7–12.
8. Rosemarie Arnold, *Baedecker's France* (Englewood Cliffs, N.J.: Prentice-Hall, 1992), pp. 52–53.
9. MacKendrick, *Roman France*, p. 12.
10. Eusebius, *op. cit.*, p. 139.
11. Werner Keller, *Diaspora: The Post-Biblical History of the Jews* (New York: Harcourt Brace and World, 1969), pp. 66–87.
12. Ibid.
13. Susan Haskins, *Mary Magdalen: Myth and Metaphor* (New York: Riverhead Books, 1993), p. 218.
14. Ibid., pp. 119, 124–25.
15. Ibid., pp. 115–19.
16. Ibid., p. 418. Also see Aedeen Cremin, *The Celts in Europe* (Sydney: University of Sydney, 1993), for discussion of the Delphi treasure.
17. Claude Marks, *Pilgrims, Heretics and Lovers,* (New York: Macmillan, 1975), p. 309.
18. Dana Facaros and Michael Pauls, *Southwest France: Dordogne, Lot and Bordeaux* (London: Cadogan Books, 1994), p. 175.
19. Ibid., pp. 36–40.
20. Ian Wood, *The Merovingian Kingdoms 450–751,* (London: Longman, 1994), pp. 6–14.
21. Baigent, Leigh, and Lincoln, *Holy Blood, Holy Grail*, pp. 250–51.
22. Wood, *The Merovingian Kingdoms 450–751*, pp. 6–7.
23. Haskins, *op. cit.*, p. 88. Origen, of course, was later regarded as heretical, although this did not stop Eusebius from defending him (Book VI).

24. Baigent, Leigh, and Lincoln, *Holy Blood, Holy Grail*, pp. 389–97.

25. Ibid.

26. John J. Robinson, *Dungeon, Fire and Sword* (New York: M. Evans and Company, 1991), pp. 223–24.

27. Ibid., p. 224.

28. Marks, *op. cit.*, pp. 282–95.

29. Zoe Oldenbourg, *Massacre at Montsegur* (translated by Peter Green) (London: Weidenfeld and Nicholson, 1961), p. 345.

30. Revelations 22:16.

Chapter 9

1. Jean Blum, *Rennes-le-Chateau, Wisigoths, Cathares, Templiers: Le Secret des Heretiques* (Monaco: Editions du Rocher, 1994), pp. 13-18.

2. Ibid., pp. 53–55. Also see Lionel and Patricia Fanthorpe, *Secrets of Rennes-le-Chateau* (York Beach, Maine: Samuel Weiser, 1992), for a review of the murder of the notary and several other local murders.

3. Wilson, *Encyclopedia of Unsolved Mysteries*, pp. 197–209.

4. Ibid.

5. Blum, *op. cit.*, p. 44.

6. Baigent, Leigh, and Lincoln, *Holy Blood, Holy Grail*, pp. 31–47.

7. Fanthorpe and Fanthorpe, *op. cit.*, pp. 139–42.

8. Ibid.

9. Wood, *The Merovingian Kingdoms 450–751*, pp. 221–22.

10. Ibid., p. 223.

11. Matthew 1:1–18.

12. Eusebius, *op. cit.*, pp. 22–23.

13. Ibid., pp. 79–80.

14. Wood, *The Merovingian Kingdoms 450–751*, p. 37.

15. Ibid., pp. 41–50.

16. Gregory of Tours, *The History of the Franks* (London: Penguin Books, 1974), p. 151.

17. Ibid., pp. 123–24.

18. Ibid., pp. 231–34.

19. Baigent, Leigh, and Lincoln, *Holy Blood, Holy Grail*, pp. 261–65.

Chapter 10

1. Norma Lorre Goodrich, *Ancient Myths,* (New York: Penguin, 1994), pp. 75–90.
2. Michael Grant, *The History of Ancient Israel,* pp. 16–21.
3. Ibid., pp. 77–83.
4. Jerry M. Landay, *The House of David* (New York: E. P. Dutton, 1973), pp. 108–10.
5. Zecharia Sitchin, *When Time Began* (New York: Avon Books, 1993), pp. 86–88.
6. Grant, *The History of Ancient Israel,* pp. 77–83.
7. James Bailey, *The God-Kings and the Titans* (New York: St. Martin's Press, 1973), pp. 130–31.
8. Landay, *op. cit.,* pp. 203–17.
9. Robinson, *Born in Blood,* pp. 111, 217–18.
10. For a discussion of the orientation of ancient structures and just how recently modern science has begun to accept "archaeo-astronomy," see E. C. Krupp, ed., *In Search of Ancient Astronomies,* (Oxford: Oxford University Press, 1994), pp. ix–xv.
11. Robinson, *Born in Blood,* pp. 274–76.
12. Hancock, *op. cit.,* pp. 44–55.
13. Robert Graves, *The White Goddess* (New York: Farrar, Straus and Giroux, 1948), p. 406.
14. Hancock, *op. cit.,* pp. 366–70.
15. Grant, *The History of Ancient Israel,* pp. 89–90.
16. Robinson, *Born in Blood,* pp. 178, 213.
17. Bailey, *op. cit.,* pp. 94–95.
18. Norma Lorre Goodrich, *The Holy Grail* (New York: HarperCollins, 1992), pp. 74–80.
19. Roger Sherman Loomis, *The Grail: From Celtic Myth to Christian Symbol* (Princeton, N.J.: Princeton University Press, 1991), pp. 24, 28–29.
20. Julius Caesar, *The Conquest of Gaul,* trans. S. A. Handford (London: Penguin, 1988), pp. 58–61.
21. Arnold, *op. cit.,* pp. 154–55.

22. Keller, *op. cit.* The story of attitudes and treatment toward the Jews in medieval France begins on p. 112.
23. Baigent, Leigh, and Lincoln, *Holy Blood, Holy Grail,* pp. 392–93.
24. Ibid., pp. 254–58.
25. Ibid., pp. 389–97.
26. Pierre Riche, *Daily Life in the World of Charlemagne,* trans. Jo Ann McNamara (Philadelphia: University of Pennsylvania Press, 1978), pp. 126–30.
27. Steven Runciman, *A History of the Crusades,* vol. 1 (New York: Cambridge University Press, 1990), pp. 10–11. On May 5 of the year A.D. 614, the Persians entered Jerusalem with the aid of the Jews. Christians were massacred, more by Jews than by Persian soldiers, which was neither forgiven nor forgotten.
28. Robinson, *Born in Blood,* p. 66.
29. Baigent, Leigh, and Lincoln, *Holy Blood, Holy Grail,* pp. 111–18.
30. Runciman, *op. cit.,* pp. 292–93.
31. Baigent, Leigh, and Lincoln, *Holy Blood, Holy Grail,* p. 119.
32. Ibid., p. 131.
33. Marks, *op. cit.,* pp. 235–49.
34. Robinson, *Born in Blood,* pp. 224–34.
35. Loomis, *op. cit.,* pp. 163–69.
36. Robinson, *Born in Blood,* pp. 224–30.
37. Baigent and Leigh, *op. cit.,* p. 151.
38. Richenda Miers, *op. cit.,* pp. 148–49.
39. Robinson, *Born in Blood,* p. 217.
40. Baigent and Leigh, *op. cit.,* p. 111.
41. Sinclair, *op. cit.,* pp. 180–91.

Chapter 11

1. Gordon Donaldson, ed., *Scottish Historic Documents* (Glasgow: Neil Wilson, 1974), pp. 55–58.
2. Pohl, *Prince Henry Sinclair,* pp. 170–71.
3. Maclean, *op. cit.,* pp. 49–50.
4. Ibid., pp. 52–53.

5. Rosalind Mitchison, *A History of Scotland* (London: Methuen and Co., 1970), pp. 59–62.
6. Ibid., p. 68.
7. Sinclair, *op. cit.*, pp. 187–89.
8. Ibid., pp. 5–6.
9. Baigent and Leigh, *op. cit.*, pp. 114–15.
10. Ibid., pp. 92, 94, and 104–5.
11. Ibid., pp. 118–122.
12. Maclean, *op. cit.*, pp. 56–57.
13. Ibid., p. 60.
14. Mitchison, *op. cit.*, pp. 60–61.
15. Morrison, *op. cit.*, p. 65.
16. Baigent and Leigh, *op. cit.*, pp. 116–17.
17. Maclean, *op. cit.*, pp. 74–75.
18. Sinclair, *op. cit.*, p. 179.
19. Ibid., pp. 179–82.
20. Baigent and Leigh, *op. cit.*, p. 114.
21. Ibid.
22. Sinclair, *op. cit.*, p. 182.
23. Baigent and Leigh, *op. cit.*, p. 109.
24. Ibid.
25. Sinclair, *op. cit.*, p. 185.
26. Baigent, Leigh, and Lincoln, *Holy Blood, Holy Grail,* p. 415. This is the primary source for the list of ruling families in the Prieuré de Sion.
27. Barbara W. Tuchman, *A Distant Mirror* (New York: Ballantine Books, 1978), pp. 343–64.
28. Henry Lincoln, *The Holy Place* (London: Corgi Books, 1991), pp. 75–76.
29. Patrice Boussel, *Da Vinci* (New York: Konecky and Konecky, 1989), pp. 5–18.
30. Ibid.
31. Ibid., p. 119.
32. Picknett and Prince, *op. cit.*, pp. 148, 149, 151.
33. Boussel, *op. cit.*, p. 119.

34. John Noble Wilford, *The Mysterious History of Columbus* (New York: Alfred A. Knopf, 1991), p. 214.

35. Baigent, Leigh, and Lincoln, *Holy Blood, Holy Grail*, p. 421.

36. Ibid., p. 424.

37. Maclean, *op. cit.,* pp. 79–81.

38. Baigent, Leigh, and Lincoln, *Holy Blood, Holy Grail*, p. 144.

39. O'Connor, *The Big Dig,* pp. 105–11.

Chapter 12

1. Clement A. Miles, *Christmas Customs and Traditions: Their History and Significance* (New York: Dover, 1976), pp. 328–30.

2. Sir James Fraser, *The Golden Bough* (New York: Macmillan, 1922), pp. 308–30.

3. Jean Markale, *King of the Celts* (Rochester, Vt.: Inner Traditions, 1994), pp. 117–21.

4. Ibid., pp. 117–20.

5. Norma Lorre Goodrich, *King Arthur* (New York: Harper and Row, 1986), pp. 13–25.

6. Roger Sherman Loomis, *The Grail from Celtic Myth to Christian Symbol* (Princeton: Princeton University Press, 1991), pp. 1–19.

7. Norma Lorre Goodrich, *The Holy Grail*, pp. 1–10.

8. Margaret Drabble, ed., *The Oxford Companion to English Literature* (Oxford: Oxford University Press, 1985) pp. 118–19.

9. Krupp, *op. cit.,* pp. 179–89.

10. Gale R. Owen, *Rites and Religions of the Anglo-Saxons* (London: Dorset Press, 1985), p. 140.

11. Miles, *op. cit.,* pp. 15–28.

12. Fraser, *op. cit.,* pp. 308–19.

13. Graves, *The White Goddess*, p. 176.

14. Fraser, *op. cit.,* p.153. Also see Barbara Walker's *Woman's Encyclopedia of Myths and Secrets* (San Francisco: Harper and Row, 1983), pp. 48–50, 503.

15. Graves, *The White Goddess*, pp. 218–19.

16. Ibid., pp. 177–78.

17. Ibid., pp. 128, 132, 176.

18. A. MacCullough, *The Religion of the Ancient Celts* (London: Studio Editions, 1911), pp. 198–99.

19. Arnold, *op. cit.*, pp. 96–97.

20. Graves, *The White Goddess*, pp. 61–73.

21. Walker, *op. cit.*, p. 218.

22. Ibid., p. 491.

23. Ibid., pp. 168–69.

24. Ibid., pp. 58–60.

25. Ibid., pp. 514–15.

26. Graves, *The White Goddess*, pp. 179–180.

27. Thomas W. Lippman, *Understanding Islam* (New York: Penguin, 1990) pp. 7–9.

28. Norma Lorre Goodrich, *Merlin* (New York: Harper and Row, 1988) pp. 41–44.

29. Walker, *op. cit.*, pp. 212–13.

30. Joseph and Frances Gies, *Life in a Medieval City* (New York: Thomas Y. Crowell, 1969), pp. 93-95.

31. Max I. Dimont, *Jews, God and History* (New York: Simon and Schuster, 1962), pp. 152–53.

32. Geoffrey of Monmouth, *op. cit.*, p. 51.

33. *The Oxford Companion to English Literature*, pp. 408–9.

34. Goodrich, *King Arthur*, pp. 117–19.

35. Ibid., pp. 113–50.

36. Ibid., pp. 202–3.

37. Robinson, *Born in Blood*, p. 217.

38. Ibid., p. 229.

39. Goodrich, *The Holy Grail*, p. 264. Goodrich further informs us that the Grail might have been moved to Scotland: p. 309.

40. Baigent, Leigh, and Lincoln, *Holy Blood, Holy Grail*, pp. 255–61.

41. Goodrich, *Holy Grail*, p. 218.

Chapter 13

1. Martin Short, *Inside the Brotherhood* (New York: Dorset Press, 1989), pp. 33–40.
2. Stephen Knight, *The Brotherhood* (New York: Dorset Press, 1984), pp. 16–25.
3. Robinson, *Born in Blood*, p. 214.
4. Fred Marks, ed., *Marquis Who's Who* (New Providence, N.J.: Reed Elsevier, 1997).
5. David Wood, *Genesis: The First Book of Revelations* (Kent, England: Baton Press, 1985), p. 218.
6. L. Resnikoff and R. O. Wells Jr., *Mathematics in Civilization* (New York: Dover, 1973), p. 25.
7. Hildegard Wienke-Lotz, "The Origin of Time Measurements," in Donald L. Cyr, ed., *Full Measure* (Santa Barbara: Stonehenge Viewpoint, 1990), pp. 34–46.
8. Robinson, *Born in Blood*, pp. 305–17.
9. Peter Tompkins, *Secrets of the Pyramids* (New York: Harper and Row, 1971), p. 38.
10. Baigent and Leigh, *op. cit.*, pp. 252–55.
11. Ibid., pp. 222–29.
12. Ibid., p. 228.
13. Morrison, *op. cit.*, p. 354.
14. Robert Leckie, *George Washington's War* (New York: HarperCollins, 1992), pp. 445–51.
15. Baigent and Leigh, *op. cit.*, p. 261.
16. Wilson, *The Encyclopedia of Unsolved Mysteries*, pp. 237–48.
17. Ibid.
18. Baigent, Leigh, and Lincoln, *Holy Blood, Holy Grail*, pp. 425–26.
19. Ibid.
20. Ibid.
21. Ibid.

22. Mary M. Luke, *Gloriana: The Years of Elizabeth I* (New York: Coward, McCann, and Geoghagen, 1973), pp. 37–40.

23. Ibid., p. 305.

24. Paul Johnson, *Elizabeth I* (New York: Holt, Rhinehart and Winston, 1974), pp. 246–47.

25. Picknett and Prince, *op. cit.,* p. 87.

26. Baigent and Leigh, *op. cit.,* pp. 187–97.

27. Robinson, *Born in Blood,* pp. 305–16.

28. Baigent and Leigh, *op. cit.,* pp. 204–29.

29. O'Connor, *The Big Dig,* p. 6.

30. Baigent, Leigh, and Lincoln, *op. cit.,* pp. 150–53.

31. Fanthorpe and Fanthorpe, *op. cit.,* pp. 6–7.

32. Ibid., p. 62.

33. Picknett and Prince, *op. cit.,* p. 72.

34. Michelle Green, "Europe's Heads, Crowned and Otherwise, Bury Zita, the Last Hapsburg Empress," *People Weekly,* vol. 31, no. 15, (April 17, 1989): pp. 50–54.

35. Picknett and Prince, *op. cit.,* p. 71.

36. Michael Walsh, *Opus Dei* (San Francisco: HarperCollins, 1989), pp. 131–59.

37. Penny Lernoux, *People of God* (New York: Penguin Books, 1989), pp. 324–37.

38. Ibid., pp. 283-301.

Epilogue

1. John Daly, "Solving Old Mysteries: A New Shaft May Reveal Buried Treasure," *Macleans,* vol. 102, no. 12 (March 20, 1989): p. 45.

2. Henry Lincoln, *The Holy Place* (London: Corgi Books, 1991), pp. 147–54.

3. Wood, *Genesis: The First Book of Revelations,* p. 98.

4. James Henderson, "In the Steps of Unrepentant Heretics," *Financial Times,* March 18/19, 1995, p. 8.

5. Sinclair, *op. cit.*, pp. 180–91.
6. Morrison, *op. cit.*, pp. 138–48.
7. Ibid., p. 164, 246.
8. Ibid., p. 247.
9. Fanthorpe and Fanthorpe, *op. cit.*, pp. 144–45.

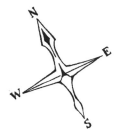

BIBLIOGRAPHY

Anderson, Rasmus B., ed. *The Norse Discovery of America.* London: Norroena Society, 1906.

Anonymous. *The Secret Doctrine of the Rosicrucians.* New York: Barnes and Noble, 1993.

Arnold, Rosemarie. *Baedecker's France.* Englewood Cliffs, N.J.: Prentice Hall, 1992.

Arribas, Antonio. *The Iberians.* New York: Praeger, 1964.

Ashe, Geoffrey. *The Discovery of King Arthur.* Garden City, N.Y.: Anchor Press, 1985.

Ashe, Geoffrey et al. *The Quest for America.* New York: Praeger, 1971.

Augstein, Rudolf. *Jesus, Son of Man.* New York: Urizen, 1972.

Augur, Helen. Th*e Secret War for Independence.* Boston: Little, Brown and Co., 1955.

Baigent, Michael, and Richard Lee. *The Temple and the Lodge.* New York: Arcade Publishing, 1989.

Baigent, Michael, Richard Leigh, and Henry Lincoln. *The Messianic Legacy.* New York: Dell Publishing, 1986.

————. *Holy Blood, Holy Grail.* New York: Dell Publishing, 1982.

Bailey, James, *The God-Kings and the Titans.* New York: Harper and Row, 1977.

Bain, Robert. *The Clans and Tartans of Scotland.* London and Glasgow: Collins, 1938.

Barber, Malcolm. *The New Knighthood.* Cambridge: Cambridge University Press, 1994.

Bingham, Caroline. *The Kings and Queens of Scotland.* New York: Taplinger, 1976.

Birmingham, Stephen. *America's Secret Aristocracy.* New York: Berkley Books, 1987.

Blum, Jean. *Rennes-Le-Château, Wisigoths, Cathares, Templiers.* Paris: Editions du Rocher, 1994.

Boland, Charles Michael. *They All Discovered America.* Garden City, N.Y.: Doubleday, 1961.

Boussel, Patrice. *Da Vinci.* New York: Konecky and Konecky, 1989.

Bowen, Catherine Drinker. *Francis Bacon: The Temper of a Man.* Boston: Little, Brown, and Co. 1963.

Bright, John. *A History of Israel.* Philadelphia: Westminster Press, 1960.

Caesar, Julius. *The Conquest of Gaul.* New York: Penguin Classics, 1988.

Campbell, Grace. *Highland Heritage.* New York: Duell, Sloan, and Pierce, 1962.

Childress, David Hatcher. *Lost Cities of North and Central America.* Stelle, Ille: Adventures Unlimited Press, 1992.

Chrétien de Troyes. *Arthurian Romances.* New York: Penguin Classics, 1991.

Christianson, Gale E. *In the Presence of the Creator: Isaac Newton and His Times.* New York: Free Press, 1984.

Cohn, Norman. *Europe's Inner Demons.* New York: Basic Books, 1975.

Collins, Roger. *The Basques.* Cambridge, Mass: Blackwell, 1986.

Cremin, Aedeen. *The Celts in Europe.* Sydney: University of Sydney, 1993.

Crooker, William S. *The Oak Island Quest.* Hantsport, Nova Scotia: Lancelot Press, 1978.

Cummings, Pete, ed. *Nordic Expedition Communicator.* Worcester, Mass.: self-publication, 1990.

Daly, John. "Solving Old Mysteries: A New Shaft May Reveal Buried Treasure," *Macleans,* vol. 102, no. 12, (1989): 45.

Daniel-Rops, Henri. *Daily Life in the Time of Jesus.* New York: Hawthorn Books, 1962.

Davidson, Hilda Ellis. *The Lost Beliefs of Northern Europe.* London: Routledge, 1993.

Dimont, Max I. *Jews, God and History.* New York: Simon and Schuster, 1962.

————. *The Indestructible Jews.* New York: World Publishing Co., 1971.

Douglas, David C. *The Norman Achievement.* Berkeley and Los Angeles: University of California Press, 1969.

Durning-Lawrence, Sir Edwin. *Bacon Is Shakespeare.* New York: John McBride, 1910.

Edwards, Samuel. *Victor Hugo.* New York: David McKay Co., 1971.

Eusebius. *The History of the Church.* G. A. Williamson, trans. New York: Penguin Classics, 1965.

Fanthorpe, Lionel and Patricia. *Secrets of Rennes-Le-Chateau.* York Beach, Maine: Samuel Weiser, Inc., 1992.

Fell, Barry. *America B.C.* New York: Quadrangle, 1976.

————. *Bronze Age America.* Boston: Little, Brown and Co., 1982.

Firstbrook, Peter. *The Voyage of the Matthew.* San Francisco: KQED Books, 1977.

Fox, Robin Lane. *Pagans and Christians.* San Francisco: Harper and Row, 1986.

Fraser, Sir James. *The Golden Bough.* New York: Macmillan, 1922.

Friedlaender, Walter. *Poussin.* New York: Harry Abrams, Inc., 1966.

Geoffrey of Monmouth. *The History of the Kings of Britain.* New York: Penguin Classics, 1966.

Gies, Joseph and Frances. *Life in a Medieval City.* New York: Thomas Y. Crowell, 1969.

Gies, Frances. *The Knight in History.* New York: Harper and Row, 1984.

Glynn, Frank. Personal correspondence. 1980.

Goodrich, Norma Lorre. *Ancient Myths.* New York: Penguin, 1994.

————. *Guinevere.* New York: Harper Perennial, 1991.

————. *King Arthur.* New York: Franklin Watts, 1986.

————. *Merlin.* New York: Franklin Watts, 1987.

————. *The Holy Grail.* New York: HarperCollins, 1992.

Grant, Michael. *The History of Ancient Israel.* New York: Charles Scribners' Sons, 1984.

————. *Saint Paul.* New York: Charles Scribners' Sons, 1976.

————. *Jesus: An Historian's Review of the Bible.* New York: Charles Scribners' Sons, 1977.

Graves, Robert. *The Greek Myths.* New York: Penguin, 1955.

————. *The White Goddess.* New York: Farrar, Straus and Giroux, 1948.

Gregory of Tours. *The History of the Franks.* London: Penguin Classics, 1974.

Hancock, Graham. *The Sign and the Seal.* New York: Crown Publishers, Inc., 1992.

Hannay, Margaret Patterson. *C. S Lewis.* New York: Frederick Unger Publishing, 1981.

Hapgood, Charles H. *Maps of the Ancient Sea Kings.* New York: E. P. Dutton, 1966.

Harwood, Harold. *Newfoundland.* Toronto: Macmillan, 1969.

Haskins, Susan. *Mary Magdalen: Myth and Metaphor.* New York: Riverhead Books, 1993.

Henderson, James. "In the Steps of Unrepentant Heretics," *Financial Times,* March 18/19, 1995.

Hibbert, Christopher. *Venice. The Biography of a City.* New York: W. W. Norton, 1989.

Hobbs, William H. "The Fourteenth Century Discovery of America by Antonio Zeno," *Scientific American* vol. 72, (January 1951).

Holand, Hjalmar R. *Explorations in America Before Columbus.* New York: Twayne Publishers, 1958.

Holzer, Hans. *Long Before Columbus.* Sante Fe: Bear and Co., 1992.

Huyghe, Patrick. *Columbus Was Last.* New York: Hyperion, 1992.

Ingsted, Helge, et al. *The Quest for America.* New York: Praeger, 1971.

Jenkins, Elizabeth. *The Mystery of King Arthur.* New York: Coward, McCann and Geoghegan, 1975.

Johnson, Paul. *Elizabeth I.* New York: Rhinehart and Winston, 1974.

————. *A History of Christianity.* New York: Atheneum, 1976.

Jones, Gwyn. *A History of the Vikings.* New York: Oxford University Press, 1968.

Josephus. *The Jewish War.* Translated by G. A. Williamson, revised by E. Mary Smallwood. New York: Penguin, 1981.

Keller, Werner. *Diaspora: The Post-Biblical History of the Jews.* New York: Harcourt Brace and World, 1969.

Klausner, Joseph. *From Jesus to Paul.* New York: Macmillan, 1943.

Knight, Stephen. *The Brotherhood.* New York: Dorset Press, 1984.

————. *The Secret World of Freemasons.* New York: Dorset Press, 1984.

Krupp, E. C., ed. *In Search of Ancient Astronomies.* Oxford: Oxford University Press, 1944.

Kufferath, Maurice. *The Parsifal of Richard Wagner.* New York: Henry Holt, 1905.

Ladurie, Leroy. *Montaillou: The Promised Land of Error.* New York: George Braziller, Inc., 1978.

Laing, Lloyd and Jenny. *The Picts and the Scots.* Dover, N.H.: Alan Sutton, 1993.

Landay, Jerry M. *The House of David.* New York: E. P. Dutton, 1973.

Lernoux, Penny. *People of God.* New York: Penguin Books, 1989.

Lethbridge, T. C. Personal correspondence (see Glynn).

Lincoln, Henry. *The Holy Place.* London: Corgi Books, 1991.

Livesay, Herbert B. *The Gunn Salute.* vol. 17, no. 3, (1987).

Loomis, Roger Sherman. *The Grail: From Celtic Myth to Christian Symbol.* Princeton, N.J.: Princeton University Press, 1991.

Luke, Mary M. *Gloriana: The Years of Elizabeth I.* New York: Coward, McCann and Geoghagen, 1973.

MacKendrick, Paul. *The Iberian Stones Speak.* New York: Funk and Wagnalls, 1969.

————. *Roman France.* New York: St. Martin's Press, 1972.

Maclean, Fitzroy. *Scotland.* London: Thames and Hudson, 1993.

Magnusson, Magnus. *Vikings.* New York: E. P. Dutton, 1980.

————. *The Vinland Sagas.* New York: Penguin, 1965.

Markale, Jean. *Celtic Civilization.* London: Gordon and Cremonesi, 1978.

————. *King of the Celts.* Rochester, Vt.: Inner Traditions, 1994.

Marks, Claude. *Pilgrims, Heretics and Lovers.* New York: Macmillan, 1975.

Matthews, John. *The Grail Tradition.* Rockport, Mass.: Element, 1990.

Mallery, Arlington and Mary Roberts Harrison. *The Rediscovery of Lost America.* New York: E. P. Dutton, 1979.

Marsh, Henry. *The Rebel King.* New York: Coward, McCann and Geoghagan, 1975.

McLeod, Roger D. "Comprehensive Evidence for Viking and Gaelic Sites in the Americas and Elsewhere (unpublished, preserved in Fletcher Library, Medford, Mass.).

McGuigan, Dorothy Gies. *The Hapsburgs.* New York: Doubleday, 1966.

McGinnis. *Canada.* New York: Rhinehart and Co., 1947.

Miers, Richenda. *Scotland.* Chester, Conn.: Globe Pequot Press, 1989.

Miles, Clement A. *Christmas, Customs and Traditions.* New York: Dover, 1976.

Millman, Lawrence. *Last Places: A Journey in the North.* New York: Vintage Books, 1990.

Mitchinson, Rosalind. *A History of Scotland.* London. Methuen, 1970.

Morison, Samuel Eliot. *The European Discovery of America: The Northern Voyages.* New York: Oxford University Press, 1971.

————. *The European Discovery of America: The Southern Voyages.* New York: Oxford University Press, 1974.

Morrison, Leonard A. *A History of the Sinclair Family.* Boston: Damprell and Upman, 1896.

Nesmith, Robert I. *Dig for Pirate Treasure.* New York: The Devin-Adair Co., 1959.

Nickell, Joe. "Pollens on the Shroud: A Study in Deception," *Skeptical Inquirer,* vol. 18 no. 4 (1994).

Norwich, John Julius. *A History of Venice.* New York: Alfred A. Knopf, 1982.

O'Connor, D'Arcy. *The Money Pit.* New York: Coward McCann and Geoghegan Inc., 1978.

————. *The Big Dig.* New York: Ballantine Books, 1988.

Oldenbourg, Zoe. *Massacre at Montsegur.* London: Weidenfield and Nicholson, 1961.

Olmstead, A. T. *History of Palestine and Syria.* New York: Charles Scribners' Sons, 1931.

Owen, Gale R. *Rites and Religion of the Anglo-Saxons.* New York: Dorset Press, 1985.

Pagels, Elaine. *The Gnostic Gospels.* New York: Random House, 1979.

Parkman, Francis. *The Jesuits in North America.* New York: Library of America, 1993.

Partner, Peter. *The Murdered Magicians.* New York: Barnes and Noble, 1993.

Payne, Robert. *The Dream and the Tomb.* New York: Stein and Day, 1984.

Picknett, Lynn, and Clive Prince. *Turin Shroud.* New York: HarperCollins, 1994.

Platt, Cameron, and John Wright. *Treasure Islands.* Golden, Col.: Fulcrum, 1995.

Poertner, Rudolf. *The Vikings: The Rise and Fall of the Norse Sea Kings.* New York: St. Martin's Press, 1971.

Pohl, Frederick J. *Atlantic Crossings Before Columbus.* New York: W. W. Norton, 1961.

———. *Prince Henry Sinclair.* New York: Clarkson N. Potter, 1974.

Prebble, John. *The Lion in the North.* New York: Coward, McCann and Geoghegan, 1971.

Preston, Douglas. "Death Trap Defies Treasure Seekers for Two Centuries," *Smithsonian,* vol. 19, no. 3 (1988): 52.

Proctor, Steve. "Island of Controversy," *Macleans,* vol. 108, no. 34 (1995):54.

Raleigh, Sir Walter. *The History of the World.* C. A. Patrides, ed. Philadelphia: Temple University Press, 1971.

Randall, Willard Sterne. *Benedict Arnold: Patriot and Traitor.* New York: William Morrow and Co., 1990.

Rees, Alwyn, and Brinley Rees. *Celtic Heritage.* London: Thames and Hudson, 1961.

Riche, Pierre. *Daily Life in the World of Charlemagne.* Philadelphia: University of Pennsylvania Press, 1978.

Ritchie, Anna, *Viking Scotland.* London: B. T. Batsford, 1993.

Ritchie, Robert C. *Captain Kidd and the War Against the Pirates.* Cambridge, Mass.: Harvard University Press, 1986.

Robinson, John J., *Born in Blood: The Lost Secrets of Freemasonry*. New York: M. Evans and Company, 1989.

————, *Dungeon, Fire and Sword: The Knights Templar in the Crusades*. New York: M. Evans and Company, 1991.

Robinson, James M., ed. *The Nag Hammadi Library*. San Francisco: Harper and Row, 1977.

Rothovius, Andrew E. "'Sword of the New North': A New Novel," *The Milford Cabinet and Wilton Journal*. Dec. 29, (1983) p. 24.

Runciman, Steven. *A History of the Crusades*. New York: Cambridge University Press, 1990.

Sandmel, Samuel. *Herod: Portrait of a Tyrant*. Philadelphia: J. B. Lippincott, 1967.

Scherman, Katherine. *The Birth of France*. New York: Paragon House, 1987.

Schledermann, Peter. "Eskimo and Viking Finds in the Arctic," *National Geographic*, vol. 159, no. 5 (1981): 575–601.

Schonfield, Hugh J. *The Passover Plot*. Netherlands: Bernard Geis, 1965.

————. *The Jesus Party*. New York: Macmillan, 1974.

————. *The Original New Testament*. Rockport, Maine: Element, 1985.

Scott, Ronald McNair. *Robert the Bruce*. New York: Peter Bedrick Books, 1989.

Seaholm, Charles. *The Kelts and the Vikings*. Philosophical Library, 1974.

Sellier, Charles E. *Mysteries of the Ancient World*. New York: Dell Publishing, 1995.

Severin, Tim. *The Brendan Voyage*. New York: Avon, 1978.

Short, Martin. *Inside the Brotherhood*. New York: Dorset Press, 1989.

Sinclair, Andrew. *The Sword and the Grail*. New York: Crown Publishers, 1992.

Sitchin, Zecharia. *When Time Began*. New York: Avon, 1993.

Snow, Edward R. *True Tales of Buried Treasure*. New York: Dodd, Mead and Co., 1952.

Swaney, Deanna. *Iceland, Greenland and the Faroe Islands*. Hawthorn, Australia: Lonely Planet Publications, 1994.

Tavell, Emille. "Rock Sketch Hints Scottish Invasion," *Christian Science Monitor*, Oct. 2, 1957.

———. "A Fourteenth-Century Riddle and Its Conclusion," *Geographical Review*, vol. 54 (1964): 573–76.

Taylor, E. G. R. "The Fisherman's Story," *Geographical Review*, vol. 37 (1964): 709–12.

Tomkins, Peter. *The History of Obelisks*. New York: Harper and Row, 1981.

Tuchman, Barbara. *Bible and Sword*. New York: Ballantine, 1984.

———. *A Distant Mirror*. New York: Ballantine, 1978.

Walker, Barbara. *Woman's Encyclopedia of Myths and Secrets*. San Francisco: Harper and Row, 1983.

Walsh, Michael. *Opus Dei*. San Francisco: Harper, 1992.

Whitehead, Ruth Holmes. *Stories from the Six Worlds*. Halifax, Nova Scotia: Nimbus Publishing, Ltd., 1988.

Wilford, John Noble. *The Mysterious History of Columbus*. New York: Alfred A. Knopf, 1991.

———. *The Mapmakers*. New York: Alfred A. Knopf, 1981.

———. "Norsemen in America—Flourished Then Faded," *New York Times*, July 7, 1992.

Willard, Lawrence F. "Westford's Mysterious Knight," *Yankee Magazine*, vol. 22, (1958): pp. 60, 61, 84, 85.

Williamson, James A. *Sir Francis Drake*. London: Crief, Lives-Collins, 1951.

Wilson, Colin. *The Encyclopedia of Unsolved Mysteries*. Chicago: Contemporary Books, 1988.

Wilson, Derek. *The World Encompassed*. New York: Harper and Row, 1977.

White, Freda. *West of the Rhone: Languedoc, Roussillon and the Massif Central*. New York: W. W. Norton, 1964.

Wood, David. *Genesis: The First Book of Revelations*. Kent: Baton Press, 1985.

Wood, Ian. *The Merovingian Kingdoms 450–751*. London: Longman, 1994.

Wood, Michael. *In Search of the Dark Ages*. New York: Facts on File, 1987.

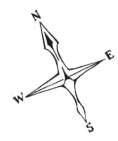

INDEX